Nathaniel Dunn

Satan Chained

a poem

Nathaniel Dunn

Satan Chained
a poem

ISBN/EAN: 9783337302009

Printed in Europe, USA, Canada, Australia, Japan

Cover: Foto ©Lupo / pixelio.de

More available books at **www.hansebooks.com**

SATAN CHAINED;

A POEM,

BY

PROFESSOR N. DUNN, A. M.,
(Of Bowdoin College, Class 1825,

FORMERLY INSTRUCTOR IN CHEMISTRY AND NATURAL PHILOSOPHY, IN WILBRA-
HAM ACADEMY, MASS., AFTERWARDS, PRINCIPAL OF HEMPSTEAD SEMINARY,
L. I.; AND LATTERLY, LECTURER IN RUTGERS FEMALE COLLEGE, IN THE
CITY OF NEW YORK.

———

"And I saw an angel come down from heaven, having * * * * a great
chain in his hand "—BIBLE.

SECOND EDITION.

NEW YORK.

PUBLISHED BY THE AUTHOR.

FOR SALE AT 805 BROADWAY.

1876.

TO MY DAUGHTER,

CHARLOTTE ELIZABETH,

WHO HAS BEEN MY CONSTANT COMPANION THESE YEARS PAST,

AND HAS EVER BEEN IN SYMPATHY WITH ME
IN MY LABORS ;

AND HAS AFFORDED ME NO SMALL ASSISTANCE IN PREPARING IT FOR
THE PRESS,—THIS POEM,

"SATAN CHAINED,

IS MOST AFFECTIONATELY DEDICATED.

NATHANIEL DUNN.

FAVORABLE WORDS.

A clergyman from Sing Sing writes :

' I am reading your ' Satan Chained ' with great satisfaction—Grand poem ! "

A lady of Rockland county, not unknown to the press, writes :

'· Full, from beginning to end, of original ideas ; many of them startling. The description of Heaven, its inhabitants, and their employments, is beautiful. The Rebellion . . . . and, finally, the chaining of Satan, is terribly sublime. It is, in short, a pen-picture, which, once read, enstamps itself indelibly on the memory.'

A lady from Brooklyn writes of it :

" Magnificent poem ! It charms, delights and edifies me.

A merchant of New York states in a note :

"I have read "Satan Chained" through twice. and with increased interest, pleasure and profit. The power and dignity of style, the elevating spirit, and the vividly drawn scenes and characters cannot fail of arresting the attention even of the careless reader; but to one who ' reads between the lines. and studies the work, it is a rich mine."

From a professor of one of our colleges :

"The sentiments of the poem are most admirable in every respect. It has never failed to afford me much interest and pleasure."

A gentleman of New Jersey, connected with the press, characterizes it as

"An admirably executed epic. . . . Am enjoying the reading very much."

A clergyman says in a note :

"I have read it with unmingled interest . . . . It was with difficulty I could lay it aside till I had reached the end of the book."

An ex-merchant of this city, himself somewhat known for his poetical compositions, writes :

' In my opinion it is a masterly production . . . . Passages in it are unsurpassed in the English language."

Another gentleman, who read the work in manuscript, said of it :

" Fully up to Milton's 'Paradise Lost;' and more readable.".

The *Methodist Quarterly* (April 1876) says :

"We cannot say the writer equals Milton. But we can conscientiously say, we think he is scarce inferior to Pollok."

A clergyman, who had it in manuscript, said of it :

" It is a splendid thing."

A lawyer of Minnesota used about the same words, saying :

"It is splendid."

A gentleman writes from Cincinnati that it is considered there,

"A master piece of work."

Those who read the poem will, of course, judge for themselves how far these favorable criticisms are just.

PREFACE.

THE following Poem, " SATAN CHAINED," was commenced in the year 1854, and was completed, as a whole, in the year 1864. During the most of those ten years, the author was engaged in giving public lectures on the subject of Chemistry, in several of the States. His mind was necessarily much occupied with the requirements of his profession. He found, however, leisure hours, though seldom whole days, to devote to the composition of it. Still, it is simply an adherence to truth to say, that the whole of it was written under a constant pressure of anxieties and cares. What it would have been, had the mind been disencumbered of other matters, whether better or not, none can tell.

It has been lying by ever since, receiving, in the mean time, numerous amendments and additions—till it is found in its present shape.

It is now offered to the public, with a desire, of course, that it may find readers : but with no expectation, however, that it will *fully* meet the taste of any single one of them. But if the major part of it should satisfy the taste of a majority of readers, the author will have attained his most sanguine expectations.

A point has been made to render the text as perspicuous as possible ; even, occasionally, at the expense of brevity, with the hope that the masses, the plainest of them, will find no difficulty in comprehending the author's meaning, and that they will the more readily derive an agreeable entertainment from the perusal of its pages.

And should this production prove acceptable to those of higher culture, and more refined taste, a double gratification will be realized by

THE AUTHOR.

NEW YORK, *December,* 1875.

Author's Note to the Second Edition.

The author need not say he feels much gratified at the reception this poem has thus far received ; a goodly number, who have perused its pages, having expressed to him, by letter, or otherwise, a high appreciation of the work.

A number of errors, chiefly typographical, found in the first edition, have been corrected in this.

One line has been expunged and another put in its place; and the rithm set right in several instances; otherwise this edition is an exact re-print of the first.

August, 1876.

CONTENTS.

SATAN CHAINED.—TWELVE BOOKS.

"SATAN CHAINED."

BOOK I.

THINE aid, Eternal Spirit, give. Instruct,
Sustain, while I attempt in venturous verse
Things past, things present, and things yet to come,
The TRIUMPH OF THE CHURCH OF GOD BELOW,
AND SATAN CHAINED.
    Among the alps of Hell,
Whose fiery peaks shoot up, and pierce and scorch
The clouds, there is a table-land. This plain,
Of wide expanse, is high uplift above
The level of surrounding lands. And here,
On jutting angle, worn with ceaseless care,
Sat Satan, Hell's great king. Behind him stretched
Immense this wide plateau ; and on his left
Far down the craggy cliffs, beneath him lay
The Stygian lake, whose darkling face was spread
Beyond the reach of keenest vision ; and
Whose billows, hoarse and dreadful as from storms
Remote, rolled sullen on the shattered beach,
And bellowed ominous through rocks and caves.
 And on his right, below this lofty plain,
Was stretched a desert drear, if desert can

Be traced in hell, where all is desert. Wide,
And wasteful was that barren tract ; and filled
With monsters dread, and vipers fierce, and asps
And adders dire, of deadliest fang.

        In front
Sprang up beyond all ken of sight, a vast,
A horrid mountain range, of adamant,
The rocks, the broken ribs of Hell.

         He saw
The prospect drear, but heeded not, for thoughts
Of weightiest moment rolled within him. He
For once forgot his sad, his lost estate,
While night falls on him, such as Hell alone
Can boast ; of pitchy darkness, only broke
By lurid phosphorescent flashes from
The restless lake, or transient threatening gleams
Of fire eruptive : rendering still more black
Night's dreadful wing, which overspread afar
That world accursed.

      Alone he sat, or paced
That area ; for none desired the risk
Of close proximity, unbid, to Hell's
Dread chief, the Hyder Ali of the damned.

 He took no rest, not e'en such rest as Hell
Affords ; but spent the night in making out
A kind of programme for the coming day,
For that day was to be a day of note ;
A memorable epoch in the books
Of Hell.

     A convocation had been called ;
The mandate had gone forth to utmost bounds
Of his domain, for all to meet on day
Appointed—all—the chiefs, the Satraps—all,

But not plebeians. What are they? ah! Hell's
A despotism—a deadly tyranny,
Beneath whose grinding wheels the common caste
Of damned spirits ever groan and bleed.
No hope to them or respite ever comes
From iron rule, and crushing weight of power ;
Except when mad rebellion frees the galled
And rising masses, for some little space ;
Though sure by force or fraud to be reduced,
And pay in blood and tears the rash attempt.

    They'd all been summoned, not by herald as
In days of yore, but telegraph ; that wrote
In one short instant, through those regions vast,
In view of every chief HIS WILL SUPREME.

    All Hell was moved at this imperious call.
None dared refuse, but instant hastened to
Prepare for flight—on speediest wing they rode,
And day and night, and night and day, impelled
By beat perpetual of pinions spread,
And strength of ocean engines, urge their course.
Through adverse winds and storms they force their way,
Nor stop for rest, though wide and ruinous
The space they pass ; for, dread of anger for
One moment late drinks up all other thoughts.

    At length the mind of Satan, as he planned,
In moody silence, wrapped in deepest gloom,
The next day's business, fierce and desperate grew.
He thought of Heaven—its bliss, once his, now lost ;
The ambrosial fields of Paradise, and fruits,
For which earth has no name, no sample ; rich
In juices, fit for gods. These ever hung
Upon the glorious trees that skirted deep

The shores of that great stream, the riv'r of life ;
Which flowed incessant from the throne of God,
And watered all the vales of Heaven, and clothed
With richest verdure ; and distilled upon
The hills and mountain-tops, and filled with fruits
And flowers.

       He thought of his renown in Heaven,
When, walking as a god among the hosts,
They did him reverence as arch-angel of
The highest rank, and standing near the throne ;
And then, aspiring, how his all he staked
Upon a single throw—and lost—and sank
To Hell.

       That instant burst a meteor, like
The sun, and showed in horrid landscape all
The wasteful desolation of his home ;
Its rocks and naked soil and desert tracts,
So far unlike the hills and vales of Heaven.
His soul burned in him with the fiercest rage,
And poured forth blasphemies that shock e'en Hell.

  The night, the sleepless night thus passes on.
And now the darkness tangible, that like
A funeral pall o'erhung that scene of death
Gives way. A fiery gleam appears, and streaks
The dread horizon, giving promise of
Approaching day ; such day as Hell can claim.
This checked his fiery thoughts and impious tongue,
And called him back, and turned him with intense
Anxiety to what the day might bring,
Of hope or of despair.

       The lurid light
Heaves slowly up the eastern sky, and now,

With clouds of blackest wing and fearful form,
Brings in the day—if day can be in Hell,
Where Darkness reigns enthroned, and ever from
Her shroud and sable locks shakes off the forms
Of ghastliest phantoms ; idly thence which flit
In silence and on dusky fearful wing
Through every cave and path ; and haunt with fear,
And freeze the spirits of the damned.

    The fiend and dreaded chief, now pacing to
And fro the wide-spread space, with visage flushed
And quicker tread, as nearer draws the hour
Assigned, betrays the intenser feelings of
His harrowed soul.

             His telescopic eyes
Sweep ever and anon the circuit of
The heavens, as if for comets new, or worlds
Unseen before.

           And now on farthest sky,
That bounds the visual circle, seen at length,
Were what appeared but specks or clouds, like that
Which caught the servant's eye on Carmel, when
The heavens refused their wonted genial showers
To thirsty Israel, grown idolatrous
From pagan Jezebel in Ahab's reign.
The servant searched and strained his aching eyes.
A cloud no bigger than a human hand appeared,
A speck above the Western sea, but which
Ere long in one dark tempest wide o'erhung
The 'thereal arch, and gave abundant rain.

    So here, what seemed but specks to Satan's eye,
Now gaining space, and wide and wider grown,
While swiftly moving on in line direct,
And shortening still the distance vast with more

Than comet speed in perihelion,
At length, in near approach, expanding and
Uniting, filled the upper regions with
One black continuous cloud.   It darkened Hell.
It was a cloud of Spirits, Captains, Chiefs,
Arrived from all the principalities
Of that vast empire ; come from every point
Of compass, centering there, the common goal,
As nebulous matter at the birth of worlds.
    They whirl aloft, with wings outspread ;
A firmament of devils.   Thence beneath
They spy the standard of their dreaded King,
And wait the signal to descend, which given,
They quit the fields of upper space, and plunge
With eagle swoop and fierce gyrations down,·
And light upon the plain on which it stood.
    'Twas more than Hell could bear.   The suffering ground
Recoiled beneath their feet, the desert sighed ;
And blasted seemed anew that blasted world.
    Their dusky wings, then folding up, they stand
In human form, a multitude, which none
Could number, none could give their names, save minds
Of highest gifts in Heaven or Hell.   Yet these
Were chiefs alone, the shepherds of the sheep ;
How numerous!   The sheep then, what of them ?
How multitudinous!   How populous
Is Hell!   Ah, spirits have gone down to death
Like autumn leaves.   How broad the way, how wide
The gate!   O, Sin, what ruin hast thou wrought!
And how cast down the sons of God ! once heirs
Of bliss, now sunk and lost, forever lost!

    They saw not Satan.   He preferred to be

Reserved, and take the most auspicious time
To manifest his august presence to
The waiting throng. He had retired unseen,
Before the host descended, to his tent ;
Which stood in front of his encampment, where
His sentinels keep watch and guard with care
His royal person when he seeks for rest
Or draws the plans of battles or of long
Campaigns ; or when he holds his council on
Affairs of state, in time of actual war.
      His marshals at command receive the host
Arrived, and in procession vast, and with
The sound of trumpets loud, and clarious clear,
Conduct them to the wide arena of
Debate.
            'Twas on the Eastern limb of this
Vast plain. The seats had there been spread and all
Been numbered with the nicest care, and named
For each one coming ; so that no mishap
Of placing out of rank should raise the blood
Of this Assembly. For in Hell respect
Of rank and title is insisted on
With bloody rigor ; and most deadly strife
In single combat would ensue for least
Infraction of the laws of etiquette,
Or code of honor. Why not even so ?
For all need something that shall give them weight :
And why not hold to rank and titles with
A dying grasp, and outward show of worth
And character, when all within is vile
And worthless ? Let the good be thrust from right,
Insulted, suffer loss of name, and be
Outcast as filth. Yet they can bear it all ;
2

For yet the inner man remains untouched.
But where there is no inner man (which long
Since like a core has rotted out), 'tis well
With nicest circumspection to preserve
The outward man, the husk, the empty shell.
In Heaven there are no duels. These are left
To men and devils, who have pressing need.
The code of honor is the code of Hell.

With nicest order all their places found ;
And sat, a vast Assembly, such as earth ne'er saw,
A prairie space from sun to sun ; but not
In open air ; for Mulciber, forewarned
An awning wide had raised to shield them from
The noisome damps and altern scorching heats
That ever vex that curse-devoted clime.
　This awning was a wonder ; spreading wide
As ocean ; high in arch above ; and graced
With lamps and gorgeous drapery ; and what
Amazed the eye beholding, had no cords
Nor stakes nor pillars. Firmly fixed, it hung
Without support, stupenduous sight! the work
Of Mulciber ; sustained by science shrewd
And devilish magic joined. Great Architect,
O, Mulciber! What skill and taste are thine!
Thy fame is known in Heaven as well as Hell.
What palaces and towers and labyrinths
Are still in Heaven, memorials of thee!
What groves and gardens and delicious walks!
What fountains, terraces and winding paths ;
And set with never-fading trees of life,
And arched with flowers, th' undying Amaranth!
O, fallen god! thy name is left behind ;

Thy works like pyramids attest thy hand,
And show what intellect went down to Hell.
Parts great secure not Heaven. 'Tis goodness ; this
Alone insures a lot among the blest.

In front a gorgeous stately throne was raised,
A wondrous piece of art, and canopied
With richest tapestry, inwrought with gold
And precious stones ; and godlier far than kings
Of Eastern climes e'er saw.

             While all admire,
Their King arrives, announced with trumpet sound
And shout that deafened Hell. The Senate, though
Composed of gods, arose at his approach,
And deference paid as due to higher rank.

He mounts the royal seat prepared, and sat
In state sublime ; a god among the gods ;
In stature vast, above the rest though great ;
As Saul the anointed Benjamite o'er-topped
The Hebrew host. His form was matchless, and
His brow—though deeply scarred with bolts of war—
Of massy mould, and full in breadth and hight,
And beetling o'er his eyes like rocky cliffs,
Or wide and darkling folds of thunder cloud,
Betokened intellect of mightiest cast,
And showed him master-spirit of that world ;
While from his gorgeous robes and starry crown
Of gems and burnished gold, the rainbow flashed
In every wondrous hue, and filled with awe
The vast admiring throng.
            They saw their chief,
And each, enrapt, forgetting for the time
His private wrongs, and inward hate, felt proud

Of such a leader. He was proud in turn.
Imposing vision! Royalty enthroned ;
And at his feet the mighty of the realm,
In countless numbers waiting his behests,
At least in semblance of submission due !
But all was hollow ; selfishness supreme,
And moral rottenness filled every breast.
None dared his fellow trust, though bound by oaths
That frightened Hell ; for each stood ready at
Some proffered good to leap the bounds of right,
And laugh to scorn his oaths and plighted faith,
And turn assassin to secure the end.
Abhorred society, unmixed with good,
Where lies and wickedness unbounded reign !
  Its salt has earth, and hence not wholly lost.
But where's the salt of Hell ? there every crime,
Uncheked by weeds of good, grows rank and yields
A thousand fold. Lot sad of spirit lost !
Unmixed result of sin, the wrath to come !
  All hated and all feared ; but Satan most ;
For though he on his gala days, with show
And royal fetes relaxed his iron reign,
And seemed a lovely prince, a father mild,
And bowed with gracious smile the gazing throng ;
Yet all but know too well what lay beneath
That semblance of attention kind : and had
Experience of his daily acts unseen :
And treasured fierce remembrance of them all ;
But, most, the keen disgrace and scorpion whip
With which at first he broke them in and bent
Them to his will. His Will! all Hell recoils!
  His word was law. And right or wrong must be
Observed. (That doctrine came from Hell, which laughs

To scorn the Higher law, the law of God.)
The powers that be must ever be obeyed.
Such is the doctrine of the Pit ; which thence
Came smoking up to earth ; the doctrine called
The lower law. They feel it there, and crawl
And lick the dust, and push through every shame ;
And fawning kiss the tyrant's feet, and shout
The lower law.
        " All hated and all feared ;"
And each stood on his guard. And Satan feared ;
And ever 'gainst surprise kept ceaseless watch.
And hence called not this concourse to be held
In his metropolis, his Royal seat,
The far, far famous Pandemonium.
He knew his men, though great, yet wicked ; knew
Their temper, fiery lusts ; and, cautious chief,
Perceived it madness to expose the weal
Of his great capital to such a host
Of ruffian spirits ; and, besides, combined
In mutinous assault they might surprise,
And wrest from him his towers, his strongest holds,
The Acropolis of Hell. And hence again,
He came not up alone ; but brought along
His legions armed ; and them encamped aloof
For what emergency might rise, to give
More weight in council, or to guard from plots
Of treason, or from bursts of passion raised
To fury in debate.

       These legions were
His own—were ready at his bid to do
Whate'er he willed. The most atrocious deeds
Were theirs. Where'er they moved all Hell turned pale ;

They sacked, they pillaged, fed their fiery lusts,
And left a lava path of death behind ;
The scourge of Hell, the Cossacks of the damned,—
Nay, worse, the "border ruffians" of that world !
　　Their midnight orgies who can tell ? The weak
Fell prostrate, and with tears of blood besought,
Besought in vain ; and mid the darkest glooms
What shrieks were heard, that made e'en devils weep !
　　They came from every province, mustered by
Conscription : (The Conscription came from Hell.)
At first they shrunk from such a service, and
Essayed to 'scape the call. They hid themselves
In caves and rocks ; or sought the bottom of
The fiery lake ; or fled to Arctic wilds
And froze, and wandered o'er the ice, or, pressed
To frenzy, lopped a hand or limb ; but all
In vain ! The marshals of the tyrant's will
Pursued them with demoniac heart, and searched
Them out from all their lone retreats, and at
The point of barbed steel removed them to
The place of rendevous ; but with a full,
A solemn promise from their chief, that each
Should be returned at stated time, and not
Again be called to serve in war. Returned !
Ah, when ? "A solemn promise !" nay, an oath !
Believe it not. It is a spider's web
To wicked power, where law can never come
T' avenge a breach ; a toy t' amuse the throng
While cheated of their rights. They ne'er returned ;
Nor wished to now ; for they had been so drilled,
And fed with blood, and made victorious in
A thousand fields ; had found such scope for all
Their passions ; bred so long to martial show,

And camps, and all the blood and smoke and dust
And death of war, that all their better tastes
Were lost ; and they transformed to devils of
The bloodiest cast.   They loved the camp, and their
Great leader, who had so infused his own
Inherent virtues through their souls, that, at
His call, they'd storm the cannon's mouth ; or brave
A wilderness of swords and spears ; or fling
Their naked bodies as a shield around   ·
Their Chief ; or cast them down a bridge for wheels,
Or iron hoofs of his impetuous steed.
Then crawling breathless, bloodless from the fight,
Would give, with first sufficient breath, the shout,
The shout, " Long live our mighty, glorious chief !"
   They were his idols, he, in turn, their god ;
His idols, while they could be used to reach
His ends ; and were provided for with best
Of care ; were flattered and caressed ; but when
Diseased or maimed, and useless grown, were left
To ruthless foes, in hospitals, or on
The wastes of burning deserts, while he pushed
His conquering march to other fields, where still
New victories could be won, new glory gained ;
But not for them, for *him* alone.   And 'tis
The same on earth.   Ten thousand sow,
And bear the toil and pain, but one proud chief
The harvest reaps.   In point of glory earth
Is much like Hell.

                The first excitement o'er
At his approach and entrance to his seat
Of royal state, with dignity composed
And kingly grace, a moment Satan sat,

And viewed with coolness but with eagle eye
The vast assembly ; slowly rising then,
Another full and searching look bestowed.
And with commanding mein prepared to speak.
  A deathlike silence hushed each whispering word
And rustling garment, e'en the breath and pulse ;
For all with eager ear sat fixed to catch
The earliest word that should reveal to them
The mystery of this call, to meet in haste
And in such numbers vast.

                          "My Lords," said he,
" The pillars of our realm, the flower, the elite
" Of Hell, and once the elite of Heaven, who drained
" That world of all her better blood when we
" Retired—a sweet revenge for all th' affronts
" Bestowed on us before we left.   It gives
" Me pleasure, yes, the greatest pleasure her·
" To find such proofs of loyalty throughout
" Our vast domain.   Receive our thanks for this
" Response.   The welfare of our realm has called
" Us here ; for Hell is yours as well as mine ;
" And all encroachments on our vested rights,
" Or those inherent, should be met with front
" Unbroken, and with firm resolve, against
" Whatever foe may rise, with ceaseless war,
" And fiercest battle to contend, till he
" Shall quit the field and leave us undisturbed.
" Or, failing this, by arts of shrewdest kind
" To circumvent and foil his every scheme,
" Till, wearied, he shall yield as if by force
" Repelled ; or, if not yielding, shall the strife
" Prolong through ages, without one success ;

" While we grow strong despite this border war.
 " But we had hoped t' advance, and gain new ground
" And hold, and introduce at will our own
" Peculiar institutions. For in Hell,
" As well you know, our institutions are
" Peculiar all." (She is the mother of
This precious brood.) " And some of these at least
" We hoped, and still do hope t' propagate
" To provinces to be annexed ; for we
" Had thought again that destiny was on
" Our side, and that we should in time annex
" All other realms, and thus our race,
" Our heaveno-hellish blood, enlarged, should reign supreme.
" But in our little province Earth, which we
" Have held these years with undisputed sway,
" Of late some tumult has arisen, which ye
" Have heard by vague report, but now, with stamp
" Official, called the cause of ' TRUTH ON EARTH
" AND RIGHTEOUSNESS ;' a scheme of our great Foe
" In Heaven."—And here the vast assembly burst
At once at sound of that great hated name expressed,
With fierce and deadly rage.—They hissed, they groaned,
They tore the suffering ground, and uttered words
Of cursing known alone in Hell.—" And," he
Continued, " this appears a scheme, a deep
" And studied plot, which bodes no future good
" To me or you. All opposition to
" Our rightful sway before, has been
" In isolated breaks, resulting thence
" In trivial harm, and easily subdued.
" So we in truth have reigned from Adam till
" The present hour.
                    Ye know how Adam fell,

" An easy prey, and how the sons of God
" By daughters fair of men were overcome ;
" And how we gathered in a harvest rich
" And unexpected at the flood.   Ye know
" Moreover, how on Shinar's plains, men soon
" Forgot the words of Noah, and began
" To build a tower to lift its head to heaven ;
" And how from thence we were adored as gods,
" And walked abroad in open day confessed,
" Bewhile the altars of our rival foe
" Were driven to rocks and caves and desert wastes,
" And his lone worshipers, the scoff of all,
" Were ever hunted down, and rooted out
" From earth."
                              And here a shout arose that tore
The concave of the infernal world, and shook
The solid ground ; a shout, compared with which,
The greatest shouts of earth, were but the hum
Of bees, or fèline purrings at the hearth
Of winter's eve.   It crashed from hill to hill,
From mount to mount, and bellowed direful through
Those regions vast ; and spread alarm among
The distant damned, and died away at last
Like warring seas.—Such relish is in Hell
For goodness overcome.
                              " But here's a plot,
" I fear," continued Satan, " tame at first
" 'Tis true, and simple, but which may evolve
" By skill and power almighty, such a play
" As earth has never known before, nor Hell.
" The first act seems beginning ; all the rest
" Is myst'ry, wrapped in darkness ; far beyond
" The ken prophetic of the greatest sage

" Of Heaven or earth or Hell ; but which the lapse
" Of years in slow succession may unfold,
" In separate acts, but yet connected in
" One grand design, till drama-like, the whole
" Shall be displayed, and end in ruin full
" And final to us all.
          " But how, or what,
" Or when, we know not. This we know, and shall
" Forget not soon, that when the curse went forth
" On man, a promise found its way therewith,
" ' THE WOMAN'S SEED SHALL BRUISE THE SERPENT'S HEAD.'
" Quite simple words, but of tremendous power !
" They rang through Hell, and shook her deep and dark
" Foundations, giving awful signs of some
" Approaching ill.
          " And should this be a plot
" To this effect, it must by counter plot
" Be met ; for war we will not now advise.
" But first, *is* this a plot, distinct from breaks
" Of isolated kind, which have no force
" Beyond themselves ? The facts will cast some light.
" Then first, in Ur of Chaldees Terah dwelt ;
" And with his household left his native land
" And dwelt in Haran, nothing strange ; but then
" His son, next called of God, removed again
" And dwelt in Canaan, far from all his kin,
" And left his gods behind ; and altars built
" To worship our great foe. Yet no alarm,
" But rather pity, and the laugh of Hell ;
" That he, who held or boasted that he held
" Omnipotent control of Heaven and earth,
" Should have but *one* to bear his name, and build
" Him altars, while we, ' conquered,' had the rest

" Of Adam's race. He *did* seduce *this one,*
" The gain to him was pitiful and weak,
" Unworthy of that boastful name 'Supreme.'
" The loss to us was but a drop from out
" Of ocean, neither missed nor cared for, but
" Resigned with ease, and richly paid in mirth.

   " A famine came and southward drove the pet
" To Egypt, where his blood had stained the soil,
" And Sarah been a princess of the land,
" His comely wife, and worshiped us again,
" Had not another fact appeared, and God
" Rebuked the king, ' Touch not the anointed one.
" Nor do my prophet harm.'
                              " This startled us.
" For Abel and a thousand others fell
" At once, but he's preserved unharmed : besides,
" Some words were dropped ; ' A blessing shalt thou be ;
" A nation great, and known through all the earth ;
" And dispossess the Canaanite ; and dwell
" In that rich land.' For what ? For aught we know
" To work our fall, and send us back to Hell.
" A thousand altars then may rise for one ;
" And worshipers in numbers as the sand ;
" And undermine, and push us from the earth.

   " Again : ' Go take thy son and offer him
" A sacrifice to me.' We heard with joy,
" And fullest throb of hope ; believing he
" Would sure refuse, and be destroyed.
" But no ! with steadfast eye and steady step
" But aching heart, he took the boy, the wood,
" The knife, and journeyed to the fatal spot ;
" Prepared the wood, and bound the child, and raised
" The knife, and would have finished the command,

" Had not his hand been held, and he released
" By God himself from this tremendous call.
  " Our hopes were dashed, and we thrown back in deep
" Perplexity at this mysterious deed.
" It seemed a freak of arbitrary will ;
" But yet a *meaning* may be couchant there ,
" A meaning that some future day may show.
  " Moreover, angels oft were seen from Heaven
" In close communication.　Sometimes God
" Himself descended, and with voice distinct
" Encouraged and approved with mystic words ,
" ' Fear not ; I am thy sun and shield.'　And he
" Was prospered, and became a prince, despite
" Our machinations for his fall.　He died ;
" And left his seed and faith behind.　His race
" Expanded, and mysteriously were sent
" To Egypt, where they might have mingled with
" That race, and there been lost as drops upon
" The face of ocean ; but they mingled not,
" But kept distinct, and grew a multitude,
" And threatened to eat out that race ; at least,
" To overtop them as the cane o'ertops
" The humble weed ; until our king, alarmed—
" I think he's here."—All eyes were instant turned
And rivited upon him as he sat
In ghastly paleness, running o'er in mind
With frenzied spirit, all his acts on earth,
His mock of God, the plagues, and Red Sea grave—
" Our king essayed to crush them and destroy ;
" But like the rebel flower they grew beneath
" His feet ; and with a high and mighty hand
" Went out of Egypt, 'mid the bitter wail
" Of mourning for her eldest born and slaughter of

" Her gods.
     " But lo ! their leader seemed to miss
" His road, and senseless marched against the sea ;
" And there pent up, was thought an easy prey.
" But note another fact.   When Egypt's hosts
" Pursuing pressed their rear, with eager scent
" Of battle, spoil and lust, the opposing sea
" Divided ; and the hosts of Israel marched
" In safety down within the depths, and found
" A path all smoothed and hardened to their feet ;
" And moved in comfort to the other shore
" Between the crested walls of ocean waves
" In light effulgent from a flaming cloud ;
" Bewhile the Egyptians making hot pursuit,
" Were wrapped in darkness, plagued and terrified ;
" And at the dawn of day were whelmed beneath
" The waves returning ; and at rising sun
" No trace of them was seen, save here and there
" A body or a garment floating, or
" A helm or shield, washed up by ceaseless wave.
" Alas ! abashed, alarmed we fled, we fled
" The field.   The gods of Egypt fell ; Jehovah reigned.
  " Again, we hoped the wide and arid waste,
" The wilderness, that lay before them would
" By thirst and hunger overcome and blot
" Them out from earth.   But no ! a tree, cast in,
" Made bitter waters sweet ; and bread distilled
" From heaven along with dew : and e'en the rock
" Gave water at the call of Moses and
" The touch of his mysterious rod.
      " Again,
" At Rephidim, we stirred up Amalek,
" A numerous host, to extirpate at once

" The hated race. But Joshua in the field,
" And Moses on the mount with hands uplift,
" O'ermastered him, and swept like chaff before
" The wind. And now a curse hangs over him ;
" The race of Amalek to be extinct ;
" And e'en his name at length shall perish from
" The earth. We sought for victory and won
" A curse. What means it ? Is there nothing here ?
　" At Horeb we had thought to make the host
" Our own ; and while their leader was upon
" The mount, in talk with God, a calf we made
" By Aaron, and the host adored, and eat
" And drank and rose to play. We thought all safe,
" And that our work was done ; and though the race
" Might keep distinct, yet *us* they would adore
" Instead of God. But 'twas in vain ; for lo !
" Their leader, after long delay, appears
" Within the camp ; and with a sharp reproof,
" And slaughter of a thousand, less or more,
" Brought back the fickle tribes to God again :
" A thing not known before since time began.
　" Ere this, when nations fell to worship us
" Through images, or beasts, or sun, or stars ;
" Or rather *rose* to worship us ;—for 'tis,
" We hold, a *rise* to worship us, a *fall*
" To worship God.—Ere this, we say, when we
" Had once gained this important point, we held
" Our own ; and ever kept the field, and laughed
" To scorn our foe, 'Almighty' called, and half
" Believed by some. We held the nations fast
" To our allegiance, never more to break
" And turn to God again. But now, what see
" We ? Why not be alarmed ? A nation won,

" And thought secure, back-sliding at a word,
" And seeking God again, and that with tears
" Of deepest degradation.   Is not this
" A new, a startling fact ; without its peer
" Within the Books of Hell ; more ominous
" Than aught befell our cause in Egypt or
" The sea ?   What's this but presage of
" Some time to come, when idols shall be thrown
" As chaff away, and we neglected thence,
" The scorn of all the servile hosts of Heaven ?"

Here Satan faltered in his speech, his lips,
Compressed and quivering, and his shaking frame
And bloodshot eye, showed rage and fury scarce
Controlled, and on the point of bursting all
The bounds that decency and policy imposed.
Amazed, all eyes were fixed, and though
The host were hardened by the scenes of Hell,
And every nerve was iron, yet all cheeks
Were blanched, and every knee its fellow smote,
Lest on themselves his passion fierce should fall,
And they be rent to fragments in his ire
For want of other foes.
                              A moment's pause
Ensued, a silence fearful, such as Hell
Alone can know.   In even scale awhile
His passion hung.   It turned at length ; a sense
Of what and where he was prevailed ; and he
Resumed ; and then the pale and speechless host
Took breath.
                         " And when the spies returned from search
" Of Canaan, and declared the land, though good,
" Yet filled with armed men, of stature vast,

" That dwelt in cities walled to heaven, to whom
" They seemed as grasshoppers ; and never could
" Subdue that warlike race, and raze those walls,
" And enter in and thence possess the land,
" And ghastly fear, and weeping seized the host ;
" And when, rebellion rising in the camp,
" The disaffected tribes threw off the yoke
" Of Moses, and proposed a leader new,
" And quick return to Egypt, whence they came :
" When this occurred, what hopes were ours ! We thought
" Again our ends obtained, that they would spurn
" Henceforth the rod of Moses, and the robes
" Of Aaron, and return, and be no more
" Enthralled with priestly rules and separate laws
" Of worship ; but be ours for evermore,
" Or if not this, if God would not resign
" Them to our power, as he has done with all
" The other nations of the earth, yet they,
" Provoking to the utmost, would be swept
" At once away by his avenging hand,
" We hoped, from earth, and thus relieve us of
" The fear of future ills from Abram's race.
  " But no : The deep could leave its bed to drown
" A world, and his exterminating wrath
" Burned hot on Sodom. We ourselves know well
" The fury of his ire, implacable
" Before, upon his foes. His ire ! We felt
" Its utmost, unrelenting stroke, when foiled
" In battle on the plains of Heaven. No truce
" To us : no gracious terms vouchsafed of peace ;
" Unasked 'tis true ; but yet, if offered, would
" Have been received, if on conditions such
" As due to vanquished foes of merit high ;

3

" As left us masters of ourselves, and gave
" Us room sufficient for our empire in
" Some spacious quarter of his Heaven. But no ;
" Instead of that, we felt the direful shock
" Of Thunderbolts, in his relentless rage,
" Tho' overthrown ; and keenest torture from
" His arrows, barbed and sticking fast within
" Our souls. No truce !—We fled, but he pursued ;
" And not content with that, his engines swift
" And dreadful on our suffering rear, and all
" The towers and bastions as we passed in flight
" Precipitate toward Heaven bounds, opened on
" Our broken lines with fire destructive, and
" In quick succession shot forth ponderous orbs `
" Of death, and lightning shafts, that spread dismay
" And direst havoc through our myriad hosts,
" And overthrew anew the overthrown ;
" Till forced, we leaped the abyss that landed us
" In Hell. And *now* no truce ! for yet his hate
" Insatiate pursues the vanquished here ;
" Pursues, although we were the glory of
" His realm, in worth his equal, if not so
" In power, the elite of Heaven. And still no truce
" To us. And yet this dastard, slavish crew,
" Toward them, how quick his anger is appeased '
" A prayer of Moses sets all right again,
" Or if not wholly right, yet so far right
" As spares the miscreant race. And though the fate
" Announced, is forty years of travel, and
" The death of all rebelling ere they reach
" The Promised Land, yet this preserves it still,
" And much to our dismay ; for who cannot
" But see that this will leave a nation young

" And vig'rous, trained by Moses, pious called,
" Though mean we deem ; but yet adverse to us,
" And far less likely to espouse our cause
" Than their devoted sires ?

                 " From all these facts,
" And others, meaning less or more, compared
" And pondered, we may further judge,
" That FIRST ; 'tis not the individuals that
" Our wily foe intends to save, but 'tis
" The race of Abram. 'Tis his seed that he
" Intends to keep on earth ; and SECOND : that
" The use is future. How far future who   •
" Can tell ? The longer time, the mightier is
" The growth. For where's the nation yet that has
" Been blessed by Abram's seed ? And THIRD : what else
" Soe'er is meant by this conjectured scheme,
" This system of events begun and yet
" To be produced, it means no good to us :
" But good, perhaps unbounded good to man.
" They say that 'mongst the attributes of God
" There's one called MERCY, which can pardon sin.
" ('Twas ne'er vouchsafed to us ; and hence we know
" It not, nor wish to ; if the knee must bend,
" And we must beg, submissive at his feet.)
" No never, never that. I'd rather feel
" Ten thousand thousand Hells than fall thus low,
" And ask for pardon at his tyrant hands.
" So say you all."—And here all bowed assent,
But with a ghastly smile, and look forlorn
That told how desolate they felt their lot,
How sure that hope to them could never come.—
" But sinful men, may-hap, will pray and seek

" Forgiveness of their sins.   And this strange plot—
" Who knows ?—may be a scheme of mercy for
" That very end—that GOD CAN PARDON SIN.
" ' THE WOMAN'S SEED SHALL BRUISE THE SERPENT'S HEAD.' "
" And who can say but from this race a seed
" May come."—And here each face throughout the host
Grew ghastly pale ; and faintness seized all hearts ;
And Satan staggered to his seat and fell
As struck with death.   A pause ensued.   And Hell
Seemed motionless and dead.   No sign or hope
Of life appeared ; a second death seemed like
A pall to settle on the myriad throng ;
While all without was trembling and despair,
As if the final judgment had arrived.
Within, it was one awful charnal house ;
A scene that Hell had never known before.
The throng had swooned, and lay in ranks immense,
Like boundless forest felled by winds of heaven.
Their glaring eye-balls in their sockets set,
Their hellish features, stiff and sunken, shot
The direst horror through the failing nerves
Of hardiest devil venturing there to view
The unwonted sight.   At length a gasp of life
Returning, sighed and gurgled through the throng.
Then all was still again : another gasp—
And still another—and at length revived,
Each silently resumed his seat ; and gazed
Upon his fellow, stupified, and yet
Alarmed.   And Satan his ; and sat upright.
   Such wondrous power inherent in that word
The SEED ; whose import none could tell, but all
Could feel.   A death-like silence still prevailed,

And Hell for once was humble and subdued.
Not long ; for burning thoughts soon coursing through
Their veins, and passion fierce reacting strong,
And waking every feverish pulse again,
Restored the temper lost ; awakened zeal
To speak, and keenest gust to hear.
  " The woman's seed shall bruise the serpent's head ;
" And who can say," continued Satan, " but
" The SEED may come from out this race ;
" Whose ponderous heel, though bruised by us, may grind
" Us into powder ? or perhaps he'll tread us down
" With foot resistless to a lower Hell
" Than we have ever dreamed.   And yet this can
" Not be ; for none but God can safe contend
" With our Almighty strength ; which once we tried
" Upon the plains of Heaven, successful, and
" Withstood the fiercest onsets of his hosts
" Angelic ; led by chiefs of mightiest deeds,
" And deemed in strength but less than God himself.
" And yet we held our ground, not one short hour,
" But thrice the space that measures day and night ;
" And had been fighting still, or, conquering, driven
" Them from their Heaven to this our Hell ; had not
" The Son, alarmed, flew to the rescue, and
" With direst arms, unknown before, the scale
' Of Battle turned.   If such could not o'ermatch
" Our godlike strength, then how can mortal man ?
" And yet the threat'ning stands, ' the *woman's seed*
" Shall bruise the serpent's head.'   What is the seed ?
" And then the bruising what ?   And whence the strength
" To do the deed ?   'Tis mystery all : for God
" Can only do, if that he can, what seems
" That threat to mean.   " It must be man, must

" Be God, else 'twill not be the SEED, or else
" Our heads will not be bruised ; be sure of that,
" In short, it must be man or not the Seed
" And then it must be God or not the deed.
" But how can it be both at once ? both God
" And man, the Seed, both God and man ? We know
" Not ; nor can e'en conjecture give relief
" To our perplexed and painful thoughts. But we
" Can see this much, that through this race our shrines
" And altars and our worship might be spurned,
" Ourselves be made the scorn of all on earth,
" And thence the scorn of Heaven. But yet the threat
" Seems something more, ' A bruising of the head.'
" Perhaps 'tis but a threat of idle words,
" T' encourage man and frighten us the while,
" And not intended to be put in force.
" Yet this is not like our great foe ; for what
" He says we too well know he means. We say
" 'Tis mystery ; and here we give it up ;
" And wait for future times to solve the doubt.
    " Meantime, we must be watchful, and exert
" Our utmost skill to thwart his every plan,
" And turn his purposes to our account.—
    " And now permit me to digress, and note
" The immediate cause of my alarm.—
                                    " I've had
" A dream."—And here an inadvertent smile
Ran through the assembly, and unconscious eyes
Met eyes, to think a dream should e'en be *named,*
Much more relied upon as ground of fear.—
Though all know well the dreams of Hell, yet none
Regard them as of grave portent ; but count
Them as mere ravings of the spirit damned

When reason for a moment drops the rein.
O! dreams are rife in Hell. They roam abroad,
With head erect, and fiery eyes ; and roll
Their snaky folds, and bare their deadly fangs ;
And dart their bloody tongues ; and hot pursue
The sleeping, fleeing wretch o'er desert tracts,
Through caverns deep, o'er frozen mountain tops,
And fiery plains.—He flees, he flees! And they
Pursue, pursue.—His vigor fails at length—
He breathless falls.—They seize him, and he shrieks,
And starts bewildered from his frightful couch,
And dares not sleep again, though dead for rest.
　　Some dreams steal softly as the evening dew,
And bear the spirit up, and gently waft him
To the fields of bliss.—He treads anew
His native Heaven. He breathes its vital air ;
And rushes fiercely to the living springs ;
And scoops the sparkling stream ; and eager brings
It to his burning lips ; *in vain!* then leaps
Impetuous to the bending trees, that hang
Exhaustless with the fruit of life. He plucks,
He eats—unsated still, till frantic grown,
He wakes, and finds himself in Hell.
　　　　　　　　　　　　　　　" I've had
" A dream," continued Satan, "not as dreams
" Are wont to come to us, a shadow ; but
" A substance tangible ; more like, it seemed,
" A living verity ; that wrought itself
" Upon my soul, and fixed it there as firm
" As thought or sense ; a dream—start not—a dream,
" If it may so be called ; or waking vision ; which
" Shall last as long as this my being lasts ;
" And which, mayhap, portends some dread event

" To me, and to us all perchance. Methought—
" But how can feeble words convey a dream?
" A dream we know can only be conveyed
" By being felt. Methought—but first permit
" Me to premise—'Twas after I had made
" The tour of Hell, to view anew the length
" And breadth of this our realm ; but more,
" To mark the state of all the posts, and view
" Official all the doings of our lords,
" To whom were given important trusts ; and to
" Allay what feuds might have arisen ; and to
" Exhort and urge to duty the remiss ;
" And to reward the faithful ; and to make
" What new arrangements time and progress might
" Require ; in short, to see that Hell was what
" It ought to be.
                    I need not here recall
" The whole ; nor could I, if disposed. Suffice
" To say, I found Hell prosperous ; far beyond
" What I had known before. I was amazed
" To note th' extent of our domain ; and could
" But take a hasty view of things ; and then
" To leave particulars to future day
" To be reported by the lord, or prince
" Who held control of each respective state.
    " Three years I spent—so vast the field !—yes, three
" Great years of Hell, on this exclusive task,
" And then the work was only seen, not done.
    " Returned, I sat within my palace hall ;
" The princes all had made report enjoined ;
" And each had brought the vast statistics of
" His charge ; and all had been recorded in
" The Books, thus kept. Amazement filled my soul

" To see the sum, the census of the damned.
  " I thought of Hell, how great, and said within
" Myself : ' Is this not Hell, great Hell that I
" Command, great Hell that I have builded up!
" If not as wide, yet populous as Heaven ;
" And promises a mightier growth henceforth.
" So, if I missed the throne of God I here
" A greater throne have found.   I envy not
" Our common foe his reign.   His reign ! how tame!
" His subjects, how devoid of noble aims !
" Fit subjects for fit king ; while here, we have
" The chivalry, the pure untainted blood,
" The aristocracy, high born, high bred,
" The choicest gems of all the universe.'
" 'Twas thus I thought, I thought within myself."
  And here a smile of approbation ran
Along the seated ranks ; and pride and self
Conceit, swelled every bosom, and induced
A kind of faith, that they, the damned, debauched
And worthless, were in excellence above
The holy angels of the living God.
Such, such the folly of the Chivalry !
The chivalry of earth, and chivalry
Of Hell.   They meet and estimate themselves,
And vote their rank without a blush.   If aught
(If pity had no place for spirits lost)
Could ever cause a smile in Heaven, 'tis such
A sight as this.
                " And while my breast was fired
" With present things, and greater yet to come,"
Continued Satan, " Sudden sleep came o'er
" Me : not indeed our usual sleep, disturbed
" And fitful, but a sleep of sound repose,

" Like that of Heaven, our former quiet home.
" (You all know that, though never tasted here.)
 " Methought," said he, " that I was on the earth,
" And stood upon a mount in Araby ;
" And saw below, the tents of Israel, spread
" In goodly prospect ; and in order planned
" With wond'rous skill.   I saw her thousands in
" And round the tents, enjoying ease, or close
" At needful tasks, as inclination or
" As duty called.   'Twas in the heat of day.
" The cloud, called shekena, was spread above,
" And gave a cooling freshness to the air,
" Not much unlike the bracing air of Heaven.
" I saw, besides, the tent of worship, where
" Of late had been set up by our great foe,
" His daily service ; which consists, as all
" Who hear me are aware, of offerings made
" Of beasts and birds of harmless kind ; the lamb,
" The goat, the ox, the dove, the pigeon, and
" What else the people bring of wine and oil
" And cakes ; all offered up by Aaron and
" The minor priests, to him they worship as
" Their God.
   " 'Twas tame ! 'twas stupid ! and I said
" Within myself, ' *And is this all ?*   Is this
" The best that God can do to raise
" Him in the estimation of the world?
" A stupid worship, offering stupid beasts
" Alone.   Some might be used, if with them mixed
" Were those of higher nature, and of powers
" Superior ; the noble steed, that scours
" The plain, the lion king, and tiger strong,
" That scatter terror through the timid herds,

"And battle ever for supreme control ;
" The eagle bold, that dwells among the peaks,
" And soaring up to heaven renews his fires
" By bathing in the sun ; the furious boar,
" That braves the forest king : and mightier yet,
" Behemoth and leviathan ; and last,
" And worthier still, a human sacrifice,
" A man or woman, or a tender child,
" Or virgin fair. If these were mixed therewith,
" As we require on earth, methought our foe
" Might somewhat vie with us in homage paid.
  " But no ! These stupid beasts, abundant found,
" And cheap ! No costly noble offering does
" Their God require.—And is this all ? if so,
" Methought, ' it is unworthy of a God,
" And will forever be the laugh of Hell.
  " But *is* this all ? the thought sprang in my mind,
" Which now seemed luminous, prophetic grown,
" ' PERHAPS IT IS NOT ALL. It may,' methought,
" ' Foreshadow something yet to come, a kind
" Of worship differing far from what we have
" As yet or seen or heard on earth ; a kind
" To which all these may be a key. These beasts
" By Aaron slain, this blood, and wine, and oil,
" These cakes, and sheaves, and fruits, and firstlings of
" The flocks and herds ; these feasts, and jubilees.
" And cleansing rites, and vows ; the running stream ;
" And goats, one slain, the other led and left
" In desert land, upon whose head the hand
" Of priest was laid ; the sacred fire, the ark,
" And vail, the mercy seat, the cloud by day,
" And fire by night, the pascal lamb, but roast,
" Not boiled ; and blood besprinkled o'er the doors,

" All spotless when alive, and slain, a feast
" For all, (but of unbroken bone ;) with herbs
" Of bitter taste, and bread unleavened, eat
" With sandals on, and staff in hand, and loins
" Begirt ; the show bread, ever ready on
" The table of the Lord ; the day of GREAT
" ATONEMENT, when the priest with blood of goat
" And bullock passes through the vail, and there
" Before, and on the mercy seat, sheds forth
" The crimson drops ; in priestly garments clad ;
" The altar, where the offerings burn, the bread
" From heaven, (the manna,) given as daily food ;
" The parted sea ; the water-yielding rock ;
" And Aaron MADE high priest ; and e'en the camp
" Itself of Israel, and the sep'rate tribes,
" With Moses at their head, commanding all :
" All these may be a key, may be a key
" To something yet to come ; and may explain
" That something when revealed, as nothing else
" Could do, a worship, mayhap, worthy of a God.
    " And as I gazed, and saw the whole,
" In doubt to fear or laugh, lo ! Aaron stood
" Before the altar.   In his hand he held
" The shoulder of a lamb, an offering brought,
" Ordained by law, to cleanse a leper vile,
" The ' heave shoulder ;' and in the basket lay
" The ' wave breast,' brought with oil and cakes. He raised
" The shoulder thus, in up-right line ; when, lo !
" It left a track in air, a shadow of
" A staff, or pillar more it seemed.   He took
" The breast and waved it thus, in even line.
" It left a shadowy track ; and both combined ·
" Produced a cross, a shadow of a cross,

" And stained with blood.   I shrank instinct with fear,
" That cross, a simple thing yet full of dread,
" I felt a pang unknown before, as if
" The fingers of eternal death, unseen,
" Were twisting out of place the cords of life.
   " Revived at length, and shattered nerves composed,
" I saw the cross, the blood, the leper cleansed.
" I spell-bound strove in vain to fly ; I thought
" What possible connection could there be
" Between a cross and cleansing of a sore
" And dying leper ?   ' Yet,' methought, ' the fact
" ' Is so, at least, to-day.'   Perplexed, I left
" To future time to solve the doubt.   And then
" ' The blood, what means the blood upon the cross ? '
" I mused, still spell-bound held, and half afraid,
" When, lo ! from out the tents of Judah came
" A lion of the mightiest strength, and crouched ·
" Beneath the cross, in attitude to spring,
" As tiger in the path of traveller
" Belate.   He sprang not then, but waiting seemed
" His own convenient time to spring, and rend
" Me as a kid.   Lost !! Lost ! I seemed ! all hope
" Of future being fled.   And next, it seemed
" I soared aloft, was worshiped as a god,
" By all on earth and all the hosts above.
" And age on age elapsed, and still I rode
" Sublime ; and ruled the spheres ; · and nested in
" The stars ; and seemed regaining fast the height
" I'd lost, of glory and of power.   And more,
" The throne itself of God, to which we all
" Aspire, seemed just within my grasp.   I felt,
" In fine, inherent power, and growing might,
" That gave full promise of eternal sway,

" And high possession of the gorgeous Heaven
" And bright and awful mount that God now holds,
" When at my feet the gods of Heaven should bow,
" Or fly on lightning wing to do my will ;
" While I should revel there in wanton ease,
" And to eternity, take in my fill
" Of every pleasure, drawn from every source
" Of luxury that Heaven affords, and given
" To me through every sense.

        " My soul was fired ;
" My appetites seemed gaining strength immense,
" And making preparation for the lusts
" Within my reach : When, lo ! the cross appeared
" Again. The shadow of a cross 'twas once ;
" But now 'twas fixed and tangible. Its foot
" Reached down to Hell ; its top reached up to Heaven.
" Its arms extended wide, as if t' embrace
" The universe of God ; a wonder great
" To earth and Heaven and Hell. And as I gazed
" The cross grew luminous, and lit with rays
" Resplendent all the works of God. The stars
" Retired unseen, and suns were swallowed up,
" Their glorious light, not needed now, withdrawn.
" The cross was all in all. A cloudless and
" Eternal sun it seemed. When, lo ! a voice,
" Me thought, ' 'TIS FINISHED ! ' and the frame at once
" Of universal nature shook, as if
" Its end had come. A crash came up from Hell,
" And groans, as if her adamantine face
" Had broken in, and she was crushed with all
" Her living millions ; crushed and ground beneath
" The ponderous foot of our great foe ; and I,
" It seemed, that instant FELL LIKE LIGHTNING DOWN

" FROM HEAVEN. And as I fell—not flew—but fell,
" Methought I saw the jaws of bottomless
" Damnation, yawning wide, with fiery gulf,
" To swallow me beyond all reach of hope.
" This woke me, horror-struck.

      " 'Twas thus I dreamed,
" If dreamed, or felt, if felt, or saw, if saw,
" As in a trance with open eyes, within
" My palace hall. And yet I feel it is
" Not all a dream, a phantom merely of
" The brain ; but has a meaning which we must
" Divine. And if portending ill, as needs
" It must, that ill we must elude ; or if
" Not that, at least defer till latest day
" Of possible extent. You have the dream,
" As far as words can show a dream ; and yet
" It is no more the dream than feeble words
" Describing pain are pain itself. I this inferred
" From what I dreamed, or felt, or saw : That ILL
" More dreadful than we yet have known, is kept
" In store for me ; and if for me, not more
" For me, than you ; for if our kingdom shall
" Be overthrown, a common ruin will
" Involve us all.

     " But still, to put beyond
" The shadow of a doubt the question of
" Portent, before I sent the call that you've
" Obeyed—(Such loyalty scarce Heaven itself
" Can boast)—I took the consecrated cup,
" The great Divining Cup of Hell. I cast
" Within, the dregs ; then whirled the cup with due
" Observance of the magic rules that make
" The future sure, from mystic signs. I quick

" Inverted it : Then paused awhile with awe.
" At length I took it up to see what there
" Might be revealed, pertaining to our dream.
" I looked within, and shudered to behold
" The self-same imagery ; the tented tribes,
" The cross, the lion, and my fall from Heaven.
" Beside, the cup ran blood, alarming sight !
" And then I took the consecrated urn."
  This urn and cup were wonderments of Hell,
The work alone of Mulciber ; for who
But he was able to design, or skill
Possessed, to execute such samples of
Amazing art ? of ample size, and cast
Of massy gold, and burnished to the height
Of art in Hell or Heaven ; and laid, besides,
With rarest gems from out the choicest mines
Of Hell. They flashed with light of richest hue,
And filled with rapture every eye that saw.
  Upon the forms of each were wrought with skill
Unequalled, many a scene in Heaven, to hold
In mind the glorious state from which they fell.
For none desire to lose remembrance of
Their former joys, though now in pain ; but all,
E'en Devils lost, find some relief, though mixed
With pangs, in counting o'er the scenes of days
Gone by, of happy days though never to
Return.
        But Satan most was wrought thereor
In acts of high renown in Heaven.
He rode sublime amidst the endless throng
That met to celebrate the birth of Time ;
Which in procession vast, to music moved ;
To music, such as Heaven alone could give,

With banners waving, and with shouts that rocked
The very hills, a prominence to him
Accorded for his worth esteemed, and deep
And searching wisdom, by assent of all.
  Again, appeared embossed in living forms,
The day to Satan most of note in Heaven ;
The day when he was placed above the Sons
Of God, the high Arch-Angels of that realm
Immense ; the highest he, though others high.
None envied, for he'd reached the goal ; he had
Excelled in all that God, or angels love ;
In might, in heart, in intellect ; and all
Were happy to concede his place ; and God
Himself from off his holy mount, distinct
Proclaimed him first Arch-Angel of the host
Of Heaven, on that triumphal day.
                                    And then
Were given him all the ensigns of his rank ;
The rich regalia of a prince thus high ;
A crown, a sword, and robes of dazzling white,
And royal purple of the richest dye,
And, last, not least, assigned him as his due,
The Urim and the Thummim ;   oracles
Of old renown, which gave responses of
Unerring truth.
                  All this, and more, in gems
And gold in high relief was wrought thereon ;
Amazing skill ! and hightened by the rich
And glorious scenery of Heaven.—" I took,"
Continued he, " the consecrated Urn."—

  This Cup and Urn were consecrated each
To serve as oracles for future times ;
4

From which events to come, or near or more
Remote, might be revealed by lot or signs
Of such significance as left no doubt
Of their approach ; and made as substitutes
In Hell, for those great oracles in Heaven,
The Urim and the Thummim, lost by him,
Alas! in his defection, when he fell.

The day was great, of consecration ; great
In multitude, and in atrocious deeds.
'Twas more like Hell than any day before.
The work had all been done, and Mulciber
Had brought them finished to his lord; his work,
The greatest yet achieved, resplendent to
The eye in living light and gorgeous hues,
And to the touch, of finish exquisite,
And mould of highest taste.

                              Th' appointed day
Had come to demonize, and place them in
The dark arcanum of the mysteries;
And must remain, and be consulted not
But on occasions rare, of import vast,
And such as should concern their greatest weal.

They both were borne on high ; and all the great,
The princes, potentates of that vast realm,
Moved after in procession such as earth
Knows not ; and then, the lower powers, in line
Of endless length. And having reached at last
The destined goal, the vessels stayed, and round
Them wheeled this line immense. And as each passed
He cursed, (such cursing earth can never know,)
And blasphemed God ; decried the Holy Ghost,
And called on Erebus, the lowest deep,
For aid, for potent aid.

This done, the Cup
And Urn, thus charged with devilish influence,
Were borne by Satan's hands, as priest of Hell—
(For there the spiritual and temporal pow'rs
Are both combined in one, one head supreme,
And Satan claims and holds that high estate ;
And thence the precedent found way to earth,
A spiritual power and temporal in one.)
The cups were borne by Satan's hands, and placed
With due solemnity from out the sight
Of vulgar, nay, of princely eyes. This done,
The day passed on with Hellish feats, of arms
And gladiatorial shows, that shocked that world
Itself ; and closed with crucifixions dire
Of thrice ten thousand thousand helpless souls
Of lower caste.

" The consecrated Urn
" I took," continued Satan, " and within—
" I, fearful, cast the fatal lots. On one
" I wrote 'The Woman's seed ;' the next, 'The Tribes
" 'Of Israel ;' and the third, 'Of Judah ;' and
" The fourth, 'The Cross and Lion ;' on the fifth
" I wrote 'The bruising of the Serpent's head ;'
" And on the sixth and last, 'My fall from Heaven.'
" Six lots in all, thus named, the rest were blanks.
" And then I shook the Urn, and mingled all
" With strictest care, until they seemed involved
" Beyond the reach of utmost chance to bring
" Them up again from out that mass, thus mixed,
" Within the number e'en of millions drawn ;
" Much less in order as they reached the Urn
" I blindly drew six times, six lots in all,

" And lo! in order as I put them in,
" The 'Seed,' the 'Tribes,' and that of 'Judah' came ;
" The 'Cross and Lion;' next the 'bruising' rose,
" And last and more appalling still, my 'fall,'
" My direful fall from Heaven.   Alarmed, I gave
" The call that brought you here.   The common weal
" Demands our care.   This race, of late but slaves,
" This race—it must be so—is kept and fed
" And nourished up as instruments of our
" Great foe to work our utter ruin, and
" Of them the Tribe of Judah, and from this
" It seems the threatened seed must come—the seed
" To bruise ; and work our final fall ; and this
" To be achieved in some mysterious way
" Connected with a Cross, and stained with blood.
" Of this perchance the blood, by Aaron shed,
" In daily sacrifice is but a type.
    " This race, this hated race then, now in march
" Through Araby to Canaan's better land,
" Must be our care ; our care or to destroy,
" And quite expunge from off the face of earth ;
" Or better, mayhap, still, to take by guile,
" And quite transfer from him, our deadly foe,
" To us, for ever bound hereafter in
" Allegiance strong.   And then the seed if sprung
" Therefrom, shall not be his, but ours, to do
" Our will and turn his strength on HIM instead
" Of us ; thus foiling this his scheme with arms
" Of his own make.   But it remains with you,
" As well as me, to judge.   Let each then speak
" His mind, in full debate ; propose, reject,
" And freely show his reasons for the same.
" The time requires our utmost thought, and cool

" Deliberation ; for a step too far,
" Or one not far enough, or made too soon,
" Or one not made in time, may work the loss
" Of all our hopes ; and leave us so involved
" That endless years may not repair the fault ;
" But like an avalanche, as each proceeds,
" Roll ruin waxing greater, heavier, more
" Tremendous still, for endless ages on
" Our undeserving heads.—But no ! this fate,"
Continued Satan,—and his form drew up
And showed its full gigantic size ; his eyes
Flashed fire ; and all his features gave full proof
Of direst rage within, a burning hell,
And deep determination to succeed—
" This fate shall not be ours," continued he,
" Shall not, for Hell has means exhaustless, and
" We'll bring to bear upon our foe and this
" One scheme of his, the skill of *all her gods*
" *Combined*, as yet untried against him, and
" We'll baffle all his efforts to destroy.
" Or failing this, we'll try another field ;
" We'll rouse the entire damned.   We'll ransack Hell,
" And scour the universe for arms, and break
" Resistless on his hosts, wherever found ;
" Or here in Hell, or through unbounded space,
" Or o'er the battlements of Heaven itself ;
" And sweep them, panic-struck, and overwhelmed,
" Like chaff ; and teach him, though he claims supreme,
" He may pursue too far a conquered foe."

And here the eloquence of Satan passed all bounds,
While he described the wreck of Hell
" Should they be wanting to themselves in care

And ceaseless effort in this time of need,
Of greatest need, this crisis in their weal ;
When all was being poised in even line ;
The scale was trembling, and 'twas theirs to sway
The beam, and cause their fate to rise, or fall,
To fall—then all was lost ! their doom was fixed !
The golden moment could not be recalled,
The haughty foe would tread upon their necks,
And drag them captive at his chariot wheels.
To rise—then they henceforth should roam abroad
As gods supreme, the victor foiled ; no more
Pent up in Hell ; but reaping pleasures full
And endless, mayhap, e'en in Heaven itself ;
With all the angels of the Living God
Subdued and subject to their will, and bound
To minister to their desires ; and God
Himself, retired and awed, should fear to let
His thunder loose lest they should storm his mount
And overcome."—Presumptuous words ! yet such
Is Hell.
            What more he said the Muse 'tempts not
To sing, as quite uneqal to the task.
For earth knows no such eloquence as Hell ;
Were spirits, lost 'tis true, and damned, but yet
Retain their mental powers but partially
Impaired : And Satan his ; most eloquent
Of all in Heaven before his fall.   Else he
Had not seduced such hosts of spirits wise
To hazzard certain bliss ; and to conspire
With him ; and risk it all in battle joined
Against Almighty God.—"The Muse 'tempts not."
Suffice to say, the vast assembly hung
Upon his words, which flowed like oil, and with

Persuasive force enchained them all. Then quick,
And breaking forth with rage, anon he starts
The wildest storm of passion. Driven to fury, all
Forth leaping from their seats, with beating wings,
And hand to hilt, and half-drawn blades
Exposed, and bloody visage, and an eye of fire,
Burst forth in tumult and the wildest shouts ;
Such shouts as only Hell could hear, or bear.
　　Again, he eased them down, as falling winds
The high tempestuous waves of ocean, lest
Their fury, overreaching every bound,
With wild delirium, should unfit them
For the call on hand, and thus defeat the cause
They came to save.
　　　　　　　The per-oration closed,
At length he sat. And then a shout went up,
Such shout as earth has never heard ; a shout,
Not made by feeble men, but spirits strong.
It rent the air, and shook the distant hills,
And rolled tumultuous over desert tracts,
And broke in echoes back with deafening roar,
Till Hell at large seemed answering with acclaim,
And fraught with furor of th' exciting scene.
　　Again, and then again the shout burst forth,
Midst waving wings, and storming feet, and shrieks
And yells, that could or would not be suppressed ;
Till wildest rage had run the round of three
Times three, and scarcely then their furious breasts
Were calmed, and order, broken, quite restored.
　　Such was the effect of eloquence in Hell.
O, Eloquence! artistic gift of God!
Vouchsafed for good, to rouse to virtue, and
The act of noble, god-like deeds ; or with

Enchanting phrase, to urge accepted truths,
Or those as yet unknown ; the power of mind
On mind ; first heard in Heaven, where throngs
Enchained by some high-gifted tongue forgot
All time and place ; and ravished by the spell
Of flowing words and clearest logic ; dressed
In richest drapery of thought, heard God
Set forth in all his wonderous ways, and high
Benificence for creature good ; or were
Engaged more firmly hence to do his will
And love and reverence him, as God Supreme ;
Or zealous made, to aim at greater hights
Of excellence of heart and mind, and make
More glorious still that glorious Heaven, their sure,
Their everlasting home.   " Artistic gift
Of God!"   But how perverted from its use
Divine, in earth and Hell! to make the worse
Appear the better cause ; to rob of right,
And move to wickedness the listening crowd.
" Such was the effect of eloquence in Hell."
    The furious current, ebbing out, at length
A calm ensued ; and all the multitude
In silence sat.   Each gathered up his thoughts,
Thus scattered, and his normal state of mind
And temper slowly gained.   Each was himself
Again ; and all took breath ; and waited what
Might next appear.—A pause.—The pause at length
Was fearful.   On that moment hung, perhaps,
The destiny of Hell.   And weighty thoughts
Began to press their spirits down ; and each
On other looked. with slow but wistful glance ;
Not forward to begin, but rather chose to hear ;
From modesty, not half so much as want,

Instinctive felt, of strength to oppose, or skill
To circumvent a foe so strong and wise
As God, th' omnipotent, omniscient God.
  Their courage sank to zero. Hell was nigh
To caving in, and would, could wisdom but
A lodgement find within their breasts ; but no :
A devil is not tamed by better thoughts ;
And brought to better deeds by reason's reign.
He runs his length of sin, and hurries on
Amain, nor stops his mad career till chains
Or thunder-bolts, confine, or awe him down.
'Twas thus with these. The ebb had run its course
And drained the spirit from their very souls.
They sat aghast, and hung their heads in deep
Despair ; not long ; for now the refluent wave
Appears, and slowly rises brimming up ;
And all again are ready to attempt
Some plan of force or fraud against their foe,
As best may be advised.
                         On Satan's right,
And near the steps that mounted to the throne,
Sat B'elzebub, who rose with stately mein,
And aspect grave ; a venerable god ;
With hoary locks, of massy giant frame,
And facial show of intellectual strength ;
But hard and wicked to the practised eye.
  " Your Majesty, and you my lords, may't please,
" I feel the force of what your highness has
" Advanced, for I am well aware our foe
" Implacable, contemplates to us some
" Dire harm, and this he fixed upon when first
" We drew to our allegiance in the bowers
" Of Eden, Adam and his youthful spouse.

" Chagrined at our success, and filled with rage,
" He swore an oath that shook the depths of Hell,
" That though successful then, the time should come
" When we should see the wreck of all our hopes,
" And find a deeper Hell proportioned to
" Our crimes : Why so ? Can we not foil again
" Whom foiled we once ? and if indeed that race
" Is destined for this use, I join with our
" Beloved Chief, that *they* must be our care.
" But how our care to work the end designed ?
" Shall we succeed by guile ? or furious sweep,
" In some unguarded moment, them from earth ?
" The mind of all should be expressed. And here
" Permit me to suggest that our high Chief
" Should put the needful propositions now
" To vote. For though 'tis true each one alone
" May err, yet all in conclave joined possess
" Infallibility." Here, here it is.
Infallibility ! first broached in Hell.
And save in Hell where could such doctrine have
Its birth ? and who but devils could or would
Bring such a doctrine in to curse the earth?
" Infallibility !" said B'elzebub.
And here each devil smiled a hellish grin ;
Instinct, forsooth, with future use of that
Infernal word. O Hell ! concoctor of
The woes of men ! This stands thy master work
Since Adam's fall ; an accident at first ;
But seized upon in after times to fill
The earth with woe. Infallibility,
Alas, alas ! through years of dreary length
With scarlet clad and drunk with blood of saints !
    Then Malcham rose and with confiding air

Proposed what all, he thought, would judge but right
To their beloved Chief, who was the head
(How great the boon to have it thus!) the head
Of both the spiritual and temp'ral powers :
'Twas this, he urged : that through all time to come
He shall be styled " His Holiness," as due
His piety and moral worth.—'Twas put
And carried with a rising vote, not one
Dissenting ; Satan, with a bend and bland
And self-complacent smile, received, well pleased,
The proffered prefix to his saintly name.
" His Holiness " shall be his style, at least
In documents of church, if not of state.
  That instant Satan's color went. He leaped
Upon his feet and drew his blade : " What's this ?"
Said he ; " What's this," I thought ; I thought I heard
A laugh suppressed.—But all were mute.—He stood.
Then Malcham, quick : " Your Holiness must have
" Mistook. 'Twas but an undertone of full assent."
  O Malcham ! falsest of the false ! " assent !"
When every devil scarce could hold his sides
From split of laughter. But " His Holiness "
Was soothed by Malcham's words, and soon resumed
His seat, and handed then his scribe, who sat
In front, a scroll, from which he, rising, read
In hieroglyphics writ, the sum of what
He wished should be proposed, rejected or
Received, as wisdom there combined might give
Its voice. For Satan, though imperious he
And haughty, ruled with dictatorial sway
For most, nor brooked advice of highest god
In Hell, or slightest interferance in
The acts of his despotic will, yet now,

Relaxed, as he perceived a crisis had
Arrived, e'en deigned to ask the mind and aid
Of all; not liberal grown, but conscious of
His want of skill and strength to meet alone the foe,
With whom the times gave warning he must soon
Contend; contend, or quit, forever quit
Perhaps, the field, belittled and disgraced
In sight of all the damned.   Two evils here
His stubborn autocractic will gave way,
He chose the least, and called on Hell for aid.
    The scroll, prepared, as read by scribe, thus ran :
" Whereas, a prophecy went forth, announced
" In Eden, that the woman's seed should bruise
" The serpent's head, the beast within whose form
" Concealed, we drew off man, and foiled our foe :
   " Whereas, portentous signs betoken some
" Dire harm from him about to fall on Hell :
   " Whereas, a race, from Abram sprung, and grown
" A nation strong, in Egypt nursed, and now
" In Araby, in emigrating march
" To Canaan's better land, in league with him
" Just now, and strangely fed by manna sent
" From Heaven, and watered from a fountain rock,
" At times, that pours out living springs at call
" For man and beast ; and strangely sheltered from
" The burning sun by an extended cloud,
" Which, luminous by night, shines forth, and lights
" The camp of Israel, through her hosts, when pitched,
" And guides them in their march, called sheckena :
   " Whereas, those signs with import not to be
' Gainsaid   seem plainly cent'ring on that race
" As source from which that harm, whate'er it be,
" Shall come, though how, or when, or where, we know

" Not : (yet our foe is wily, and may take
" Us by surprise), by us in conclave joined :
 " Resolved ; as giving full the sense of all
" The gods of Hell, that this impending harm
" Is nothing else than that intended blow
" In Eden threatened, called the bruising of
" The head, beyond all hope to crush us : and
 " Resolved again, that from that hated race
" That seed will come (if let alone) to do
" The bruising deed. And here again be it
 " Resolved, that Hell is virtuous, and Heaven
" Corrupt, CORRUPT! And further be it here ·
 " Resolved again, that Hell is amply worth
" Preserving ; and that we will never yield ;
" But to the last withstand him with what means
" Soever we can ply, of force or guile ;
" First guile, but failing this, then force ; yes, force ;
" Hell meeting Heaven in direst battle joined ;
" Jehovah foiled, mayhap, and Heaven our own.
 " Resolved again, though Heaven in some respects
" Might be preferred to Hell, yet only when
" Possessed by us, the chivalry : for 'tis
" The people makes the place. For who would dwell
" Of us, high bred, high born, among the tribes
" Of serviles found in Heaven, on equal terms ?
 " Resolved again : if from defence we should
" Aggressive prove, (who knows what chance of war
" Might bring about ?) and repossess our Heaven,
" Then our ' peculiar institutions ' shall
" Be planted there, and we amended for
" Our risk, and martial toil ; and lastly be't
 " Resolved, that here we pledge ourselves, whate'er
" May come, to prove us worthy of the Hell

" We rule ; to leave no means untried for our
" Defence, defence if but no more, or our
" Advancement should the fates decree.—And if
" We perish, it shall be at night-fall of
'' The bloodiest day that gods have ever known."
O, godlike courage! worthy, worthy of
A better cause.—Though wanting virtue, yet
The chivalry can fight.
            The reading done,
A move by B'elzebub, preceded by
A short but cogent speech, was made that these
Resolves at·once should be adopted as
The sense of this august assembly, and
By Chemosh seconded ; 'who had at heart
The weal of all beyond the love of life
Itself.'—The rest sat waiting for the word
To vote. For none dissented from the views
Of their high chief ; or if dissenting, cared
Not then to make it known ; but silent sat
Or called aloud for "question! question!" to
Be put, which put, was answered by a loud
And thundering "aye" in lowest octave of
Their devilish throats.
        . So much was gained. ALL HELL
Had now combined to overthrow the race,
The chosen race of God.—O Israel! where's
Thy refuge from the coming s'orm ' Flee, flee
To HIM, thy only hope! as Noah to
The life-preserving ark.
            Then B'elzebub
Again arose, and with distinctive voice
Announced a proposition for the faith
Of Hell, a dogma in her creed. 'Twas this :

" That our beloved chief, our saintly guide,
Is,from his wisdom sure *infallible.*"
There's nothing like a dogma new within
A creed ; it gives such life, such life and strength,
As late th' immaculate conception gave.

This pleased them all ; but Satan most, who
Bowed with kingly grace toward B'elzebub,
His high assent. The same appeared throughout
The whole assembly. Each, unconscious, with
A slight, but simultaneous bend, declared
His full accord. 'Twas plain that Hell again
Would be unanimous. 'Twas put at once
And carried with a rising vote, not one
Dissenting, each declaring thus his mind,
His public mind. What each believed within,
May not be told ; nor mattered much, for not
For them did most subscribe their vote, but for
The common herd without, who soon would find
It heresy of deepest dye to doubt.
But B'elzebub believed, believed the whole ;
A fossil devil of the slowest kind.

Now Hell had gained new strength.—A dogma to
Her creed, like magic, would effect, mayhap,
What arms had failed to do before ; but both
Combined, success was sure. Proclaim it then,
Throughout her vast domain ; let all now hear,
The masses hear, and know what is decreed ;
And hearing, with implicit faith believe.
('Twas once a sentiment, but now defined.)
Some think this rendered Hell rediculous ;
Not so the poet sure, for he conceives
A dogma added now and then to creed,
A stroke, master-stroke of policy.

'Tis thus in Hell, a few, compared, make faith
For all the rest.
     A momentary pause,
And Proteus rose, a most unstable god.
A coat he wore of different colored sides,
And so contrived that either could be worn
Without, as suited best the times, or those
In power. In time of revolution, when
The masses ruled, and red was all the rage,
His coat was red ; and none so loud as he
For people's rights. All kings were tyrants, not
To be endured. The aristocracy
Must all succumb and find a level on
The common plain. "Vox populi" was on
His tongue forever.—But upon reverse,
When war or fraud had changed the scene,
And some successful chief had leaped to power,
Though red with blood and perjured to the soul,
(As late O, Gaul! a villian reached the throne)
And blue had now supplanted red, his coat
Was blue. With oily tongue he talked of kings,
And their inherent rights, and went abroad at call
On embassies, or planned at home to prop
The recent throne. Now Satan ruled again,
He was for Satan in the fullest sense,
And first among the fawning court, with hope
Of place and power, to pay him def 'rence due
As god supreme ; whose right it was to rule.
In fact he was the Tallyrand of Hell.
He rose—his coat was blue, the color of the
Time—and with a gracious smile and bend
Of courtier mien towards Satan, spoke with bland
And flattering words of all the excellencies

Of Satan's rule ; his wisdom, gentleness ;
His care for all, and last not least, his high
Integrity.   He said not piety,
But meant it ; for it is in Hell as on
The earth.   It must be told that here, O shame
The most abandoned villians, if they have
But crowns or miters on their godless heads,
Are heaped with every sacred adjective
The language owns, of " holy," " pious," and
" Most Christian," e'en till devils, if not men,
Are nauseate and hang their heads.—His high
Integrity —It was not irony ;
He was sincere, sincere as courtiers are,
Who make a trade of words and sentiments,
As merchants do of wares, nor care who buys,
Provided that the price desired is paid.
   This smooth and gracious speech concluded, he
Desired to read for their approval what
In haste he had committed to the scroll
He held in hand, and knew would please them all.
   " Whereas, in times gone by, rebellion hath,
" Of direst kind, disturbed our grateful peace,
" The lower orders rushing from their sphere
" Assigned by fate, with maddening fury, and
" With blindest zeal o'er-sweeping Hell with one
" Resistless deluge wide and wasting, and
" With surge terrific lifting from their base
" The firm supports of order, sweeping down
" The edifice of state, and mingling all
" In wildest, deepest wreck," continued he ;
   " Whereas, our chief beloved, permitting first
" The wave to spend its strength, (what barriers could
" Withstand such elements combined ?) and then
   5

" By nicest diplomatic skill, and casual force"
(The muse asserts, the blackest perjury.)
" Obtained at length the throne, thus lost, and now
" Reseated firm in lawful power, vouchsafes
" Again his former mild propitious rule :
  " Resolved, that we rejoice in such a prince ;
" And deem his reign most suited to the wants
" Of Hell. And that we cherish in our souls
" The most sincere affection for himself,
" His royal person ; and the warmest wish
" For his perpetual, universal sway."
  Apolyon moved, and Baalim seconded ;
The question put, a deafening " aye" received
And placed it in the register of Hell
Unanimous.—What loyalty and love
Were thus expressed ! But all was hollow, not
A devil there but did detest his reign ;
A devil there, whose bosom was not filled
With fiercest hate, and would not throttle him
With keenest gust, but for the lack of arm,
Or danger of the deed, or loss of place
And power for time to come. 'Tis thus from fear
Or selfishness the throne of Hell is propped :
Not patriotism. This can never grow
In such a soil. It needs the light of Heaven,
The genial warmth of better skies, and air
Of purer breath. Though none so loud as they
In all God's works, in patriotic show
Of words, in praising Hell, and ranking it
Above the Heaven where God presides, and " which,"
Say they, " though lost is not much loss. The clime
" Enervates, and the luxuries destroy
" The highest elements of soul, and lead

" To indolence and loss of noble aims.
" Not so with us ; our hardy clime, our fare
" Of coarser kind, nerves up to action, and
" Evolves a spirit fraught with noble deeds.
" We envy not their residence, and ease
" In that voluptuous world. But here in our
" Beloved Hell we choose to stay, and build
" An empire worthy of our chief, and of
" Ourselves. And now we pledge our all for this
" Great end, nor would accept the gift of Heaven,
" With all its hills and vales and gentler toils
" And far-famed rich repasts : while here
" Our wants are met to our desires ; abstemious
" 'Tis true, but yet well met ; and we can add
" Renown to this our cherished home. We lay
" Upon her altar all we hold most dear,
" And make the sacrifice for her best good.
" Nay, would not shrink, if called, to yield up life
" Itself." Fair words, and spoke with show of zeal,
Yet hollow ; not a devil there but would
On offer sell out all he boasts so dear,
This cherished Hell of his, her vast domain,
Her millions, future prospects, chiefs and all,
At once, for one, O faith ! one single mess
Of Heavenly pottage.—Thus, in Hell ; so loose
The tie, so starved are all the damned !
    But one there was must not be overlooked.
He came, 'tis said, from regions of the north.
He had a seat among the rest, and held
His head as high ; whom all despised ; and yet
Refused him not, but rather welcomed him
A place ; not for his worth, but for the work
He would perform ; such work as would be done

By not another devil of the throng.
In fact, he was the scavenger of Hell ;
And ever lived, 'tis said, and moved, to please
His betters.   And 'twas doubtful if had
A soul.   He fawned like Proteus, but he lacked
His shrewd and inward depth of thought, that planned
Far reaching some perceived and selfish good.
His mind was dull.   The chivalry at will
Would wind him round their fingers.   Yet he thought
Himself an equal in their midst, and deemed
His seat accorded and the bows and smiles
Vouchsafed, as tokens of the inward worth
They found in him.—And thus he talked and smiled
And acted, as a peer among his peers ;
When lo ! he was the secret laugh of all.
Besides, his face was of unusual kind ;
Not fixed in form—(alas, he knew it not !)
But soft and plaistic as the clay upon
The potter's wheel or yielding loaf beneath
The baker's hand ; and hence his masters had
But little task in moulding him at will.
    And yet he found rewards for all his acts
Of menial kind.   (Rewards but not respect.)
He rose to place, by the appointing power ;
And once, 'tis said, (for truth of which the muse
Declines to vouch,) he filled an embassy
Abroad, and there for three long years disgraced
E'en Hell.   What sad materials compose
That nether world !   And some such kind are found
E'en here on earth.
                    Next after him arose
From where he sat in savage thought, and look
Of desperate deeds, the fiercest, deadliest god

That Hell produced ; and far more cruel he
Than Moloch ; long, long worshiped here on earth
In Indian climes, and Sciva named ; the dread
Instinct, of infants ; from whose shrieks and dying wail
His ear drank Hellish joy, as from the breast
They fed the crocodile, or plunged the stream
Of sacred Ganges to a wat'ry grave ;
And painted there with bloody mouth and tongue
And reptile jaws, fit emblem of the god.
　The widow on the funeral pile was his,
And deeds besides that make e'en devils blush.
In stature tall ; his head behind was wide
And massy, and in front 'twas low and scant,
And brutish in extreme.　His eye was small
And snaky ; and betokened passion and
Self-will to boiling heat, but not a spark
Of intellectual light.　He rose, and held
His ear for cries, and snuffed the air for blood,
Bedecked with gewgaws ; and the laugh of all ;
The god, in fine, of every savage tribe.
And as he stood, a thrill of dread instinct,
As from a serpent coiled, bechilled the whole
Assembly.　With assurance bold, " With leave,
" Your Holiness," said he, " and all these gods,
" I see, methinks, the surest way to gain
" The point desired, to bar the dangers deemed
" About to come from Abram's race.　Be mine
" The task to execute, should you approve
" The thought.　Let's send the plagues, the direst plagues
" That Hell can boast.　Let's send them teeming in
" The evening dew, and breathing in the winds
" Of Heaven, and pregnant in the water from
" The rock, and unsuspected mixed within

" Their daily bread, the Heavenly manna, sent
" From God, least likely to be deadly in
" Its use, but which we'll sow with seeds of death,
" As tares among the wheat.   Their babes shall nurse
" The poison from the mother's breast, and death
" Shall lie in ambush, lurked in every cup.
 " Thus unperceived, methinks, but sure in aim
" We'll come upon the host not roused to know
" Their danger till too late.   For if they pray
" Their God will hear and save.   We will destroy
" At once ; or if not that, their intellects
" Shall be deranged ; and pangs of direst kind
" Shall seize their frames ; and maddening pains shall drive
" Them frantic to unearthly deeds.   Each hand
" Shall rise against its neighbor to destroy.
" The father, red with blood, his son shall slay,
" The child, the parent, and the mother, from
" The breast shall dash her babes against the stones ;
" Or seek their blood, or strangle them with shouts
" Of maniac joy.   Give me but one, one day,
" With all Hell joined in league, and come to aid
" When once our plans are laid, and all this race,
" The boastful care of God, shall be no more ;
" But blood instead ; and one delightful field
" Of wide-spread death.   The vulture there shall seek
" His prey, unscared, among the silent tents.
" Thus all shall perish ; not a trace of them
" Shall be preserved, but blotted from the rolls
" Of earth ; and God abashed, and we avenged
" For this his effort to disturb our peace."
　　He sat, and from his look none doubted that
He had the will to do what he proposed.
　　Then Ashtaroth arose, and with a sneer

Looked out on Sciva ; and extolled to Heaven
His wondrous scheme. " How sure !" and set
The very day and hour for all to be
Achieved. And then with smile, and courtly bend,
He begged him to comply with one request, but one
Besides, and that " to give a programme of
" A battle-day to storm the skies and cast
" Out God, and seize anew their long-lost Heaven.
" For him 'twas easy ; since to execute was but to plan."
    This Sciva heard with trembling frame ; but sat.
All eyes were fastened on him, as he changed
To fiery red with sudden gathering ire :
While Ashtaroth, in scalding irony,
Took sweet revenge for some old grudge that long
Had rankled in his breast. It was enough.
The bloody fiend could brook no more ; but sprang
In fury to his feet, and headlong plunged
Towards Ashtaroth with tomahawk, and shriek
That curdled blood. Each drew ; and Hell was in
A blaze. Sword flashed on sword, eye glared on eye ;
And direst battle then among the gods
Seemed imminent. Some leaped for Sciva and
Withheld his arm, while others shouted for
An open field, and fair and equal fight.
    But Satan's steel was seen among the rest,
With light terrific, and an arm that none
Could view unawed, and voice that sent dismay
To every heart. He called to order, and
The host complied ; and Sciva sat again ;
Now pale with rage ; and sworn to be revenged.
    Next Peor rose, with od'rous curly locks,
And visage trim, a soft licentious god.
He stood in fair proportions to the eye,

And graceful far beyond a spirit lost.
His ways were winning, and his look serene ;
His speech was smooth, and seemingly sincere ;
And guarded well with cautious words, that won
At once upon the heart ; and gave no note
To innocence, of deep design, and dark
Depravity within.   And yet he was
A whited sepulchre.   His blasted soul
Was rottenness itself. ˙His plans were deep,
And laid for future use ; and ere aware,
The fairest angels, tangled in his folds,
Fell victims ; lost their virtue and their all.
And in his fall, seduced and won, he dragged
Them down to hopeless days of shame and pangs
Unceasing of remorse.   The heartless god
Stood up.   All knew his tastes and upmost thoughts,
And hence his mind was known before he spoke.
    " Send women !" spake the lecherous god.   "Let them
" Be called from every nation to the camp,
" The sacred camp of Israel ; let them come
" With songs and dances, and with wanton smiles.
" And sure these sons of God, when they behold
" The daughters fair of men, will laugh to scorn
" The holy law, proclaimed upon the mount ;
" And take them wives, not wives ! of all they choose.
" And God, besure, will straight destroy them, as
" The world before the flood.   We've tried this once
" Before, with full success ; and only eight
" Remained alive of all the peopled earth.
" If God spared not the world that was, but swept
" It bare for sin, this sin ; why not this race
" When sinning to the full in light so clear ?
" If we succeed at all, methinks, it will

" By this be done.   Let's try the heart of this
" His people Israel, and end our care.
" For God is great in anger as in love.
" And when his ire is roused, his vengeance knows
" No bounds."   To this all bowed assent, for they
Knew well the wrath unmixed of God.   Thus hard
It is for devils or for men, grown blind
By sin, to comprehend the ways of God
To man.   His great designs shall in the end
Succeed.   Though sin may hinder, and the day
Defer, and thousand thousands " die without
The sight," yet all shall bend at last ; his plans
Shall triumph, and his foes shall find that e'en
Their machinations to defeat his will,
Have served but to defeat themselves ; to dig
A deeper pit for their more deadly fall ;
While God unharmed shall still be all-in-all.
Nay more, his moral problem, solved with full
Success, shall show him God all-wise, as well
As God supreme, before admiring worlds.
    " We know," continued he, " their God is strong,
" And naught can pluck his people from his hands.
" But they can pluck themselves, and scatter from
" His fold ; and be devoured as sheep astray
" Upon the mountains ; nay, he will himself
" Destroy them ; for 'tis written in his book
" That all are cursed that fail to keep his law.
" His curse will fall upon them and destroy.
    " Then make them sin, all sin to such
" Extent that he will swear an oath that not
" A soul shall enter in and see the land,
" The promised land, reserved for Abram's seed.
" And when the oath is sworn, tis sure ; for God

" Will keep his word in wrath as well as love.
" We know this truth, who lost our Heaven, and found
" This Hell, and we will use it sure upon
" Our foes. And let them know as well as we,
" That God will keep his word in anger sworn.
  " Send women then, the fairest of the earth,
" And draw them off from God. For this will lead
" To every breach of law ; not one of his
" Commands will then be safe ; no longer God
" Adored, nor Sabbaths kept, nor parents feared,
" Nor murderous hands restrained, nor thieves unknown,
" Nor truth be loved, nor covetous desires
" Repressed ; but this one sin shall break the mound,
" And like a flood, o'erwhelming in its course,
" Shall let all others loose ; and death, disease, .
" And lust, and Hell itself, shall reign uncurbed
" Within the camp ; till our great foe with rage
" And shame shall sweep them from his sight.
  This pleased them all, save those whom jealousy
Forbade to approve. For some there are in Hell,
And not a few on earth, who're sure t' oppose
The wisest schemes for public good, because,
Forsooth, to others, not themselves, the meed
Of praise will come, of first proposing. And
Whatever plans for general weal might seem the best
That Hell could bring, yet each great chief, corrupt,
And false, and deep debauched within, would
Let Hell " slide," and all the state be wrecked, unless
Some selfish interest of his own could be
Advanced.—Of course then Peor's plan would meet
With foes. And so it did. No sooner had
He sat, than scores of envious devils scrambled for
The floor, with voices loud, and fiery zeal

That scarce could be restrained. The wildest scene
Of uproar now prevailed. Each "patriot" claimed
The right, the prior right, of being heard ;
Which was, at length, accorded Rimmon. "He
" The greatest good of all had nearest to
" His heart, his own the most remote. For what
" Was he, or what his weal, provided Hell
" Was safe ? His hand upon his breast, he called
" To witness Erebus, and all the powers
" Below, that Hell had all his thoughts, and all
" His love ; and to unceasing days should have
" His labors and his zeal. Her car should move,
" Though he and all his hopes were crushed beneath
" Its wheels." What patriots are in Hell ! And some
We have on earth of self-same stamp ; who "serve
Their country for their country's good ;" and yet
Forever block the wheels, unless themselves,
Or their own interests can be first. How cheap
Professions ! and how rife in earth and Hell !
" He doubted not the noble lord just up
" Had full belief in what he urged ; but still
" Himself had doubts, and serious doubts, of its
" Success ; and rather would that naught be tried,
" Than aught be tried in vain. He hoped that none
" Would be misled ; but all would wait till some
" One should advance what all could choose ; and then,
" In truth, 'twould be a *trial* mere, and might
" Not work the good that they designed. But still
" He granted that a trial must be made ;
" For all results were hid, though fixed in fate ;
" And none could know them till divined, or brought
" Matured, by real action into light."
    Another noble lord upon the left

" Accorded with the peer last heard ;" and one
Upon the right, and one in front. In fine,
The foremost peers were clam'rous, though in terms
Polite. (Politeness is an attribute
Of Hell as well as Heaven, but differs thus :
The first is hollow, and the last sincere.)
" Were clam'rous," (though the cause was hid from most)
Lest Peor's plan should be received, and full
Success should follow.—All the leading peers
Oppose ; and so affected many more,
That when the vote was put, 'twas lost
With voice o'erwhelming, and chagrin and rage
Within of Peor ; who full clear perceived
The reason why his plan had failed.
He bit his quivering lips, and inward swore
To blast with might and main, whatever scheme
Should be advanced ; " to blast, come then what would,
" Though Hell thereby should sink, and every hope
" Be lost, forever lost, his own among
" The rest." Such, such is Hell ! Though one
In aim, chief envies chief, and thwarts his course ;
And direst hatred rankling in the breast,
O'erthrows the wisest counsels ; and betrays
The hopes of all. Among the wicked, and
The damned, a bond of concord is a rope
Of sand. 'Tis wisely so, else earth would have
No spots of green, no flowers ; but waste and bleak,
One desert drear would stretch from pole to pole.
   Then Satan rose, himself not free from fear
Within, that he should act a second part
In conclave, and thus lose the prestige hoped
Forever his, of first in council as in war.
" He liked the plan of Peor, but preferred

" The trial first of one more likely to
" Effect, he judged, what all desired ; and that
" Would he propose. Those tribes, you surely note,
" Are under laws to God ; and men, called priests,
" Administer the laws, and teach them to the host
" In place of God himself. Now Aaron holds
" The chief appointed lot. He leads their minds
" With easy sway, and closer still allies
" Them to the God of Heaven ; and builds them up
" In virtue, ' virtue ' called ;" and here a curl
Of scorn ineffable upon his lip,
Evinced that virtue had no quarter there
With him. " What wait we for ? Why not at once
" E'en seize the priesthood, and thus place ourselves
" 'Twixt God and man, the channels of the law
" From him to them ? And if the law shall flow
" Through us, we'll sure corrupt it in its course,
" And bring it to their hearts not pure as when
" It came from God, but mingled with our own
" Strange waters, as shall seem us good. Let this
" Be done ; and then, forsooth, we have within
" Their camp a foothold nothing can destroy.
" The priests secured, the teachings first shall be
" As heretofore, the pure and perfect law
" Of God. But, in the stillness of the times,
" And while men sleep, the tares we'll sow, which shall,
" Ere long, produce abundant yield. The priests
" Shall learn of us, and stealthily, as fall
" The shadows of an evening sky, shall trench
" Upon the law, and step by step, at length,
" Shall fritter it away ; and, in its stead,
" Shall place a code replete with man's
" Device, by us inspired, traditions rife,

" And false philosophy imbibed. The plan
" Of Peor, noble lord, and those besides,
" Of equal worth, will then come in at once,
" Harmonious ; and will join to give one grand
" Result ; and make the Tribes our own till time
" Shall end. We'll see, then, that from them no harm
" Shall come ; no lion strong to tear, nor arm
" To shake the firm set throne of Hell."—He sat :
And instant rose a murmur of applause,
Like hoarse and distant booming of the sea ;
Which loud and louder grew, as ocean tide
Approaching from afar in mountain wave,
And goaded on by winds of Heaven through rocks
And straits and steadfast bars. So swelled this tide
Of voice subdued, which broke ere long in one
Amazing shout, that echoed back anon
From verge of farthest Hell. A smile ensued
Upon the face of Satan ; and he thought,
He vainly thought the victory won. Alas!
The wicked, both in Hell and earth, insane,
Forever overrate their strength, nor count
The cost of conflict with the might of God.
    He smiled. His stern and savage features bent
For once ; while visions started o'er his mind,
Of power and glory and revenge to come.
    How vain ! Their house is set on sand ; they toil
For years, and in a single night find all
Demolished, and their hopes a wreck.—" But who
" Shall win the priests ? Shall Aaron and his sons,
" Seduced, and Moses, and in fine the house
" Of Amram turn from God to us to work
" Our will ? or shall we move rebellion in
" The camp, and raise to power another line,

" With better hopes for us ?   Our worthy head
" Must this decide.   And then, our leader there,
" Why not our Chief beloved, whose wisdom, skill,
" And foresight well compare with His of Heaven ?"
This Proteus said, the soft fallacious god,
The flatterer of Hell.   He saw it pleased,
Then moved, forthwith, that " Our beloved chief
" Repair to earth, and there, by choice of means
" As seems him best, bring over, if the thing
" Can be, the priesthood to the side of Hell."
'Twas carried with a thundering aye.   And yet
'Twas doubtful who were there sincere ; or wished
A fatal snare to spread, unseen, for his
Detested feet.   Yet Proteus was sincere,
With many more.   He propped the powers that be :
He only changed, when those in power were changed ;
And sought the good (for selfish ends of course)
Of each one holding sway.   And others were
Sincere, and wished him all success ; but not
From love ; the damned can never, never love.
They hated Satan with unceasing hate,
But hated Heaven more.   And this is all
The concord Hell can boast ; made only to
Agree from stress of circumstance ; or fear
From some despotic arm.—Then Satan rose
With soft imperial words, and thanked them for
The confidence reposed in him ; and made
Full promise, on return, to publish his
Success, the priesthood won, the Tribes secured,
And all avenged.   And then put forth a word,
By way of counsel, to his "loyal peers."
" He knew they would be faithful on return
" To their respective posts ; and see that all

" Was kept as should be, and not one be slack
" In duty due." And here he slowly drew
His trusty sword, that flashed with diamons, from
A diamond sheath ; his sword, appalling sight !
A burnished fiery blade, the terror of the damned,
And gently laid it on the *rest* in front ;
A hint significant, to give more weight
To his paternal words. Thus princes oft
Betray their doubts of all the loyalty
And love they boast of in the public breast.

He then assured them " He would soon be there
" Among the Tribes, and should his utmost skill
" Put forth to compass all they wished ; and they
" Must stand as minute men at call, to come
" Up singly, or in numbers vast, as need
" Might be. Perhaps this would decide their fate
" At once ; and none must shrink from any post
" Assigned, however hard ; for though he went
" Alone, 'twas but to plan unseen, then give
" The signal for whatever aid might be
" Desired, from one to numbers such that earth
" Would reel beneath their feet, and God himself
" Be taken quite aback at their approach."

And here he rose in stature, and in rage,
And uttered words that none but Hell must hear.

'Tis hard for devils to be calm, whose breasts,
Abandoned to the darkest deeds, and thoughts
Of desperate cast, have no restraining grace
To curb them in. 'Tis so for most with men.
The nearer devils they approach in heart
And life, the more unbridled are their wills
And passions fierce. God leaves the wicked oft,
On earth, an awful sign of what they'll be

Alas! in time to come ; and Hell is not
Confined to Hell, but is foreshadowed here.
    Let men beware ; and mend their ways perverse
Through aid implored, ere all is lost.
                          And now,
The spark of rage once struck, it ran like fire
In fallen stubble. Devil kindled at
The rage of devil, till one blaze of wild
And fearful fury swept o'er all. They cursed ;
They hurled defiance at the skies ; and shrieked
And shouted and looked upward, filled with spite
Untold ; now flushed, now pale, then flushed again,
As passion o'er the current of their veins
Held sway.—A sudden flash is seen ; and ghastly fear
And paleness gather in the face of all.
And Hell is mute.—Another flash.—The pall
Of death seems settling down, no more to be
Withdrawn. What? Why this sudden, awful pause?
    Behold yon western sky! 'Midst mirky glooms,
A cloud is rising there; of portent dread ;
As far as spirit eyes can reach, a cloud,
A harbinger of God's judicial wrath ;
A cloud, impenetrably dark, and fringed
With fire.—A flash.—The cloud still swells, and rolls
Its direful folds upon itself.—A flash—and now
A sound far off, scarce heard by spirit ears.—
A flash.—Another sound.—A jar! the waking bass
Of God Almighty's voice.—Subdued the assembly sat,
Benumbed. None silence broke ; an hour of dread
Suspense! No usual tempest frowns afar.
But such as threatens earthquakes, bursting fires,
And yawning earth ; and e'en disruption of
The crust of Hell ; and hurricanes, beside ;
6

The like unknown in all God's works, except
That clime, that torrid, God-forsaken clime.
The dire phenomenon! They know the sign;
Though ages have elapsed since last beheld;
Now seen, the fresh remembrance, fixed as fate,
Portrays the dreadful day, long gone, when that
Same scourge swept over Hell, and changed its face,
And wrecked anew the damned. O, Hell! Sad, sad
Abode of spirits lost! Yet 'twas their choice.
Forewarned, they heeded not. God proffered life,
But they refused. They would have sin though death
Was sure to follow in the end. They loved,
'Tis true, the thought of life, but would not pay
The price. The will was free, unhedged by God's
Decrees; and life was free to all. WAS FREE!

O God, thy goodness hath no lack or stain!
But justice cries aloud and must be heard.
And he that treads thy laws beneath his feet,
Shall find thy threatnings, as thy promise, sure.

'Tis o'er! 'tis fixed! The harvest that they sowed
They now must reap. 'Tis well if these be all.
Let worlds beware, that are or may be made,
For God hath set these forth, example sad,
That all for times to come may fear, and choose,
The way of life; nor fall as erst they fell.
Then cease from sin; be sure God changeth not;
Its wages must be death ere long. Though sweet
The present draught, the pain, the deadly pang,
Is sure.—All Hell is withered up. Alas!
Their boasts how vain! how impotent their threats!

Thick folds o'erspread the skies, and fires and glares
Of direst form. The distant awful war is heard,
As coming of the flood in days of Cain's

Devoted race ; of mountains falling, and the crash
Of hills ; while thunder, clap on clap, bestuns
The ear.—The stroke is nigh. All wait in dire
Suspense, with visage pale, and nerves unstrung ;
And scan with sinking heart the nearing storm ;
And dread the smiting of its power. They brace,
And hold with grappled hands, and grinding jaws,
And half suspended breath ; and wait the shock.—
It strikes.—Their canopy, the pride of Mulciber,
Receives the blast ; and but a moment holds ;
Then yields, and, stripped to ribbons, vanishes
From sight, and like a vision leaves the crowd
All naked to the storm.—Hell groans and reels
Beneath the blow ; and hail descends amain,
And lightnings cleave the air in fearful streams,
And run along the ground, and rend the rocks,
And plough the earth, and fill with fulgurites
Immense that arid soil. And bolt on bolt
Besmites the spirit lost ; and tells him God
Will not be mocked impune ; nor cease to rule.
    And fires below reply to fires above ;
And what was solid ground just now, and fixed,
The rocky face of Hell's unyielding orb,
Now, cracked and heaved, rides up in billows like
The liquid wave. Now mountains sink ; now rise ;
Now sink again ; and caverns yawn, of depth
Unknown, and central fires break forth, and shoot
In forked spires and fearful sheets beyond
The reach of spirit eyes.—God's arm is bare.
He looks from out the cloud in fiery form,
As on the Egyptian host ; and plagues the damned.
    Now night sets in, such night as only Hell
Can know, while howls and roars the storm unchecked

Throughout that wide domain. The direst shapes
Are seen ; the deadliest shocks are felt ; and winds
And hail and bolts bepeel the face of Hell ;
And hurl the spirits like the lightest chaff,
In fury to the clouds ; and fling them far,
In darkness wrapped, and lodged on tracts unknown.
　　Such night the unblessed passed, who dared defy
Their God, alas ! and measure arms with him.
A lesson this if devils could but learn.

BOOK II.

The night wore off at length.—Such night before
Was never passed in all God's works. The dawn
Appears, the dawn of Hell, mid clouds and gloom
And howling winds. The tempest still is high,
But spent its fiercest rage.—The work is done.
A feature scarce is left, a land-mark of
The day last gone.—Where sat th' assembly mid
The pomp of regal state, and, haughty, held
High council on their future weal, and planned,
Secure of ultimate success, unawed,
The overthrow of God's designs,—a lake,
A sulphurous, stenchy lake is seen. It rolls
Its sullen tide, ejecting slime and scum
And pestilential fumes. How changed! Where now
That matchless host that threatened war on God?
O'erthrown, and scattered to the winds of Heaven!
Where now that gorgeous canopy, out-spread
By Mulciber, a sight for angel eyes?
The throne of Satan where? and wide plateau?
All, all engulfed; ten thousand fathoms sunk;
As Admah, Sodom, and Ziboim, gone!
  New devils now are seen of ancient type,
Whose forms for ages of remotest date
Had lain encrushed within the crust of Hell,
Or deeper still, within her central fires;
Now thrown aloft by this eruptive chance

They gain once more the freedom of their limbs,
While myriad others, 'mid the shocks of that
Disastrous night, had sunk in pitfalls of
The gaping ground, which, closed, shall hold them there
In jaws relentless, till some distant age
To come, mayhap, in turn, shall set them free.
   But Satan had escaped, and many more ;
With life, 'tis true. but bruised and wrenched and torn
In every limb. They lay for days forth-cast
On deserts lone, and mountain tops ; bestunned
And stupefied, from that resistless blast
That swept them out. Then crawled like idiots prone,
And gazed, and laughed, and lolled, and licked the dust.
Alas, for gods that late in council sat,
And boasted high of deeds to be achieved!
How weak! how low!—Their minds at length restored,
They gain forthwith their furious passions lost ;
But now increased to tenfold rage.—The strokes
Of God's chastising rod may bring the good,
The erring good to humble thoughts, and lead
Them to review their ways, and mend for time
To come. But not so devils. They, chastised,
Become more deadly in their hate ; and change
Not, save from bad to worse.—Thus Satan with
His crew, recovered from their lapse of mind,
Swore double vengence 'gainst the God of Heaven.
Their words and frenzy earth must never know :
When they beheld the wreck that God had wrought,
And felt the stings his stripes had left behind ;
Nor thought nor cared how much deserved.
Revenge, revenge, impenitent, their souls
Demand.
        But time is precious ; earth requires

His care, and Hell must now be left,—to whom?
His "faithful lords." O, faithful! Devils to
Be trusted? Never! And he knew the risk.
But nothing better could be done. He knew
What timber Hell produced ; and chose the best,
The best that could be found,—what best in Hell?—
To make his statesmen of ; and could no more.
'Tis so on earth. The tyrant knows his tools ;
Though lifted to the highest seats, and praised
In documents of state, as " High in worth,
A blessing sure to any reign," he eyes
No less, with greatest care, their every way ;
Nor feels secure within their power ; detests,
And uses them, and dreads ; and pines for men
Of trust.—Thus Satan, could he have a few,
O! but a few, of honest devils, whom
No bribes could move, no selfish ends seduce,
With whom to leave his vast concerns so dear ;
And feel secure when far away, that all
Was safe at home, and faith was kept in Hell!
Alas! an honest devil! When, or where?
As incompatible as heat and cold,
As light and shade. Ah, vain desire! He first
Corrupted them, and then, forsooth, would have
Them honest. Strange! Had they been honest they
Had not been there. Another realm had held
Them ; other fields and climes had been their range ;
And other interests claimed their care.
Yes, yes, an honest devil, when, or where?
Had they been honest they had not been there.
                                        Next day
He calls his greatest peers around him, and
With speech parental takes his leave. 'Twas on

The highest peak of highest mountain range.
His royal words were few, but full of hope ;
And bland as breath of summer morn. " Adieu ! "
Said he, " till I in triumph come."   " Adieu,"
Said they, " our Prince beloved."   Then spreading out
His wings like sails of battle-ship, with wave
Of hand, shot off, in downward sweep for sake
Of speed ; which gained, he rose balloon-like to
The upper air.   They gazed and gazed ; yet prayed
In heart, that they might never see his face
Again ; while still he held his way in course
Direct, and lessening to the view, at length
Evanished from their sight.   Alone he sped,
In ceaseless surge, 'mid outward solitudes
Of frightful breadth ; a cheerless, blasted soul !
A vulture bent on prey.   How drear his flight,
The muse recordeth not ; what wilds he passed,
Or angels scarcely shunned ; or voids of space
He crossed, where God's creating hand is still
Unknown ; but night primeval reigns alone,—
The muse recordeth not.   At length appeared
In distant view the nebulæ, those flakes of suns outspread
That God has granted mortals to descry ;
The outskirts of those distant heavens, whence light
For ages wings its way ere it can reach
The searching gaze of nightly sage.   These passed,
The glorious scenes of suns and flaming worlds
That lit his path, the ursæ of the poles,
Arcturus, Sirius, Lyra, Doneb, and
The host, that time would fail, though seen before,
Yet now, as then, unbent his devilish mind,
And made him half devout.   But what avail ?
A mind depraved rejects the works of God,

Or views them to derange and to destroy.
He passes these on furious wing, and drives
Afar through fields of living light ; then down
He plunges by the sun, and grazes 'mong
The planets, Neptune, Herschel and the rest,
In slackened speed, and lights upon the earth,
With gentle touch.   An earthquake yet was felt.
He folds his wings, those devilish engines that
Had brought him there ; and eager gazes round,
As eagle eyeing for the helpless fold.
   'Twas on a mount in Araby, from which
He saw the camp of Israel, stretching out
In wide proportions to the eye, in hopes
Of better days, the land of promise, and
The Seed to come.   'Twas evening ; and the smoke
Of sacrifice just made, by law enjoined,
Ascended up before the God of Heaven,
A savor sweet.   And here and there within
The tents, unseen, was made by pious souls
A sweeter offering of a humble heart.
   In Korah's tent was bowed a lovely form,
A rose full blown from childhood's opening bud.
The rest were walking in the freshning breeze.
God's spirit rested on her from a child ;
Had filled her soul, and sweetened all her life.
A pious mother had the daughter trained ;
Who saw the promises afar, and bade
Her hold them with unyielding grasp.   She prayed
For all, for Israel, that " They might be kept
" Unharmed, and see full soon their destined rest ;
" Her father's house, might that be owned of God,
" And like a tree by water-brooks refreshed,
" Forever green in leaf and branch, tower high,

" Bear fruit, and bless all time to come.   And O !
" O ! haste the day when Shiloh shall appear,
" The hope of Israel, and the Nation's joy."
And then with fervent quests that " God would shield
" Her from the ills of life, and ever be
" A guard about her path," she offered praise
With an o'erflowing heart.   She ceased, and rose
From suppliant posture ; and with face serene
As summer eve, awaited their return.
Arrived, the father asks, " My daughter, why,
" Why thus alone !   We missed you not till half
" Our walk was o'er.   You've lost the joys, the joys
" Of eveningtide, the breeze, and setting sun,
" Which glorious sank below the western sky.
" You are not ill, I trust ?   Then why alone ? "
    " Not ill, my father, nor insensible
" To charms of evening walk.   But joys are found
" In solitude at times.   Though quite alone,
" I've not been lonely here."   She said it with
A modest mien, and chastened smile, that showed
A humble heart, and full possession of
An inner life : an inner life, in reach
Of all, attained by few, discredited
By more, unsought by most.   " I love to see
" The works of God ; for sure if these are such,
" So glorious to the sight, how much more He,
" The God that made them all." " What, child ? but what
" Is God ?   Is not the earth a part of God ?
" The sun, the moon, the stars and clouds and winds
" Of Heaven ? all these combined, my child, are God.
" Apart from these no God exists."   " Permit
" Me to inquire," rejoined the child, with glow
Of cheek and kindling fire of eye, " Can these

" Produce such plagues as Egypt saw ? divide
" The sea, or speak from Sinai's mount, in voice
" To make earth tremble to its base ? or shower
" Down manna daily for a starving host ?
" Or bring forth water from a smitten rock ?
" Or hang this cloud of mercy o'er our heads,
" To cool our sultry days, and cheer our dark
" And gloomy nights ?"   He answered not again,
But placed his hand upon the silken head
Of Rachael, youngest one, whose childish glee
Had filled with life their recent walk, and said,
" 'Tis time your were asleep my child."

       An hour
Passed on.   The hour of rest had come, and all
Was hushed throughout the camp ; save hourly voice
Of sentinel in watch for outward foes.
The cloud hung o'er them, with its softened light,
Which shielded them by day from burning heats,
And cooled the blasting breath of desert winds,
Called Sheckena in Hebrew tongue, forth spread
Of God, a symbol of his presence to
The host, and to his church throughout all time
To come.   But one slept not, within his tent.
'Twas Korah ; whose ambitious mind refused
The balmy antidote of toil, to man
Vouchsafed.   He tosses wild upon his couch,
With features flushed, and heavy beating heart ;
Whose every throb, distinctly heard, threw up
The vital current with a rush and roar
Internal, to the fevered brain.   " Must it
" Be so ?" said he in whisper au liblc.
" Must I and all these mighty, worthy ones
" Obey ? and learn our duty at the mouth

"Of Amram's sons? and more, have Mirriam,
"A woman! teach us songs and dances for
"Our festal days? Why this? And Amram, who
"Is he, that these his children should thus wield
"The rod of church and state? Enough, methinks,
"That one, that Moses should possess the rank
"And power he holds, of Captain of the host;
"But he must call a brother to be priest,
"And, not a brother left, must needs for lack,
"Appoint a sister to be prophetess,
"A woman stepping from her proper sphere;
"And thus the offices and honors place
"Within his father's house."   The night wears on,
While thoughts the like disturb his heated brain.
      He sleeps at length; and now is Satan's time.
For he had viewed aloof the restless bed
Of Korah; and with practiced eye perceived
The soil prepared for any 'mount of tares,
The seed that devils sow. Ah, sown too oft!
      Unseen he stealthily approached the bed,
In shape of nightly vampire, and with wings
Outspread, hung o'er his prey, the deadly fiend!
And closer settling down, and closer still,
Came quite in contact; and with gentle fan
Of wings, but dark and ominous, induced
Continuous sleep; while direst venom was
Infused through all the sleeper's soul.   What thoughts
Sprang up! What dreams were clothed in flesh, and walked
The earth! What castles built in empty air!
He sees himself the king and priest of God's
Elected host; to whom the promises
Belong; whose number should the stars outvie;
In whom the nations should be blest; whose power

And rightful sway, thought he, should over sweep
The world ; himself the founder of the reign ;
His kingdom everlasting ; and his heirs
Perpetual in descent, a line of kings
And priests unknown in earth before, upheld
By ancient right, till time shall end.　　He woke.
And all had vanished.　Moses still held sway
Supreme ; and Aaron, mitered priest, had lost
No power from this injected dream ; and he
Was Korah still ; the leader of a house,
But not of that great host ; now doubly moved
To compass that great end.　　" What wait we for ?
" Why, why not rise at once, in multitude,
" And holy zeal, and sweep these Amrams out,
" As chaff before the equinoctial storm ?
" It shall, it shall be done.　I'll move a plot,
" And others call as leaders, who shall share
" With me the honors won.　My bosom friends
" I'll sound upon this scheme, and cautious try
" Them—Dathan and Abriam.　They shall have
" The offer first, as worthy of high rank
" In such a move."
　　　　　　　　At length the morning shone.
The glorious sun now burst the op'ning gates,
And pierced the misty clouds, that ever hung
O'er Israel's path ; now rolling through the tents,
In silver sheen and healthful cooling spray.
The dews, distilled, lay thick in richest pearls
And Eden seemed restored to earth again ;
And life awoke throughout the vast encamp.
And daily tasks, begun, and songs of joy
And praise, made vocal many a tent.　The herds,
Discharged from nightly watch, spread lowing to

The distant plots of grass and foliage green,
That marked the gush of springs and scanty streams ;
Refreshing sight! a God-send in that waste
Of drouths and burning heats. The dew, dispersed,
The manna shone beneath, as hoar frost on
The face of earth ; as coriander seed ;
A small round thing ; in color, white, in taste,
Like wafers made with honey, food for gods,
Yet loathed, O shame! by that ungrateful race,
But Korah noted not the glorious morn,
Nor grateful felt for manna showered by night,
Perpetual bread for Israel's daily food.
Far other thoughts his mind had now possessed.
Ambition goaded, and the gifts of God
Were trampled under foot. All peace was lost,
And, 'mid the thousand blessings God had given,
He was a mariner at sea, bestormed,
And floating on a single plank.   He sought
For Dathan, whom he found alone within
His private tent, and wrapped in deepest thought.
For he had seen a dream, of import strange ;
Of sharing kingdoms, and dividing spoils.
As Satan had not stayed ; but gone
From tent to tent; and hung in influence dire
O'er many a couch ; had started hopes that ne'er
Could be attained ; and hidden fires had lit,
That rivers could not quench.   He entered with
An Eastern bow, and comely grace, and talked
Awhile of health, and friends, of Egypt, and
The promised land ; of Moses, Aaron, and
The general weal. "And why," said Korah, "is
"This long delay in tents ; and even life
"Itself worn out in hope deferred? Our food,

" This everlasting manna ; while the fields
" Of Canaan call, and richest fruits invite ?
" What full contempt upon our heads is pour'd,
" While we, the race for Canaan's land designed,
" As boasted by our leaders when we passed
" The Egyptian bound, delay to seize by force
" That land, that trembles at our very name,
" Whose bowels melt within them at the sight."
  " 'Tis passing strange ; 'tis folly," Dathan joined,
For he had restless grown from long restraint,
" A kingdom waits us, and we linger here ;
" A land with milk and honey flowing o'er ;
" And yet we starve on manna, this vile bread.
" Let those accept it whosoever will,
" As gifts of God, if God there be ; a God
" Who keeps his chosen ones in durance vile,
" In this cursed wilderness, to waste our strength
" And lives in wand'ring here, and making chests
" Of gold, and gorgeous tents, and princely robes,
" To be enjoyed by those who call themselves
" Our leaders. Yes, let those accept who will,
" But as for me, I seek a better fare,
" And better region for my life to come ;
" Nor be forever held in leading strings
" By those our chiefs, so called, who false pretend
" That God—and who is God ?—has bid them say and do."
  Then Korah, inward pleased at this response—
For he perceived a spirit there for him
To mould at will in his designs,—rejoined ;
" Our years are wasting as a Summer's day ;
" And age will come at length, and we shall seek
" The dust, and leave no trace behind ; unknown,
" Shall perish from the rolls of earth ; and e'en

" Our graves·be lost : for if indeed our sons
" Shall ' enter in,' and hold the promised land,
" Yet none will e'er return to view the spot,
" The spot forever lost, where we repose :
" A life of toil, and an ignoble grave !
" But here's Abiram.   Lo ! he cometh from
" His tent, in thoughtful mood.   ' Thrice welcome here
" But why so thoughtful ?   Has some ill befall'n
" Thyself, or father's house ? or does some care
" Oppressive weigh thy spirit down ?"   " No ill,"
Quoth he, " but I have had a dream, a dream
" Of double form.   Methought I saw on earth
" An Eden springing up, with flowers profuse,
" And fruits of richest hue ; the olive, grape,
" And thousand more, inviting to the taste.
" The waters sparkled as they leaped in sport
'· From crystal rocks ; then silent sped away
" In bowers of living green.   The balmy breeze
" Up-swept from spicy groves, and filled the sense
" With odors as of Heaven.   The skies serene
" Gave never threat of storm ; but fleecy clouds
" With silver sheen enriched the azure arch.
" Mid spreading branches of perpetual green,
" The notes, the richest notes enrapt the ear,
" From plumage rare ; and this, methought,
" Was mine ; and at my feet the nations bowed,
" As lord of all, and piled their offerings rich
" From every clime.   My soul expanded ; and
" I touched not earth, but seemed above, and looked
" E'n downward on the seat of kings, who paid
" Me homage, with the rest of men ; and while
" Thus crowned and sceptered and enthroned, methought,
" The vision waned ; a dimness came o'er all ;

" 'Till all had vanished quite, and left a void,
" A desert drear.   And then a voice, ' beware !'
" I heeded not.   ' Beware ' again ! but still
" No heed I took.   ' Beware !'   But all in vain,
" And then a gulf I saw beneath my feet,
" Down which I plunged immeasurable depths,
" To rise no more."   " We all have had our dreams,
Quoth Korah, with assurance doubled now ;
" 'Tis ominous.   Some great event awaits
" Us.   Sure the times are full of meaning ; and
" E're long the signs shall have their end.
" We must bestir ourselves, or plunge the gulf you saw ;
" Must rule, or feel the foot of power full soon.
" Yes, surely.   The fulfillment shall appear.
" And happy he who stands where fate
" Invites, to catch th' auspicious hour, and make
" The prize his own.   A kingdom may perchance
" Be plucked with ease, as comely apple from
" A hanging bough ; or picked as ruby rare
" From rubbish vile.   Let us be present then,
" For few can win, what all would fain achieve.
" A scepter has been promised Israel's race ;
" But who shall bear it never full declared.
" It may as well be ours as others' lot,
" For fortune frequent throws her favors blind,
" The ready seize them, while the laggards miss.
" The moment passes never to return."
    And, starting up erect, and drawing near,
With hand uplift and eyes of flashing fire,
" Let's seize the reins at once," said he, " while all
" Is weak ; before these Amrams seat themselves
" In power ; and laugh us all to scorn, 'mid tow'rs
" And walls of adamantine strength.   A crown

7

" Will soon be won, and lost. The struggle sure
" Will come. The mighty princes of this host
" Will try their strength in time ; nor leave
" A boon so tempting to us all, to fling
" Itself by chance into the lap of *one,*
" Unreached for by the rest. These Amrams have
" The field 'tis true, but they must battle, or
" The field be lost ; and, battling, prove themselves
" More mighty than the rest, or still the field
" Be lost. 'Tis worth the toil, 'tis worth the risk,
" A prize like this must never be contemned ;
" A people to be numerous as the sand ;
" A kingdom stretching to the utmost bounds
" Of earth ; a name, an everlasting race
" Of kings, and families of princes high
" In power." To which Abiram quick replied :
" These things are worth our care, I full accord,
" For Israel shall be mighty in the earth.
" Before his sway, the nations one by one
" Shall bend ; the thrones of earth shall crumble to
" The dust ; and Israel,—why not *we ?* be all
" In all." Nor Dathan sat unmoved, but felt
Within the kindling of a fire, a fire
Unquenchable till quenched in death. " He fain
" Would stake his all upon this throw ; and reach
" A kingdom or his ruin find." For he
Had thoughts that all might not succeed ; as chance
Of war might foil their wisest schemes ; and yet
Would not but try. " I'll take my chance with you,"
Said he, " and strike for empire while the times
" Invite. The blow shall lift us up as gods
" On earth, or cast us down as devils sunk
" To Hell ! but naught without some hazard e'er

" Was won." Then Korah, flushed with his design,
And sanguine of success, enjoined them to
" Await the silent evening hour, then seek
" His tent, where further views could be disclosed,
" And plans of action formed, and made mature."
" Meanwhile, the lips of each be sealed ; no friend,
" The nearest friend apprised ; but silent as
" The foot of death let us proceed, till all
" Our schemes are laid. But where is On ? Must he
" Not have a part with us ? A braver man
" Lives not among our tribes ; nor one more fit
" For offices of state ; nor one to whom
" A kingdom, should the lot be his, would be
" A prize more worthy of regard, or who
" Would wear a crown with better grace. But all
" Shall have their chance, the kingdom won ; and fate
" Shall guide the lot within the urn, and make
" The king. The rest shall win, not crowns,
" 'Tis true, but titles high, and offices
" Of priests and princes near the throne.
" Let him become aware of our design,
" He will accord with us ; fear not, His mind
" Is cast for elevated aims, and deeds
" Of effort high. Let him be called to meet
" Us in the eve." They parted ; each to con
Within himself, and plans devise, and more,
To sap the virtue of the church of God,
And turn them from their only hope, to seek
Their good in man. Work sad ! and oft performed
Too well ! Behold yon temple proud ! in form,
And size, most comely, and stupendous, to
The eye ! Its columns vast were heaved with skill,
And wond'rous toil. And stone on stone was laid,

The work of years; and men grew hoary as
The building rose. The time and toil how great,
To build! but to destroy, how quick the work!
A day shall full suffice to cast it down.
But when demolished and bestrown in dust,
Ah! who shall build again? With aching heart
The ruins we may scan; and pause and weep;
But they are ruins still.   'Tis even so
In morals as in art. A day may waste
The piety of years; and hence are sprung
The devastations of our moral world.
But woe to him who mars the good of earth!
A millstone round his neck were better hung,
And he down-cast to ocean's lowest depths,
Than draw a single soul away from God.

Ah! who can tell what mischiefs were achieved
That day? what vows were broken, and what soul
Seduced? Seditious thoughts sprang up where e'er
These evil men had passed. They sowed the seed,
And ere the sun went down,—so quick the growth,—
A harvest ripe was ready at their hand.

They meet at eve with highest tide of hope.
'Twas in Abiram's tent. The rest had gone
To visit friends hard by; so planned, that all
Might still be kept a secret. There they spoke
Of what the day had done; of hints thrown out,
That caught like sparks in stubble ground and swept
Through half the host : that disaffection was
Abroad; the times were calling, and they must
Obey. They there defied their God; those men
Of atheist heart : and vainly thought to foil
His high designs; and God looked down and laughed
But let them run their length : that in the end

A warning might be given through future time.
From night to night they meet. 'Twas now within
A tent prepared aloof from passing feet.
They here mature their plans, enroll their host,
And make all ready for a coup d' état.
The morning came at length, the day prescribed,
And one grand muster startled all the camp.
Aghast the faithful stood. Sedition is
On foot! Distrust and fear fill every breast.
The stoutest heart grows faint ; and cheeks turn pale.
And gathering multitude at central point
Betrays the faithless crew. There princes stand,
Of high repute, and unsuspected till
That hour. From tent to tent the terror ran ;
And wildest uproar spreads amain ; and God
Frowns awful from the threat'ning cloud, that rolled
In wrathful folds above the *Tent*, and scarce
Restrain its all-consuming fires. Stood there
Abiram, Dathan, Korah, joined with On,
The atheist chiefs, in bold relief, with sword
And buckler, spear and helmet armed.
They stood unawed, and marshalled that false host,
Which to their standard flocked, and with disdain
Defied the host of God ; blasphemed his name,
And laughed his law to scorn. Alas! for all
The sons of God ! the faithful few, that now
Remained, before this mighty rebel host,
As trembling kids before the lion's rage,
The hungry lion, roaring for his prey !
The rebels stayed not, but impetuous rushed
With shouts and hellish rage, in broken ranks,
To seize the consecrated tent of God,
And all the treasures there, with those whom God

Had placed as captain of his host, and priest
Of holy things.   The tumult still increased ;
And prayers and curses mingled, rise to heaven,
And shrieks and trampling sound.   All, all, combined,
Bestun the ear, and tell that all is lost !
    But no : the fiery form of God is seen,
As never seen before.   That cloud ! that cloud !
The awful shekena, now fierce in wrath,
Hangs dreadful in the upper air ; then stoops
In forked flames and tempest roar quite down
To earth, and overspreads the Tent.   The sight
Appalling terror-struck the recreant crew,
That back recoiled, as ocean waves opposed
By steadfast rocky base of mountain range,
Or hasty traveler from the glaring eye
And naked teeth of deadly lion, crouched
And waiting in his path.   This Godless mass,
At length, still reeling backward, fall to earth.
    Recovered now, a pause ensued ; a pause,
A stillness as of death.   As well the friends
Of God, as foes, stood gazing fearful at
The sight, the darkling folds and shooting spires
Of flame, uncertain what the moment might
Bring forth.   The temper now was changed.   Instead
Of slaughter round the tent of God, of heaps
Of slain, of reeking blades, and gory earth,
The rule of God o'erthrown, and ruffian rule
Unchecked, the holy place defiled, the ark
Itself a prey, and all the treasures seized,
And vilest passions glutted through the camp,
A calm,—how changed !—a calm remonstrance fell
From Korah's lips.   " Ye take too much upon
" You.   Every one is holy ; and the rule

" Might come to all by choice or lot ; at least
" To all the princes, who of right should share
" With you in turn the offices of king
" And priest, usurped till now by you alone.
" Ye take too much upon you ; wherefore lift
" Yourselves above the congregation of
" The Lord ?"   Then Moses fell upon his face,
And worshiped God ; and there besought him to
Restrain his wrath.   Then rose and with a firm
Rebuke to Korah and the princes there,
Announced : " To-morrow shall ye know whom God
" Hath chos'n for his priest to minister
" In holy things.   This do ; your censers take,
" With fire therein, and incense place thereon,
" Then come yourself and all these princes, thus
" Prepared, before the Lord ; and Aaron shall
" Be there ; and he whom God shall choose shall be
" Elect.   Ye sons of Levi, hear : You take
" Too much upon yourselves.   To you doth it
" Appear but small that ye are chosen from
" The tribes, the sons of Levi all, to stand
" Before him in his house, to do from day
" To day the service of the law, before
" The congregation when convened?   Thus marked,
" But, not content, the priesthood seek ye too ?
" This rebel act is not to *us*, but 'tis
" Against the Lord ; for Aaron, what is he ?
" Or Moses what ?"   He ceased ; and forthwith sent
A messenger to call up Dathan and
Abiram to the tent, to answer for
This bold rebellious act.   For they'd retired
And sought their tent again.   But they, secure
Of their own strength, defied him, ruler of

The host. They came not; but a message sent
Of highest insult. "Back," said they, "and tell
"Your leader prince, to make his promise good,
"Of Canaan to these weary tribes, with which
"He first seduced us while at ease, to leave
"The happy land of Egypt, filled with all
"Delights,.and for a better promised, to
"Forego those present sweets; a promise made
"With ease, but not fulfilled. No longer shall
"He blind the eyes of this becheated host.
"He must needs be a prince, though all of us
"Should die, for which he brought us to this curst,
"This death fraught wilderness. Fine land! Are these
"The vineyards promised? this the goodly land
"Of fertile fields foretold, and olive groves?
"Of richly waving grain, and flocks and herds?
"Let that be first fulfilled. Fine land! Go tell
"Him, we're our own. We scorn his message and
"His rule alike." Unrighteous charge! It was
The people's sins that shut them out, when erst
The twelve went up to spy the land. Returned,
"The land was rich," said they, "as God had said,
"A land of milk and honey running down.
"But ah! the people were of stature vast;
"Too mighty to be overcome by them.
"Hence all their labor and their care were lost."
Then all the people raised their voice and wept,
In unbelief of God's assurance given:
That they should pass the bounds, and take the land,
And hence he closed the door; and sware that they
Should perish there, and never enter in.
And now the blame they cast on Moses, and
Accuse that truest man that earth has seen,

Of want of faith, of reckless wish to rule,
And selfish ends. He heard in agony
Of spirit, and prophetic prayed : " Regard
" Not thou their offering. ' Selfish ends !' An ass
" Have I not wrongfully required, nor harmed
" Them in the least." To Korah then he said :
" Be thou and all thy company before
" The Lord to-morrow. Thou and they shall come,
" And Aaron. Every one shall have in hand
" His censer, twice five score and fifty ; one
" For each revolted prince."   He bowed assent,
Nor spake, but stern retired, resolved to push
His claim to any test that might be sought ;
His claim, to be relinquished never, till
His life should end ; alas, how soon ! Thus men
Resolve, resolve on wicked deeds, and count
On length of life to come, when lo ! the call
Is at the door, the messenger to take
Them hence to face a righteous God, the Judge
Of all the earth ! Where now the deeds devised,
Of wickedness to come ? Unwrought, 'tis true,
But still the sin remains.
                              Now night o'erspreads
The camp. The cloud had lost its fiery hue,
And soft, as wont, shed forth its lunar light.
The air was cooled ; and fresh and spicy breeze
From distant Oases sprang up, and filled the sense
With rare delights. The outskirts now
Were still, the herds at rest, and all was hushed,
To outward eyes and ears, but deep within,
Was agony and sore distress. They feared ;
The faithful feared, the faithless feared ; the first,
Lest God should sweep them for this daring sin,

As Sodom and Zeboim erst, or as the race
Before the flood ; the last, lest they should fail
By some mischance, to reach their hopes, their hopes
Of place and power ; but feared not God.   They'd lost,
Those atheist grown, had lost all fear of him.
    In silent wakefulness the millions lay,
Excited by the scenes just past and those
About to come.   For on the morrow, who
Could tell what issues would be tried?   What fates
Be sealed?   What tears were shed that night the muse
Can ne'er record, the tears of pious ones!
What prayers besieged the throne of God, the muse
Can never tell.
                    In Korah's tent a form
Of manly mould, and ripened years, with step
Of hasty tread, strode too and fro, in deep
And agitated thought.   The hoar frost had
But touched his locks.   His well developed front
Betokened intellect ; and lineaments
Of face showed fixedness of purpose, and
A mind that might achieve results, untold
Results of good, if trained to virtue ; but,
If left to sin, might even wreck the weal
Of empires.   He reviewed in thought the day's
Proceedings, and had naught to change, or to
Retract.   His course was fixed ; and, "life or death,
" The trial should be made.   And if that cloud
" Of fire, the pest of all the camp, would but
" Preserve its place, nor interfere to thwart
" His high designs, next day should see a change ;
" A change of rule, a change for Israel's good ;
" A change that soon should bring them from that waste,
" A change the Canaanite full soon should feel

" To his dismay, and utter rout, with loss
" Of all his fertile hills and vales : While they,
" No longer duped, and held at bay by sad
" Misrule, and coward councils, should at once
" Rush in resistless to the promised land ;
" And seize, and hold to farthest end of time.
" The brave make speedy work, and soon enjoy,
" While cowards linger, and the chance is lost."
    'Twas done, 'twas settled, nothing to be changed.
His mind here rested, and he sought repose,
And slept till morn ; and rose refreshed :
But not his household.   They had found no rest ;
But agony.   The deadliest fears had held
Them sleepless from the evening's hour.   And tears
Had coursed their cheeks ; and prayers gone up to God.
    They rose bewildered, sad and pale, and gave
No salutation as they met.   A funeral scene! but looked
In silence at each others face, as if
Expectant of some sudden, dreadful ill.
Which Korah seeing, quick the silence broke.
    " My spouse, my children dear, why sad ?"   His spouse!
She'd been his bosom friend, from early youth.
And fresh and fair in days gone by ; still fair,
Less fresh.   The bloom of youth had waned, but rich
In years mature, a mid-day sunshine from
The blush of morn ; a noble matron of
A noble house ; of upright heart ; who trained
Her children in the fear of God.   " Why sad ?"
He said, with slight misgiving as the words
Went forth.   Then Jochebed, for such her name,
With Eastern deference her lord addressed.
    " My husband and my lord, ask not why we

" Are sad, while we can not but hold in mind
" The acts of yesterday ; a bold revolt
" Against the rule of God ; a questioning
" His right to make his rulers of the men
" He will, and call upon the rest to mind
" His law as uttered from their lips : His law,
" With signs and wonders given, the awful mount
" With lightnings crowned, and thunders riven, and smoke
" And darkling flame ; the quaking earth,
" And awful trumpet, sounding long and loud,
" And God Almighty's voice distinctly heard,
" As never heard before : a scene so dread
" That even Moses trembled ; and exclaimed
" ' I have exceeding fear.'   Is this so soon forgot ?
" The law thus given, is that so soon contemned ?
" And shall my lord and spouse be leader in
" The sin of war on him ? and shall he hope
" T' escape, with these loved ones, his wrath awaked ?
" What has been once, be sure may be again.
" Remember days gone by : how Pharoah warred
" With him, and where is he ?   Go ask the sea
" For him and all his host.   And them that but
" Complained at Taberah, the fire of God
" Consumed, nor ceased till Moses prayed.   And them
" That only lusted for the taste of flesh,
" (Ungrateful, true, when filled to full desire,)
" The plague, that dreadful scourge of God, destroyed;
" Kibroth-Hatavah, let us not forget!
    " See Miriam leprous by the stroke of God
" At Hazeroth, for only words in haste
" With Aaron uttered in reproach of him
" Whom God had chosen.   And the ten that brought
" A bad report of Canaan, and induced

" Rebellion in the camp, again the plague
" Smote down at Paran. And shall we escape,
" Thyself and all our house, if we provoke
" His wrath with acts of treason, and a rush
" For power ? Nay, nay, my lord, such thought
" Be from the far ; a better mind come o'er
" Thee ; and retrace thy steps at once. By all our loves,
" By thoughts of children dear, and future hopes
" Of rest in Canaan's happy land, at least for them,
" If not for us, (for we, perhaps, shall fall,
" As God hath said, in this lone wilderness,)
" I pray, I do beseech thee, to forbear ;
" Nor madly risk the censer test ordained,
" Alas ! for thee this day, and Dathan and
" Abiram and the princes in that league.
" Forbear, my lord and spouse, the father of
" Our sons and daughters. Do not waste our house,
" By *ill advised* attempts (to say the least),
" Against the powers that be, installed by God
" Himself, by him, be sure, to be sustained.
" Unequal contest ! how can you succeed ?
" But rather turn ; with penitential tears,
" And broken heart, implore the mercy that
" May be vouchsafed before the time is lost,
" To come no more. Methinks I see the wrath
" Of God, in store, held back, in mercy held,
" Till latest moment, that forgiveness may
" Be sought and found ; and Israel saved the stroke,
" The awful stroke of an avenging God.
    " Behold yon cloud of fire, where God resides,
" The shekena, a cloud out-spread for good
" To Israel, to shield us from the heats
" Of torrid suns, to light our darksome nights,

" And guide our wand'rings in this desert-wild
" While we obey ; but sinning, let us fear,
" As warned by yesterday, that God will break
" Upon us and consume.   Retract, my spouse,
" And pray as Aaron prayed at Paran ; and
" Perhaps the wrath of God will stay, and we
" Be spared."   She ended, pale and tearful, for
She had but little hope.   She knew the man too well :
A loving husband, kind and gentle sire,
But *will* of iron, and a heart untouched,
Unsoftened by the grace of God : in whom
Ambition reigned above all law.   Such, such
Was Korah.   Such he took the field ; but not
Till Adah had entreaties tried, in turn.

She was his fav'rite child, now scarcely grown
To womanhood ; had seen but eighteen suns
Of summer light ; a pious heart, of staid
Deportment, and of temper mild ; a child
Of prayer, a conscientious keeper of the law ;
And cheerful as the lovely hours of morn ;
A living radiance of the livelong day ;
With mind and intellectual strength beyond
Her years ; her mother's image ; and though young,
Her great support in arduous household cares ;
A guide to younger ones, a blessing, sure.

He loved her for her mind, her heart, but most
Her heart ; for wicked men lack not delight
In piety at home.   They love sincere
The loveliness it lends to all, though seek
It not themselves.   She'd heard her mother's plea,
A plea in vain.   The hour drew nigh when who
Should stand, who fall, should be revealed.   He took
The censer from its place, and incense put

Thereon. His hand shook not, his will was seen
In ev'ry lineament of face. His loins
He girded up, as soon to leave ; while tears
Of anguish flowed from every eye, save his.
His hand on Adah's head he laid.—" My child,"
Said he, " fear not. I'll soon return, if not
" In triumph, yet in safety come ; and you
" Shall see that all your fears were vain."
    She rose then up to plead.—" My father, pray
" Forgive th' offence, but I must speak. Forbear !
" Nor doom thyself and us to perish. See
" Us here, thy helpless ones, and this our dear,
" Our faithful mother ; and thyself, revered
" And prized above all price ; our house in hope
" Of rest in Canaan's land, our talk, our talk
" By day, our dreams by night ; now blasted nigh ;
" Our sun about to set ; a night, a night
" Of darkness setting in, whose gloom shall hang
" Upon us till the last of time ; our house
" No more, our very name, a curse pronounced
" By all. Can these not move thee ? Must thou go
" As ox to slaughter led ? as bird to snare
" Of fowler, nor perceive 'tis for thy life ?
" Stay ! stay ! "—Her hand convulsive grasping his,
Her face begushed with tears. — " Nay, stay !
" O, be persuaded ! Stay, my father dear !
" How can we give thee up ? how see thee bleed ?
" Or, smit with pestilence or plague, behold
" Thy dying face ? or, blasted from the breath
" Of God, receive thee back, a blackened corse ?
" And, O ! thy sin !—forgive me—O, the sin
" Of him that lifts his hand against his God !
" Our father, stay ! our light, our joy, our hope,

" Our staff!—Poor reeds, bruised, broken! E'en if spared,
" The storm shall beat us down. Thy sons behold,
" My brothers dear, of tender years ; who, who
" Shall guide them, and prepare for life? Be sure,
" If reft of thee, though spared this stroke, our lives
" Shall waste away, and, one by one perchance,
" Yet surely, shall we fall, and find our graves
" In this lone wild, unblest with Canaan's rest.
" But shouldst thou stay, perhaps"—" Why all this fear?"
Replied the desp'rate man, now slightly pale,
" These many tears? Think not that God will smite.
" We're ten to one in this our noble cause.
" And God is always on the side of those
" Who have the greatest strength ; and hence we shall
" Prevail ; and e're the sun goes down, rejoice
" In vict'ry over traitors, won, the rule
" Secured, and Isr'el saved. Cheer up ; you weep,
" But you shall laugh ere long."—Then all was still.
A pause ensued ; but tears still flowed, and pale
And hapless Adah sat again.   He held
The censer, and with half misgiving smile
Departed to the holy tent ; whereat
He found in tumult wild the populace,
Unawed, and clamoring loud and fiery for
The blood of Moses and of Aaron ; which
Perceiving, quick he stirred them up to rage
Of tenfold heat. The princes all were there,
And censers held, with incense and with fire
Thereon.
            Meantime there stood on highest peak
Of Horeb's distant mount, a dusky form,
With wings about him cast ; what seemed in shape
A vulture, perched, but of gigantic size.

His presence startled all the birds of Heaven,
That sang or sported high, or far below.
They crept to thickets, or, in clefts of rocks
Concealed, bestirred them not. There fell besides,
A sad penumbra, fearful shade, on all
The region round. The eagle screamed afar,
The monarch of the skies, whose hoary head
Had marked the track of ages as they passed ;
Whose fiery heart had never quailed at foe
Discried. He screamed, and wheeling from his course,
Gave this phenomenon the widest berth.

'Twas Satan ; standing there where God himself
Had stood ; presumptuous! Nay, a devil knows
No awe ; defies the law of God, and treads
His very paths with impious feet. He stood,
With eye intent on Israel's camp. His plan
Was ripe ; the time had come ; the priesthood just
His own ; and one short hour would make the full
Transfer from God to him. What hopes sprang up!
What visions sweep along! The priesthood his,
Religion would be his ; and man would then
Be his, the world at large to end of time.
And when the SEED should come, the seed be his.
And he in earth and Hell be all in all.

Salvation should be given to the priests.
And they shall sell it as a thing in trade ;
The while be keepers of the keys of Heaven,
To shut and open, damn and save at will ;
And men shall thence confess their sins to men
Instead of God, and find forgiveness at
A stated price. The priest, above the king,
Shall rule ; and tread the people down ; a priest
And king in one, shall do the same ; and earth

8

Shall drink their blood as early rain.   The priest
Himself shall riot at his ease, secured
To me by wine, and cloistered women, and
Debauch.   The law of God shall be withheld
From vulgar eyes, and used by priests themselves
To lead astray, and conscience-bind the race
Of man to me.   "Hail happy moment!   This
Shall be achieved! "   And filled with thoughts like these,
He waved his wings unconscious as he stood,
As if in act to fly ; his wings, that cast a wide
And dreadful shadow over all the mount,
And down, far down the cliffs and vales below.

Composed again, he stood, and eyed the camp.
There fiercest tumult reigns.   The masses, like
The surging of the sea, sway to and fro ;
And every surge brings up a higher tide.
What can withstand?   The barriers soon must yield,
And, overswept, be lost beneath the flood,
And one wide ruin overspread the whole.

The incense smoke ascends.   The shekena
Displays a fiery hue, and fearful roar
As of devouring flame, not heeded now
Through passion fierce, that boiled in every vein.
The voice of God is heard for Moses to
Depart, and leave the impious crew to death.
But Moses prostrate prays, as wont, and God
Forbears again, and tells him : "Let them flee
Who will, and leave the rest to meet their fate."
And Moses rushes through the crowd, and prays
Them, " Separate yourselves from out among
" These wicked men, lest you be swept away
" With them."   Some flee, some stay and clamor
For his blood.   He speeds to Datham's tent and gives

Th' alarm ; Abirams then, and warns his house ;
And then, to Korah's, praying all to flee.
But Dathan and Abiram heard in scorn
His warning words. Their Atheist wives delay,
And little ones. But Korah's fled.   A shout
Is heard that Moses has escaped.   " He's fled
" The camp ! "   A rush is made to overtake
His flight ; and Korah's voice is heard above
The rest, " Pursue ! pursue ! his blood, his blood
" Shall answer for his base misrule."
    He'd gone to warn and save his house.   They left
The TENT.   The dogs of war had slipped the leash,
And furious on the scent of that best man,
The meekest of the earth, swept through the space
That led to Korah's tent, he in the van—
    But hush ! a shock is felt—a voice is heard
Of subterranean thunder—all is still—
And cheeks grow pale, and passion cools—
And lo ! the shekena, unseen till now,
In darkling, forked flames appals the sight—
An arm is heaving up the pillars of
The earth.—Another shock, that mingles earth
And skies, long, lasting, till the stoutest heart
Is sick.—Now tears of penitence begin
To flow, from eyes that never wept before ;
But all in vain.   For God's not mocked.   The time
Is passed ; the judgement now is come.   They chose
Their portion, and it shall be given.—A shock !
A shriek ! a wild tumultous shriek ! a shriek
That earth shall never hear again, till God
Shall raise the wicked dead.   The earth is rent,
The heaving earth ; her crust is broken to
The very core ; and headlong down the abyss

Are hurled the recreant crew ; their tents, and goods,
And what pertained to them! But Korah saw
The fearful gape, and turned to flee. How vain!
How vain! The quaking earth divides before
His feet ; and down the chasm dread he plunged,
With frightful groan, to share the common death.
Another shock—and earth had closed again ;
Her jaws forever shut upon the slain,
Till God shall call them to their last account.
Then earth shall cleave again and give them up,
What time the graves and sea shall yield their dead,
When God shall square accounts with Adam's race.
    No trace of them was left ; no signal of
Their fate, save scars and furrows deep where earth
Had closed ; and spaces blank where once their tents
Had stood.
                Behold yon battle-ship, of size
And form majestic to the eye, with sails
All set to take the favoring breeze, but wrong
In course, and near a dangerous reef ; and warned
And signaled to return without delay,
While all was safe, and save the precious ship
And still more precious freight ; but all in vain ;
And plunging onward still till all is lost.
One shock—one shriek—one reel—the ship is gone!
A blank is left, a momentary whirl,
To tell the tale. The fleet is stayed, and mute
The seamen stand, with tearful eye, and mourn
Their comrads lost.   'Twas so with Israel. Deep
And still their grief, while awe-struck at the wrath,
The dreadful wrath of God.   At length the eye
Was turned to where the princes stood before
The holy tent with censers, filled, in hand,

But they were not. A heap of ashes lay
Where each had stood, the censers near. A smoke
Arose as from the site of Sodom when
It fell, that told, too plainly told their fate.
The fire of God had broken forth, and none
But Aaron spared.   Let sinners then beware,
Nor brave that Power, that waiteth long, but will
At length avenge.

> 'Twas done—'twas o'er—the camp
Was eased of its rebellious load ; and law
And rightful rule restored.

> Now Satan from
The mount on which he stood, had viewed the whole.
He saw the tumult and the fierce revolt,
He heard the cries for blood, with highest hope ;
And saw the rush for Moses through the camp,
And scarce retained his footing from delight.
Anon his visage changed, and hope gave way.
He looked and looked, his staring eyeballs from
Their sockets strained, and now grows deadly pale.
Such paleness none but devils e'er can show ;
A death-set visage that despair begets ;
Despair, a sense that none can feel as they.
   The earth had swallowed all his hopes ; alas !
He rose in agony, and took his flight, away,
Away ; his cheeks becoursed with scalding tears ;
Such tears as spirits shed, that spring from hopes,
Destroyed, and burning shame. He rested in
A vale in south-sea isle, collected thought,
Reviewed the whole, and sought if hope remained.
   At length from his obdurate fate a spark
He struck, that lit his soul anew. " Let all
" Arise and slaughter Moses for the day

" Last past. ' He's killed the people of the Lord.
" This thought shall take their souls. I'll raise a fire
" That shall not stay till every branch of this
" Detested race shall be consumed : for God
" Will smite them if they will but sin."   He's gone,
And like electric spark is in the camp
Again. A shadow fell ; none knew the cause ;
The day was shortened e're the sun went down.
He labored till the flush of morn, from tent
To tent, from heart to heart, and furious rage
Provoked and deadly hate.   The sun was up,
But scarcely up, when, lo ! a tumult rose,
Like ocean's boiling waves. The masses are
In arms again, untamed, untameable,
And fiercely called on Moses for redress.
    " You've slain the people of the Lord. Your blood
" Shall answer for the deed ;" when, lo ! the cloud
Of fire appeared again, and fearful hung
Upon the sacred tent. And God was heard,
Again, to Moses, and to Aaron : " Flee
" This wicked race, and save yourselves ; for I
" Will sweep them from the face of earth." But no :
That man, that had the weal of all at heart ;
That sought the good of them, and not his own,
Fled not, a shepherd true ; but risked his life
For them, the sheep. He stayed to plead. Both fell
To earth in suppliant prayer, that God would spare.
(The plague was smiting then its thousands down.)
Then Aaron seized a censer where it hung,
And incense flung thereon and fire, and ran
With haste among the dying host.—The plague
Gave way, from camp to camp, from tent to tent.
At length, the whole was stayed. But, lo ! before

The atonement came, what slaughter had ensued!
What cries were heard! what loved ones were no more!
Alas, for Isr'el that they will not heed!
But ever sin, and reap the bitter fruit!
'Tis so with men, throughout the length of time.
Though warned, they sin, and risk the wrath to come.
Twice seven thousand fell, and more, for that
Day's folly.—(What a breach in Isr'el's camp!)—
Besides what died in Korah's train.—Let men
Beware, and think and fear!
      Then rods were brought,
And laid before the Lord, to see whom he
Would choose, of all the tribes.   And Aaron's brought
Forth buds and blossoms, even ripened fruit
Of almonds in a single night, while theirs
Were dry and withered as before.
        Then all
Perceived that God had chosen Aaron to
Be priest ; and here forever rested down
Upon this stable fact.
      The priesthood shall
Forever run within his line, till God
Shall change it, and induct another, who
Shall be a priest enduring to the end
Of time, and not a priest for one, one nation of
The earth, but priest for all in every land
And clime, not bound to years, or line of birth,
A priest forever, as Melchizedek.
And he shall enter through the vail, his flesh,
A great High Priest to offer blood, his own,
That shall atone for sin ; whereof the blood,
By Aaron shed, was but a type, and had
No power beyond ; but was a prophecy

Of blood to come, that should redeem the world.
And he shall stand before the throne, the seat,
The mercy seat in Heaven ; a faithful priest for all.
And plead his blood for those who shall believe,—
A Priest and King.   Then, then be changed the law,
And Gentiles be received on equal terms ;
And worship be reduced to simple forms ;
And knowledge shall increase, and fill the earth,
As ocean waters spread the mighty deep.

But Satan's hopes were blasted here anew ;
The priesthood not obtained, and Aaron fixed
More firmly than before, and Isr'el's race,
Though scourged full sore for sin, yet not extinct.
He now departs, and soon is found in Hell.

END OF BOOK SECOND.

BOOK III.

Now Satan, foiled on earth, had gone to Hell ;
And sits alone amid his towers ; and broods
In moody silence o'er his fate.   Alas,
Great filibuster on the works of God !
Like that great filibuster from the land
Of Gaul.   Both went with highest promise of
Success.   Both failed, and, shattered to the hull,
Returned with prestige gone, and dead with shame.
    Throughout the city first, and then the realm,
The rumor spread that he had come.   But why
This silent, stealthy creeping in ?   Why not
A triumph held at his approach ; and he
Received as conquering hero comes ?   Alas !
This tells the tale, of his defeat.   He dared
Not ask a triumph ; but if asked, it would
Have been decreed ; decreed in every style
Of pomp.   He needed it full sore, but could
Not face the ridicule of Hell.   So he
Forbore.   But 'tis not always so on earth.
A recent filibuster has arrived
From tropic climes, to which he boastful went,
A humble imitator of the last.
He made a run for life, a desperate run,
In view of hemp ; and as he ran, he felt,
Or thought he felt, the fatal noose about
The spinal column just below his head,

So sure the one was for the other made.
This quickened pace, and he escaped, with loss
Of all. But, on our shores again, is made
A hero all at once, is toasted high,
And carried on the backs of men, or what
In shape appear like men ; and he receives
It all without a blush, because his soul,
His stolid soul is lacking in the shame
That devils have.
                    The day had now arrived
For his report ; for he had telegraphed
From earth, the day before his desperate rout,
That " all was well, and more than well."   O, fool !
How sanguine Devils are ! and ever cast
Accounts without their host ; had telegraphed,
In shortest phrase : " To-morrow night 'tis o'er ;
" The priesthood ours ; the Tribes secured ; the sons
" Of Amram slain.—Appoint a day for our
" Report ; no more till I arrive."—The day
Was set at once, and now had come.   And what
A concourse at the early dawn !   But what
Report could he advance ?   What triumphs tell,
When foul defeat had wound up every scheme ?
    The assembly waited, and he must appear.
They clapped, they roared, and yelled, and rent the air
With loud unearthly sounds, and still his feet
Were slow.   He lagged behind the scene, and seemed
Half stupified : while all was uproar wild,
From gallery to pit ; and greatest fear
That all would be demolished at a stroke,
From devilish fury raised at his delay.
    At length his fiery temper rose at the
Insufferable strait in which he found

Himself, though King and Autocrat of all
The Hells.   And now erect he shows his hight
In full, and with a savage frown upon
His darkling brow, and full determined step,
Walked sullen to the royal seat prepared.

  A loud and boisterous clap and shout ensued,
Of outward welcome, running round and round
The noisy maze of three times three ; which he
Of course acknowledged in the usual way
Of bow and slight unbend of features, that
Displayed, or half displayed the twilight of
A smile.   Then music quick and glorious filled
The air, with sweetest sounds of instruments,
In nice accord, and voices, rich as those
In heavenly bowers.   It was the self-same tune
They gave when he was crowned in Heaven.   Alas !
How changed !   *Then,* he resplendent shone in all
The virtues of the upper world ; and on
The topmost step of God's creation, cast
His eye o'er all ; and cared for all ; led out
The myriad hosts, and gave them charge of worlds,
And suns and constellations wide ; and built
Them up in moral worth, by word and deed.
To him a future then was spread, of bliss,
Of endless years of bliss, and higher flight
In excellence forever upward towards
The throne of God : *Now,* wreeked in happiness,
And hope ; a blasted soul ! depraved, debauched,
And seeking to destroy the very things
He once was building up.—O Lucifer !
Thou morning star ! how fallen, fallen now !—
" It was the selfsame tune," and sung in strains
As in the days of Heaven.   The airs, the chimes,

The symphonies, and solos rich, that for
The time unbent each devilish mind, and caused
Each heart to melt ; and drew forth tears from out
The hardest eyes.   The enchanting sounds were heard
Afar without, and stayed the footsteps of
The wand'ring damned.   Such power has music, e'en
In Hell.—O music ! gift divine, throughout
God's works ; the high delight of Heav'n ; and heard
By angels and archangels, rapt alike :
To man, a solace in the storm of life ;
And softener of the heart grown hard in sin ;
And e'en to devils not denied ! the thing,
The only thing retained, of all the Heaven
They lost.   It ceased ; and Hell returned to Hell
Again.   The bars are shut, forever shut ;
God's spirit never moves ; and hence reform
Is never known in that deserted world,
Whatever cause may act.   The day of grace
Is past.   They had their day ; they made their choice ;
The cup they chose is ever at their lips,
And must be wholly drained.

                     Then Satan rose,
And with assurance forced, professed to give
An outline of his doings, and success.
" The cause was onward, though with speed less great
" Than he had hoped.   The priesthood nigh was won ;
" And would have been outright, and all the Tribes
" Secured, had not the elements and fate,
(He spoke not once of God, but elements
And fate,) " his planning thwarted, and thrown back
" A little his designs.   But all was full
" Of hope ; and time would show that he, their chief,
" Had gained a foothold that should not be lost ;

" And laid his plans so deep, that all would yet
" Be theirs."   'Twas thus in generalities
He spoke.   Then drew them off by flatt'ries ; and
Befogged their minds by fulsome praise, bestowed
Upon them all, his " trusty ones," his " loved
Constituents "—for virtues that he knew
Not one of them possessed.   And they believed,
The most of them believed his false report,
As if a filibuster, foiled in his
Designs, returned, could speak the truth ; and would
With honest heart reveal the whole.   Besides,
The word of Satan never was the best
For truth at any time since first he sinned
In Heaven, as all well knew.   And yet, how strange !
The most believed.   But some there were had doubts,
And dared their doubts express.   This raised a storm,
Which, fearful scene ! nigh wrecked them all.   Enraged,
The direful fiend upleaped and drew his blade.
All shuddered, paused, and instant from their hearts
Believed.   No shadow of a doubt was left ;
They *knew* 'twas true.   Such sympathy there is,
'Twixt minds and metals, sentiments and swords.
   'Tis so on earth.   Poor Galileo, at
The sight of steel, grew skeptical, renounced
His former creed of earth and skies, and swore
The earth stood still.
                  The furious chief then sat,
With sword in sheath, that priceless instrument
Of priests and kings, the maker of the faith
And loyalty of Hell, and not a small
Amount of both on earth.   The assembly then
Broke up ; and each departed to his post,
If then on duty ; and if not, as chance

Or choice his footsteps led ; with silent lips ;
But all with inward hate, and some with full
Contempt of him, the worthless scoundrel that
The scepter swayed, and filled a throne, attained
By force and fraud, but not to merit given ;
(As thrones on earth were lately held, O Gaul!)
  And Satan left ; but not in private way,
But in the style of kings ; with officers
Of state on either hand ; and bowed to by
Obsequious courtiers, and admired by throngs
In eager gaze, for his majestic mein,
And robes and gems of richest dyes and hues.
  'Tis so.   And who could think such show
Concealed within, such sum of rottenness
And villany as lay beneath those garbs?
  Alas! 'tis so again on earth.   "He holds
"A throne."   But this no proof the man has worth.
Go seek the greatest villain earth can boast,
The most depraved, debauched, and blood-stained wretch,
Plunge downward to the lowest depth of life,
The sinks of cities and the mire of earth,
There find your man ; then upward rise to thrones,
And seek one there.   Then tell me, which more vile,
More wicked and debased, when stripped of all
The gild that rank and wealth and state bestow ;
And judged by rules of everlasting right?
(Not all indeed, but such there sometimes are).
  The shadows fell ; and darkness closed around.
And in a lone retreat, mid palace walls,
The royal fiend was sitting, deep in thought,
His forehead leaning on a diamond hilt.
His thoughts now clothed themselves in words.   "And is
"This all?" he sighed, "for this is Heaven lost ;

" And all my former purity and bliss?
" And my renown through all the works of God?
" Once loved, now hated, I a wanderer roam,
" Out cast from all that's good. I would be first ;
" And, striving, fell thus low. I won a realm,
" 'Tis true, but 'tis the realm of Hell. This curs'd
" Unmanageable crew, that keep not faith,
" (I kept it not myself,) but full of show
" Of loyalty, with fairest speech, yet false
" Within, stand ever on the alert to thwart
" My plans ; and strike me down with open force ;
" Or stealing on me unawares, enthrust
" My spirit with assassin blade ; and leave
" Me welt'ring from the treach'rous blow. O Hell!
" For this lost I the realms of bliss? The cup
" Of life, that brimmed forever at my lips,
" I drank, and drank, and drank again ; now changed,
" The cup of death is mine ; and to the dregs
" Must all be drained. What end, what end shall come,
" What respite e'en, to this my wretched lot,
" My choice? My choice! What madness seized me in
" That evil hour, to let slip Heav'n with all
" Its range of joys, and choose this Hell
" With all its bitter woes? God's universe
" Had not the like before.   'Tis done! the price
" Is paid, the empire won, I'm first in Hell,
" But 'tis not worth the cost. Yet I must strive,
" Forever strive, to keep my place and power.
" Not outward foes alone, but foes within,
" Are mine. By day, by night, within my halls,
" And round my couch, they stand, and wait their time.
" What days of endless watch! what nights devoid
" Of rest! what never ending cares! to waste

" My strength, and crush my spirit down
 " O could I rest!—What rest? If resting found,
" My empire would be lost. Those ruffian chiefs
" Now curbed with iron bit, would rush for power,
" And one most brave, or false, of all, would seize,
" And hold the whole. And then, no rest to me ;
" But, once dethroned, despoiled of power, I should
" In dungeon lie, and only see the light
" When brought forth chained, to feel the tread
" Of his disdainful foot upon my neck ; or, worse,
" Be dragged, the gaze and scoff of all, in his
" Triumphal train, for victory won. So, watch
" And care must ever be my lot; and hence
" 'Tis Hell to reign, but would be doubly Hell
" To serve. There is no backward step to peace,
" No hope! my fate is fixed, forever fixed!
" O! wretched spirit, wherefore didst thou sin ?"
      He ceased; and sighs broke forth. What sighs! Such sighs
As only come from bosoms damned. Seek not
Their import. Earth can never know what pain,
What anguish spirits lost endure. And yet,
Not penitential in the sight of God.
He'd sinned ; but not so much for that he sighed,
As sighed because his sin had found him out,
And lost him Heaven.
                      His plans on earth had failed.
The priesthood, lost, which he regarded won ;
A HIGHER POWER, he saw, had intervened,
And now the withering thought remained, with fear
Ten-fold, *the Seed, alas! should yet despoil*
His power, and wreck him somehow from the reach
Of hope. This pressed him sore. Dismayed, beset
On every side, he felt the meshes of

The net in which he'd wound himself. Each surge
To rend the toils, but bound him more. And all
But Satan would have sunk subdued, no more
To strive ; and yielded all for lost. But he,
The master-spirit once of Heaven, and now
Of Hell, her proud uncompromising chief,
Yields not, till yield he must. While life and arm
Remain, he battles strong. Though vanquished in
A thousand fields he battles, battles still ;
And gathers courage from despair. He roused
Himself from revery of thought, and stood
Erect, and wiped the spirit tears from off
His careworn cheeks ; and sternly placed his sword
Within its sheath, and paced the hall with firm
Defiant tread ; and head upthrown, as beast
Inclosed to leap the walls that held him in.

He left ; and walked abroad, the Autocrat
Of Hell. And none surmised his tears and sighs
In secret given. Thus greatness often weeps
Alone, when joined with sin ; proof sad that show
Of outward good is not an index sure
Of peace within.
9

BOOK IV.

MEANWHILE the church of God
On earth was safe, though thinned in rank, and hemmed
On every side ;—the church, a wand'rer in
The wilderness ; alone ! but fed from Heaven,
And watered from the rock. The church ! the hope
Of man ; the stone from out the mountain cut
Without the aid of hand, that shall in time
Enlarge, and still enlarge, and fill the earth.
  She journeyed from the fatal spot, the grave
Of Korah and his host, Makhelath called.
And after years of discipline and toil,
Emerged from out the wilderness, not dead,
As all her foes had hoped, but young and fresh
And vigorous ; and pitched upon the plains
Of Moab ; better far prepared than erst,
To enter in and take her long sought rest.
  Her tents were spread afar ; a goodly sight ;
A terror to her foes. And Moab saw,
And feared. For Arad, where was he ? and where
The haughty King of Heshbon, Sihon called ?
And Og of Bashan ? all, o'erthrown, and swept
From earth ; who dared in battle join with God's
Elect. And Moab feared, and durst not take
The field ; but sought enchantments to effect
His end ; and hence, the prophet, called
To curse ; to curse whom God had blessed. How vain !

He came, but warned of God ; and stood upon
The hights of Moab ; whence he saw the tents
Of Isr'el spread in goodly sheen.   And while
The altars burned, and all the princes and
The king stood near, announced the truth,
The appalling truth, " that no enchantment could
" Prevail ; that God had blessed ; and who should dare
" To curse ? that he whose eyes were closed, had seen
" The vision of Almighty God, entranced,
" With opened eyes.   From rocky tops I see
" Him, and the hills, and he shall dwell *alone ;*
" And not be reckoned with the tribes of earth.
" His number who can tell ? as dust his seed
" Shall be.   O ! could I live his life, and die
" His death!"   He blessed ; and blessed alone, from hights
Of Baal and from Pisgah's top, and mount
Of Pe'r that looks to Jeshimon. "He saw
" His strength, as lion rising on his prey ;
" His beauty, as the gardens of the vales
" By river side ; or aloes, planted by
" The Lord ; or cedar trees whose roots are laved
" By ever living streams.   His KING shall come,
" Above the kings of earth, a Star, a Prince
" Of Jacob.   Moab then shall fall ; and Sheth
" Shall perish ; Edom be a prey ; and HE
" Shall reign ; and Amalek be blotted from
" The earth.   And lo ! the Kenite, nested in
" The rock, shall be a captive, borne away
" By Ashur, never to return.   Alas !
" And who shall live when God doth this ?   And then
" Shall Ashur, and shall Eber fail ; (when ships
" From Chittim come ;) and perish ever from
" The face of earth."   He said, the prophet, and

Returned ; and Balak went his way. A snare
Was laid for Isr'el ; and he fell to lust
And idols. And the plagues of God beswept
The camp, and twice ten thousand slew.   'Twas done!
The host was purged ; the sinners slain ; the last
Of those who had rebelled so oft ; of whom
'Twas said, that they should never enter in
And see that rest. And now a race was left,
Far other than that grov'ling crew that left
The Egyptian land,—a people young, and strong ;
And trained to virtue, and obedience ; true
To God's commands ; a race of higher thoughts
Than flesh pots, leeks, and all the fare possessed
In bondage ; and enjoyed, if that can be,
Beneath the whip, the daily scourge that called
Them forth to toil ;—a race that ready stood
To enter in, and take the chance of war,
At God's command, to give their children rest ;
And leave a home for them in after times.
A patriotism here, not seen before
In Isr'el's ranks : which gave full promise of
A nation, high in aims and power, in time,
From them to spring ; a glorious presage this !
  But Moses still remained ; though faithful found,
Yet he must enter not, for one, one sin
Alone. He smote the rock unbid, and smote
It twice, at Meribah. A flood poured forth ;
The thirst was slaked, but God, displeased ; for he
Was not extolled in Isr'el's sight ; and hence,
Another should the honor take, and bring
Them in. And he must tarry there ; and find
His grave on this side Jordan. Such is sin ;
Abhorred of God in all alike. Then sin

Not, O my soul! lest thou come short at last,
And fail of REST ; but hasten! flee at once
To Him who hath atoned, and will forgive.

His *work* was not yet done, and he was spared,
But Aaron, Miriam, both had sinned in face
Of all, and both were gone.   Their work was o'er,
And Eleazer wore the priestly robes
That Aaron erst had worn.   Now, what remained?
The time was full ; the forty years expired ;
The camp was cleansed ; the land in sight, so long
To Abram's seed bequeathed.   (How faithful God,
To all his promises!) The number must
Be cast, and all prepared ; and then the REST
Obtained.   The host is written down ; and lo!
How true the word of God! Not one of all
The names enrolled on Sinai's plain is left :
(Save two   of twelve that went to spy the land.)
But all have perished, swept from out the host
By death, and plagues, and fires ; fruit sad of their
Rebellious ways, and unbelieving heart!
A lesson this in after times to those
Who disbelieve, and disobey.   They said
" Their little ones should be a prey, and die
" In that lone wilderness."   But here they were,
To manhood grown ; preserved, while they themselves
• Were dead, who had no faith in God, his word,
Or power.

                    Now Moses, warned of God, bestows
His last and fervent charge ; recounts the law,
Their sins, and blessings, o'er ; and shows them what
Shall be in after times if they forsake
Their God ; " Cast out and scattered to the ends
" Of earth ; their lovely Canaan lost ; and they

" Shall dwell in lands unknown ; their sons no more ;
" Their daughters fair to others giv'n ; and they
" Shall mourn their loss ; and long for their return.
" Their eye shall look, and look, the live-long day ;
" And fail : their heart grow sick, and far away,
" Shall bow themselves to gods of wood, and stone.
" A wonder shall they be in every land ;
" A proverb and a by-word there.   In thirst
" And hunger shall they serve ; in nakedness,
" And want, and sore distress.   The plague shall smite
" Them ; and their numbers, few, be scattered as
" The chaff, in ev'ry land on earth.   And then,
" No ease ! no rest ! but trembling there of heart.
" And every eye with sorrow shall be full.
" Their life, in doubt from day to day, shall hang
" Upon a thread.   In morning, they shall pray
" For night ; at night, shall wish the morning come ;
" And they shall in the market stand, and there
" Be sold away, till none shall deign to buy :
" Because they left the Lord their God, and gave
" Their hearts to gods of earth."   Thus Moses spake
Inspired ; and warns them to beware, and cleave
To HIM ; and drive the nations out ; and hold
Their rest, forever theirs if lost not by
Themselves.   Then shows what blessings shall ensue
If found obedient to God.   " The heavens
" Shall give their timely rain ; the mines their wealth ;
" And bursting harvests crown the lab'rers toil.
" And they, abound in every good, desired,
" In gold, in flocks, and herds, and wine, and oil.
" Their multitudes shall be as stars of heaven ;
" And they be head of all the nations round,
" And shall possess the land to end of time.

" Then teach your children in the ways of truth ;
" Rehearse the law, and wonders God hath wrought :
" When rising up, and sitting down ; at home,
" Or in the field ; or journ'ying far away.
" And write them on thy posts, and on thy gates :
" That they remember and obey. And thus
" Preserve the Rest vouchsafed to them ; a land
" Forever blessed of God. Preserve my word
" Untouched ; add not thereto, nor take therefrom ;
" Nor worship idols, sun or moon or stars,
" The host of Heaven ; nor divination use,
" Nor seek for charmers, as the nation do,
" T' unravel mysteries and things to come ;
" But know, the Lord shall raise a prophet up,
" Like me, within your midst, and of your tribes :
" Such things shall he reveal : and him
" Shall ye obey. And it shall be, that who
" Will not that prophet hear, shall be destroyed
" From out among the people. Take good heed !"
　　The time is come at length. The number cast,
The charges given, and leader named to bring
Them in, the work is o'er. And Moses now
Must yield command, and leave the field. But first,
He shall behold the Promised Land.　　From top
Of Pisgah, stretched in length and breadth, he views,
Enrapt, with vision cleared by power Divine,
Its lovely hills, and vales, and silver streams,
And gushing springs ; its forests, fruits, and fields ;
The future home of his relinquished care :
Which God had promised long in days elapsed,
And now would soon fulfill.　　He died ; and there
Was buried, by the hand of God. He found
Another *Rest*, a better far, for him

Prepared. His faithful, God will never leave,
Be sure. How much they fail on earth of their
Desires, th' amend shall be in Heaven ; and all
Be well. Yes, God fails not in his rewards ;
If failure, 'tis the fault of man. The day
Had come ; the host must cross that Jordan. Though
Its tide is high, from harvest rains, and all
Its banks are 'whelmed, a way shall be prepared
For God's elect. The priests go forward with
The ark in charge ; and as their feet in-dip
The stream, its waves divide, as erst the tide
On Egypt's coast. They stand a heap above,
A lake outspread at length ; o'erflow the vales
And all the works of man ; and menace death
And ruin to the region round : while far
Below, the waters fail ; surprising sight !
And all in wonder gaze ; and cross dry shod.
And children sport upon the pebbly bed,
With keen delight, and dip their hands within
The crystal wall. They pass the stream, and spread
Their flowing ranks, with all their flocks and herds ;
And pitch their tents upon the plains beyond,
The verdant plains of Jericho ; and there
The tribes were circumcised ; the feast of God
Was kept ; the corn of Canaan eat ; and lo !
The manna ceased ; no more to fall : save that
Great Bread that cometh down, whereof the man
That eats shall never die. O ! haste the time ;
When all shall eat and live. The nations saw.
Their hearts within them failed ; for who can stand
Against the God of Heaven, the God that shakes
The earth, divides the sea to make a path
For his redeemed ; and dries the rivers up ?

Their gates were shut ; their walls, their only hope.
How vain ! What walls can save us from the wrath
Of God ? Their time had come ; their sin was full ;
" The Amorite shall be extinct !" A race,
Another race ensue, more likely to
Obey the laws of God. And if they fail
They too shall be expunged ; and lo ! the land,
The promised land, again be trodden down
Of Gentiles ; yes, till God shall bring a race,
A people in ; all circumcised in heart ;
That shall forever keep his law, and hold
Their land, to end of time, " the Christian's rest,"
Prefigured by the Canaan then possessed.
   'Tis thus the Lord will purge the earth of sin.
The nations that forget him shall decline,
By slow decay, or be o'erthrown at once ;
While those, more loyal, shall increase in power
And multitude. And thus the work go on ;
Supplanting and supplying, till the dark
And deadly haunts of sin shall be no more ;
The habitations of the cruel fail ;
Oppressions cease ; and righteousness at length
Succeed, and triumph through the earth. Let all
Beware ! let nations fear ; nor dream them safe,
Though great in power, amidst their public sins.
He waiteth long, but will at length arise,
And scourge ; or sweep the guilty people from
The earth. Go search the past ; go read
The tombs and stones of hundred gated Thebes ;
Or Shinar's plains ; go brood o'er guilty Greece,
Or still more guilty Rome ; and ask for all
Their glory and their might. Their days were marked
With blood. The rankest crimes were crimes of State.

The millions groaned beneath th' oppressor's arm.
And man became the prey of man. *And they*
Are not. It ever shall be so, till men
Shall heed the righteous laws of God. Beware!
Let Albion beware, the sea-girt isle ;
And Westerland beware, our home beloved!
Where much is giv'n, sure much shall be required
   Behold our land! we boasted free ; and yet
One man of six, one woman out of six,
One babe of six were late but things in trade ;
Dispoiled of rights ; without the pale of law ;
And given over to the will, the fierce
Ungovernable will mayhap, of some
Despotic lord. For them no justice held
The scales, though claimed for all ; O tell it not
In Gath, nor let the sound reach Askelon!
No cry was heard in law ; the ear was deaf ;
Their plea was all in vain ; their groanings reached
To Heav'n ; their tears bedewed the earth ; the book
Of knowledge closed ; and e'en God's word, denied :
The man thus made a brute, for lucre or
For lust ; and *saints* of God approved the deed!!
Such saints ! O how of late we've seen our sin!
And loathed it from our very souls.
                    The church
Is safe ; has entered in ; and stands upon
The land to Abram giv'n : but still her foes
Remain to be subdued. Her trust is all
In God. His arm alone can be their strength.
The captain of the host of God is in
The camp, by Joshua seen, with sword unsheathed,
To lead the armies on. The walls, so sure
And firm, of Jericho, are leveled with

A shout ; and Rahab only, who concealed
The spies, and all her household, spared, at God's
Command. The city was accursed, accursed
From God for all their sins ; nor man, nor beast
Should live. The site was cleansed by fire, that left
A blackened heap where palaces had stood,
And princely halls, the seats of revelry
And sin.   And let none build, none dare to build
" Those impious walls again ; a curse be on
" Him. In his elder born he shall begin,
" And in his youngest son the gates shall rise."
    This Hiel did, in after times ; and lo !
The curse was his.   Now Ai falls at length,
And Gibeon lives by wiles. Makedah's cave
Conceals the flying kings ; and sun and moon
Stand still at Joshua's command ; and storms
Arise, and hail-stones sweep amain, and death
And slaughter reign o'er Gibeon's plains.   He falls,
The Amorite. He melts like snow before
The sun. At night the kings are slain. What change
A day has made ! When God arises who
Can stand ? The nations vanish as the dew.
Let them be humble then and keep his law.
    The land, subdued at length, is sorted out
By lot among the Tribes. And now they have
Their " Rest," as God had said. But will they keep
It ? Will they cleave to him, and be a praise,
A glory through the earth, a way-mark to
The wand'ring lost, an ever-burning light
To ev'ry gentile tribe ? Ah ! no. The muse
With tearful eye must meditate their sins ;
Their lapse from God ; and thraldom to their foes ;
And, after long forbearance on the part

Of him, their final scattering to the winds
Of Heaven. Their tears shall water every soil ;
Their wand'rings, witness ev'ry clime ; their groans
Shall sadden ev'ry breeze : Because they failed
In their high calling to a darkened world.
   Their leader gone, and thus restraint removed,
And ease secured from foes subdued or awed
To silence by their mighty deeds, there sprung
At length defection from the law of God.
The heart grew cold, the stealthy leaven of
Their pagan foes still left, was seen full soon.
Idolatries came in, and every sin
The law forbids ; and they were sold to serve
And cringe as bondmen to some heathen lord.
   At times repentant grown, they cried from out
The depths ; and God vouchsafed to hear.
Their foes were scattered ; they, redeemed. But lo !
They sinned again ; uncircumcised in heart,
Forgot the Lord, and all deliv'rance wrought.
Not all. A few were ever found who feared
The Lord amid that sinful race ; the true,
The real Abrahamic seed ; the church
Within a church ; the salt of earth ; to whom
The promise of a better rest was sure,
If faithful to the end ; a Heavenly, meant
For all, but reached by few. O Isr'el! Why
For ever sliding back, and wrecking all
Thy hopes ? But yet, the purpose high of God
Shall not be foiled, to bring a Saviour from
The Hebrew race. Though they may fail of good
To them ; of good untold ; of blessedness,
Of earth and Heaven within their reach ; yet they
Shall be the bearer of the Son-of-God,

A Saviour to a lost and dying world.
How sad ! to make themselves but scaffolding
To build the pile, then cleared away, instead
Of pillars fixed forever in the house !
They have their choice, to bless the world, to bless
By good received, and then imparted to
The ends of earth ; or bless, a beacon-light,
A warning to the end of time.
                                    The years
Sweep on, and judges yield to kings ; who reign
In righteousness, or sin, as seems them best ;
And empires crumble from the foot of time ;
And nations new arise ; and slowly shape
The moral face of things for that great time
When earth shall see her Lord.
                                    Meanwhile, the church
Was rocking to and fro, 'midst fearful surge
Of warring nations as a bark bestormed
At sea ; now strong, now weak, as right, or sin
Prevailed ; now great with David, and his son
Of glorious name, who built the House, and saw
The shekena appear : and nations bend
In homage at her feet ;—then broken as
A rush, and thinned, and far away. She sat
Alone, in sackcloth clad, by chilly stream
Of Babylon ; with harp unused, and on
The willows hung. No song of Zion there
To cheer her lonely hours ; no heart to sing ;
But tears instead, and ever longing for
Her native land. The rod was sore upon
Her, but she lived. Chastized, and penitent,
She learned, no more to serve the gods of earth.
What other sins she had in after times,

She had not this. Returned, she built the walls
Anew, and raised the HOUSE, less costly, far,
Nor Ark was there ; nor Cherubim ; and lost,
The Urim and the Thummim ; yet, be sure
That this, this house, so far beneath in show,
Shall be more glorious than the first ; shall see,
Shall see the great Messiah, come, so long,
Desired, and yet so long delayed. But, O !
How weak ! a remnant only saved ; Tribes ten
Are lost ; forever gone ; their lovely land
To strangers giv'n ; their wand'rings, who shall trace ?
Their sorrows, who shall tell ? The Judgment shall
Reveal the whole. Till then, a mystery,
A vail impenetrable shrouds their fate.

The years still roll ; events are rip'ning fast ;
The time draws nigh ; the signs are full, and clear ;
The nations sheath their swords, and hush their jars.
—The gate of Janus, closed—and silent stand,
And breathless wait the coming of their King.

MESSIAH COMES ! A shout rolls round the earth,
And echoes through the universe of God.
Within the church his birth ; of woman made ;
The Son of God, and destined to redeem
The world ; a Prophet, Priest and King, to sit
Forever on his father David's throne.

The shock went down to Hell ; and spread alarm
And jarred that orb, that vast, uncompassed orb,
That God-forsaken orb, where devils dwell.

END OF BOOK FOURTH.

BOOK V.

TIME waited not. A thousand years and more
Had swept along since Satan, foiled, had slunk
To Hell, at death of Korah and his crew.
But Hell meanwhile had not been still. That world,
Intent on wrong, can never rest. They'd eyed
The church of God, as eagles eye the lamb,
The tender lamb, and wait their moment to
Devour. The gods of Hell had roamed the earth,
And conquests made, and trophies won ; had turned
The people from the living God. But yet
Had failed in their great end ; and rout and shame
Had marked their course at last. And all were chafed
And harrowed to the quick, at thought of what
They'd promised, and of what performed. And now
A council must be called for measures new ;
And each look other in the face, and there
Give in that all their boasting was but wind.

    And Satan ventured now to give the call ;
The first since his defeat at Korah slain.
The gods were humbled. They had tried their skill
A thousand years, as seemed them best ; at times
With sanguine promise of success. The Tribes
Were at their feet, and angry bolts on high
Seemed waiting to destroy. Each had his time,
But mostly Peor, Baal, Ashtaroth,
Astarte, Moloch, Baalberith, and
10

A host from Egypt come.   These all, with more,
Had had their fields, and failed ; and had their turn
In coming back to Hell, as Satan did,
Chagrined, and branded to the soul with shame.
   They skulked, long time in caves ; and daily heard,
Unseen, the secret mirth, and blistering laugh
Of devils at their fall.   But they must now
Come forth to meet the call.   " A Son is born,
A child is given," that spreads dismay throughout
Their ranks, and augurs aught but good.   They meet,
(Not all the States are called, those near, but not
Those most remote.)   The cause demands dispatch.
They mingle with a courteous air, and smile
Of gracious mein, that speaks of harmony
Supreme.   How false ! judge not the wicked by
Their outward mood ; and that when all is calm.
   Now Satan, seated on his throne again,
Surrounded by those goodly peers, afresh
Feels courage lift his soul.   " It can not be,"
Thought he, " such wisdom, such angelic might
" Combined, should fail.   The cause, though long delayed,
" Shall yet be mine."   He rose, and spoke with hope ;
With buoy'nt hope ; with confidence ; that roused
The whole ; and each forgot his shame, and foul
Defeat.   " 'Tis noised," said he, " through earth and Heaven,
" And echoed down to Hell, the Seed is born,
" The Shiloh come ; the King to rule : whose sway
" Shall have no bound of space or time ; to whom
" The nations all shall bend, and angels of
" The highest grade in Heaven—yes, let them bend,
" But never those in Hell ; no, never !   We
" Acknowledge no supreme beyond our realm ;
" No rule called higher law ; and wo betide

" The Son should he attempt to force it here.
" But he shall yet be ours, if we combine.
" (Combine, we must, or sink, forever sink.)
" For 'tis our strifes, our discords 'mong ourselves,
" That foil our schemes.   We toil apart, and thwart
" Each other's plans, and look with jealous eyes ;
" And each the selfish honor seeks ; and hence
" We're weak.   At first, we aim aright ; then all
" Is wrong again.   Now B'elzebub lifts up,
" With might and main, and Ashtaroth pulls down ;
" And Chemosh forward moves, and Jupiter
" Holds back, that wise and thundering god.   Is this
" Befitting gods ?   So weak and blind ?   How wise
" In times gone by, when erst in Heav'n we dwelt !
" Has Hell thus robbed us of our better thoughts,
" And higher aims ?   For shame !   The angels will
" Deride us, and avouch that Hell benumbs
" The intellect ; and strips of fairest gifts
" The angelic mind ; lets loose in wildest form
" The storm of passion, rendering each unfit
" For good.   We wish to prove them false, and show
" That Hell is better far than Heaven for all
" That's lovely deemed.   Dismiss, then, jars ; the dome
" Will never rise of our success.   Like those
" Who built the pile on Shinar's plains, our fate
" Is sealed.   From discords loud and long the work
" Must cease ; and we be scattered to the winds
" Of Heaven.   But firm combined in phalanx strong,
" All petty jealousies expunged, and our
" Great work at heart, in all as one, we shall
" Achieve success, that e'en shall frighten earth,
" And startle Heaven.   The Son—mark this—shall yet
" Be ours, a second Adam called.   The first

" At once in toils complete, and uncombined,
" We bound. This second, stronger true, but we,
" Combined, shall yet o'ercome : and then the field
" Be ours throughout all time ; for this, observe,
" *Is man's last hope.* If he saves not, then all
" Is lost with him. He has no other hope,
" No refuge left. Then how? Let every god
" Bethink himself ; and each propose the best
" His mind conceives : that we in council, of
" Our wisdom may select the surest means
" To reach our end. Shall we destroy? let that
" Be settled first ; or but seduce, and bring
" Him to our part? "—" Destroy," said Sciva ; and
The savage god stood up, impatient for
The work. " He's but an infant ; let the task
" Be mine. I'll straight to earth, and soon report
" The deed achieved, and all secure."

                                          Each eye
Was turned upon him as he stood ; uncouth
And fiery in his mein, and half a brute.
   " But how? " said Satan.—" He's of Bethlehem,"
In quick reply said Sciva. " Let me go.
" The infants there shall die ; and with them he
" Shall meet his fate." " By whom? " " By Herod," said
The god. This pleased them all. They bowed assent
And voted Sciva master of the field,
To try his hand.   And hope revived. Each face
Was cheerful. Such a sight in Hell had not
Been seen before for ages. But how short
The sunshine to the wicked given, ere clouds
Ensue, and darken all their sky, and hang
Forever o'er their fate!   It shall be so
With these. Their joy shall turn to gall ; and they

Again shall learn, if devils e'er can learn,
There is a higher power, that still shall foil
Their well laid schemes, and show that he will reign.
 Th' assembly o'er, the proud unlifted god,
With self-complacent smile, retires from out
The throng : is soon prepared, and on the wing
For earth ; with fiery speed and keenest scent
Of blood ; of infant blood. It nerved his flight,
And urged him on. O mother, clasp your child !
Its time is short. A bird of omen dread
Is on the wing ; a vulture from the deep.
He snuffs its life, and swift and swifter speeds
His direful way. In Rama shall a voice
Be heard ; and tears shall flow, and hearts shall bleed,
And Rachel shall refuse relief. Her babes
Are not. He voyaged now as Satan had before ;
With dire intent, and fierce impetuous wing.
The track, the same ; the space, the same ; the deep,
The same ; the awful deep above and deep
Below ; where stillness reigns, far out from all
The works of God, save roar and dismal howl
Of storms and doleful winds, that ever and
Anon arise, and sweep in tempest high,
Or direst hurricanes,—through all that waste,
That barren waste ; and frighten Silence with
A ghastly fear. For, Silence there holds sway ;
One hand uplift to hush ; the other on
Her lips forever sealed. These awful storms,
Unknown on earth, now crossed his path, and woke
His fears, and veer'd him from his course afar.
But instinct led him on ; and scent of death,
A luckless gift, and brought him safe to earth ;—
Though shattered as a ship bestormed at sea

With shivered sails and spars, and battered hull—
And near his fated, fair and helpless prey.
What errand for a god! yet such the gods
Of Hell.   He seeks out Herod, and the work
Begins.   O Bethlehem! what scene was thine!
The mothers flee, like doves before the fierce,
Determined eagle's grasp.   Each bears her babe
Upon her breast, and flies to cave, and lone
Retreat.   But all in vain !   The ministers
Of death pursue, and seek with care ; if foiled,
In ambush wait till want shall bring them forth ;
Or wail of infant voice, not full suppressed,
Shall guide their deadly feet.   The mother, fierce,
And mad to desperate deeds, defies them in
Her lair.   But what avail ?   The ruffian blade
No mercy knows ; but strikes her down, and all
Is o'er.   The mother and the babe are wrapped
In death.   Their blood is mingled warm upon
The cavern's hearth.   But yet shall have a voice,
And call down vengeance on the guilty head.
     Another, and another bleeds.   From hill
To vale, from copse to streamlet's side, the search,
Pursued, its victim finds, which, ruthless dragged
By murderous hands from out the fierce-clenched arms
Of ghastly, shrieking mother,   dashed against
The stones, or pierced with brutal steel—yields up
Its tender life.
              O God ! why suffered such
Atrocities on earth ?   The strong devour
The weak ; the guilty live ; the innocent
Expire ; O ! why ?   The judgment shall declare,
Shall make it plain.   Is it that sin shall write
Her chapter out, shall solve her problem first,

And grave it on the marble face of time ;
Then righteousness, brought in, shall write out hers,
And solve her problem to a judging world :
That all may see, and to the end of time
Declare the grand results, compared ?—Then haste
The day. The heart is sick, the longing eye
Grows dim. We wait, we fail.
                    The slaughter o'er,
The weeping heard, the deadly god retires,
Refreshed as from a vernal, morning walk ;
And telegraphs to Hell, that " all is o'er ;
" The deed is done ; the Son destroyed ; and Hell
" Forever safe." This took them by surprise
So quick, so sure the work. A shout arose,
And Hell was wild with joy. The dread was gone,
That gnawed their vitals through, and broke their rest,
What little rest that world can give. The fiend,
Elate, is speedy on the wing ; and flies
The abyss again, and lands at home full soon
Among the damned. They crowd around him, and
Demand the news in full. He scarce replies ;
Impuffed with pride ; but simply said " 'twas strange
" No other god could gain success on earth,"
And then retired for rest and due repair
Of damages, incurred from voyage wide
And dang'rous.   Soon in conclave, duly called
To hear report, the god explained the whole,
With ostentatious air, and ill-judged phrase,
That half conveyed offence ; and then desired
A triumph to be given, on day prescribed,
To him as savior of the land. He sat.
This Satan deemed " but just "—from policy,
That devils might be true.—The day was fixed ;

And great the concourse warned to be on hand ;
And arches rose, adorned with wise device ;
And fiery steeds, prepared ; and chaplets gay
To press the victor's brow. The day arrived ; the day
Triumphal for the victor god. The lords of Hell
Appear ; the often baffled lords, to yield
The palm to Sciva, doubtless due, yet grudged
Full sore.   The stir was great ; the multitude
Immense, which spread and thickened as the day
Rolled up. And Sciva's heart beat high. From thence
Forever should he sit, a god above
The gods, the savior of the damned : when lo !
A voice was heard, an awful voice, that stung
In every ear. " From Egypt have I called
" My Son." This struck them dumb, and ghastly pale.
Their spirits sank amain ; their souls grew sick ;
And faintness came o'er all. They reeled to fall.
An earthquake raved throughout that wide domain,
And cast them down, and ripped the very crust
Of Hell ; and shattered all their hopes. Vain ! vain
The efforts to o'erthrow the plans of God !
    They strive, the wicked, and forever fail ;
Yet strive again, not forced, but of their own
Accord. The stone they labor to the top,
Recoils, and seeks the vale again.
And still they toil it up, and still it seeks
Again the vale. It ever will be so.
    But none so much dismayed and stunned at this
Announcement as the inflated Sciva. All
His hopes were dead, of eminence among
His peers ; and he reduced to what he was
Before, a savage, half-respected god :
Nay, worse, the laugh of Hell. 'Twas on him now.

For though they felt full sore the dreadful truth,
" The Son still lives," recovered from the first
Appalling shock, they half rejoiced, as freed
From everlasting insolence and pain
Of Sciva's pride.   They laughed, at length, and clapped,
And tore the very ground on which they stood.
And Sciva heard with shame and crimson spite.
Not daring to avenge, he fled the throng
With speedy wing.   Another shout, and still
Another rose, as he escaped.   He heard
The roar behind ; and far beyond the verge
Of horizontal sky, he sought retreat
In some secluded nook ; and, found at length,
He fled again their haunting, devilish shrieks :
Till far from Hell, he 'scaped to earth, and thence,
The bitter god, he roamed the isles ; but chief
In Indian clime, the direst scourge ; and there
Demanded infants as his daily due.

   O Ganges! goodly stream, but sacred to
The dread, exacting fiend ; what thousands hast
Thou slain ; whose lovely forms and tender limbs
Have wasted in the slime upon thy bed,
Or fed the direful crockodile within
Thy wave !   The time shall come, be patient, earth,
When he shall scourge no more ; but when
The Son in plenitude shall reign, and purge
The earth, the long, long suffering earth.—O day!
Roll on thy speedy orb, and bring the much
Desired, the glorious morn.

       " From Egypt have
" I called my Son."   The Son appeared again ;
A Galilean now ; in stature grew,
And favor both of God and man ; a child,

A holy child, and Jesus called ; a name
To save the people from their sins ;—a youth
Without one fault, one blemish in his life ;
His daily walk, affectionate and kind ;
Of temper mild ; of rarest wisdom full ;
A wonderment on earth.—To manhood grown,
The same ; but firm in teaching, and the cause
Of truth.   The Pharisee and Scribe, corrupt,
And proud, and selfish, heard with lip of scorn,
And inward spite.   His stern rebukes upstirred
Their inmost gall : while all who sought for peace
And righteousness, hung ravished on his words,
And drank them in as living waters to
A thirsty, dying soul.   The poor were his,
The halt, the blind, and e'en the leper, and
The vile, the penitent, returning vile ;
And all the sick, from babes to hoary years.

These came, these sought, and found relief.   He took
Their sicknesses and bare their pains ; and called
The erring from their wand'rings home.—He shunned
The ways of state, and sought the humble roof
As his abode.   His simple truths fell on
The ear of waiting souls like dew ; and still
Majestic rose in life and power, that shamed
The lifeless scribe, and waked his wrath.   No pomp!
No state ! a meek, a lowly heart, a friend
Of all, of publicans and sinners, sent
To gather in, and save the wand'ring sheep
Of Isr'el's race ; nay, nay, of other folds,
The sheep, astray, of all the world.—So long
Desired, the reign has now begun, of peace
And righteousness throughout the world.   This, this
The prophet saw ; whose eye, unvailed, looked down

The vista long of coming years ; " begun ! "
It shall not fail.   The culminating day
Is sure.   His people shall be one, and fill
The earth.   And Ephr'im's envy rise no more,
And Juda cease to vex.   The wolf and lamb
Shall lie in peace, the leopard and the kid ;
The fatling and the lion, join ; and asps
And adders be the sport of infant hands.
   The sons of Africa no more shall bleed,
And Russ and Gaul no more in combat join ;
Nor Albion's thunder fright the distant isles ;
Nor armies sweep o'er India's eden plains ;
Nor race nor caste a barrier be to love ;
Nor ocean groan with armaments and death ;
Nor China's gates be closed against the world ;
Nor Japan isles be sealed, and bar approach
With jealous battlements, and frowning guns.
   These all shall be among the things that were ;
And works of peace shall crown the happy year,
The jubilee of earth.
                    Then science, bright,
Shall shine ; and knowledge shall increase ; and art
Shall rise, to bless the earth.   Man's greatest toil
Shall cease ; the harnessed elements shall break
The sod, shall sow, shall till, shall reap the fields,
And gather into barns ; and e'en the beast
Shall find his rest, and be partaker of
The joy.   The wastes of earth shall be redeemed ;
And lovely harvests wave o'er bogs and fens,
That now steam up with poisonous breath, and load
The air with dire disease.   Our race shall swell,
And spread from shore to shore ; from isle to isle ;
Till every nook shall have its man ; shall yield

Its fruit; and earth throughout her wide domain
Shall hold her billions, and shall flourish as
The garden of the Lord. Sahara too
Shall shine in green, an oasis become,
Redeemed by duct of Nile, mayhap, and art
And science joined, and waters, springing from
Her arid soil, from their imprisoned depths
Below,—who knows?—and made the happy home
Of man. Such, such the sequel sure of wars
And human jars subdued, and vice extinct,
And love and righteousness triumphant on ·
The earth. 'Twill come. But long the contest first
Twixt light and shade, twixt true and false.
And years by thousands shall elapse ere it
Be done.
            Now Satan, come to earth, like pard
In ambush for its prey, belurked the Son
Of man where'er he went, with hope not dead,
That he might still be snared, or slain outright.
He found him in the wilderness alone,
And there assayed to draw him off from God.
Then on the temple's peak, in sport he fain
Would have him leap the dizzy hight. Mayhap
The stones below would crush his hated life.

He failed, retired, but not from out the field.
The struggle shall not cease, e'en after hope
Is dead. The garden next he seeks, and there
The Son of Man besets, in struggle fierce
And desp'rate. Close the contact; spirit foul
With spirit pure. A suffering indeed.
Alone the Son appeared, but spirit eyes
Discerned the whole, withheld from human sight :
Saw Satan hang, like deadly serpent on

A virgin's chest, and writhe him round and round
His sacred limbs, as if forsaken of
His God. Amazed they saw, and wondered as
They gazed. 'Twas then that he was bruised, for our
Offence. His soul was sorrowful to death ;
And while the strong and loathsome fiend held grasp,
The blood, astart, came oozing from his flesh,
And fell in sweat-drops to the pitying earth.
He sought relief, and to his brethren came ;
But what could they? Ah! who could ease that pain?
The sin, the sin of worlds, and ages long,
Was summed in that dread hour, in all its weight.
He then returned, and agonized again ;
And cried, " O Father! let the cup go by,
" But yet thy will be done." Again, again,
He prayed, and said the same, and he was heard.
That moment Satan fled ; and angels flew
To his relief, withheld before, they knew not why.
O man! forget it not ; it was for thee,
That pain was felt, that bruising done.
  Still, Satan sought his life ; and used the priests,
Corrupt, for his design. They clamored for
His blood ; and stirred the people up to join
In the demand ; and feeble Pilate quailed
Before their voice. Though warned, he gave him to
Their will ; and he was bound, and scourged, and spit
Upon, and mocked, and led to Golgotha,
A place of skulls, and there was crucified !
  Now Satan's hope was brimming up. He *had*
Prevailed ; and telegraphed to Hell to that
Effect. " The Son, so late the dread of all,
" Is now o'ercome, his kingdom not set up,
" But is in dying pangs upon a cross,

"With thief and robber." Then a shout arose
That shook the firmament of Hell ; and lived,
And rolled, and rolled throughout her wide domain.
 A weight again had ris'n from their souls,
That, like a mountain-incubus, had crushed
Them down. They ran, they flew, they laughed, they beat
The suff'ring air with devilish wings ; and hurled
The arid soil in whirlwinds to the clouds.
 Ah ! little thought they that the *death* of him,
So much their joy just now, would prove ere long
The death of them ; that *death* was in the plan,
The programme of redemption of the race
Of man. They erred, as devils always do,
And wicked men.
                          He hangs upon the cross ;
The Son of God. The sun looks down amazed,
And vails his face ; and distant suns withhold
Their light ; and darkness hangs in fearful shade
Through all the vast unmeasured universe
Of God! "I thirst," he cried ;—and, soon again,
" 'Tis finished ! "—and he yielded up his life.
 The earth is shaken to her very core.
The mountain rocks are rent ; and other orbs
Receive the shock ; and trembling spreads from world
To world, in sympathy with earth. But who
Can tell what ruin swept through Hell ?
That orb was rocked with direst throes ;
Its mountains leaped from off their seats, and sought
With headlong plunge, the vales ; and devil, dashed
On devil, ghastly pale, and helpless, strowed
The ground : and Satan's head was bruised ; a wound
Forever to remain !
                    " 'Tis finished ! " all

The types arc dead ; the sacrifices, o'er ;
The Aaronic priesthood, gone ; the holiest place,
Unvailed ; the middle wall, struck down ; the Jew
And Gentile, one.   The priesthood changed, the law
Itself is changed ; and life vouchsafed
To man on better grounds.   A sepulchre
The lifeless body holds ; is sealed with care,
And guarded by a Roman band.   How vain !
The third day dawns ; an angel from the skies
Descends, with lightning visage and with robes
Of white ; terrific scene !   The keepers fall
As dead.   He backward rolls the stone, and sits
Thereon ; while Jesus leaves his tomb and walks
Abroad ; the first fruits now of them that sleep ;
An earnest of the harvest of the grave,
The great in-gath'ring of a day to come.
    He takes his life again, a proof in full,
Blest proof ! that man's redemption is achieved.
    He closes up his work on earth ; a cloud
Receives him up to Heaven ; where now he sits
At God's right hand, the Great High Priest, foreshown
By Aaron's line ; appearing with his own
Shed blood, for us ; a Mediator there,
'Twixt God and man ; " a priest forever " to
Espouse our cause ; who knows our ills and pains,
And feebleness of frame ; and can be moved
To pity, and can save to uttermost
The sinful sons of men who come to God
By him.   The Church, cut loose from rites and forms,
Is ready, now, to spread throughout the world ;
Without the lumber of the Jewish law ;
With simple worship, fitted to all states
Of men, all climes of earth ; the rich, the poor,

The bond, the free, the high, the low ; or 'neath
The torrid sun of middle zone, or skies
Of milder air ; or 'mid the arctic snows,
And ice, eternal, of the poles.   All now
Can rear their altars in their huts of mud
And straw, or palaces of ivory   .
And gold ; and there, in spirit and in truth,
Can worship God.   Blest, blest deliv'rance from
The Jewish yoke ; which they could never bear !
    Alas for Satan !   He has failed again ;
And failed when he was certain of success.
And this besides, a wound is on his head,
Which shall forever show ; shall tell his shame,
How much soe'er he may desire to hide ;
And devils, through all time, shall look and laugh ;
Shall inward laugh, and joy at his chagrin.
    And can he show himself again in Hell ?
And show his wounded head ?   He stays on earth ;
He stays, in hopes to yet retrieve his loss,
And gain his prestige, gone, by vict'ries won.
    He roams Judea like a rav'ning wolf ;
And eyes the scattered lambs of Jesus' fold ;
And waits the favored moment to devour ;
And gathers hope, forlorn, again.—Thought he,
" The shepherd safe, the sheep, may they not yet
Be mine ? "   The sheep, how thin the flock ! how weak !
And who shall shield them from their deadly foe ?
    A promise had been left, of foreign aid,
A spirit coming from on high, which should
Indue with light to know, and vigor to
Withstand direct assault.   It came ; 'twas on
The day of Pentecost.   A sound was heard,
A rushing sound of mighty winds, that shook

The house from roof to sill ; and then was felt
An inspiration never known before.
   'Tis done ; the promise is fulfilled ; the strength
And light arrived, to last to end of time ;
A promise to all flesh that shall obey
The Lord.   'Twas this the prophet saw.
" In after times," saith God, " my spirit will
" I pour upon all flesh, your daughters and
" Your sons shall prophesy, your aged men
" Shall dream, the younger, visions see."   Then spake
The ministers of Jesus, as the pow'r,
Infused, gave utt'rance, in the tongues of earth,
To them unknown before.   And tongues of fire,
With double flame, amazing sight! sat on the
Apostles' heads ; and thousands saw, and heard,
And turned to God.   The Elamite was there,
The Jew, the Parthian, the Mede, and those
Of Rome ; and men, devout, from every wind
Of Heaven.   The Church had now received her strength,
And each could view unmoved the mightiest foe.
   And Satan was again alarmed ; and hope
Nigh fled.   " It must be stayed, this tide of life
" And truth ; or 'twill o'ersweep the world.
" The ruler must be called, the priest invoked,
" The scribe and pharisee, and all must join,
" Or all is lost."   He stirred them up to fierce
And deadly rage.   But all in vain.   The threat
Of council, or the sight of chains, or dark
And loathsome dungeon, nay, of death itself,
Deterred not.   " JESUS " was the theme of all,
" The RESURRECTION and the LIFE."
   11

END OF BOOK FIFTH.

BOOK VI.

AND now
Sprung war in Hell ; such war that hostile realm
Had never known before. The effort was,
To rid themselves of Satan and his power ;
His power, that chafed and galled each devil
High and low. The elements had been at work
A thousand years and more ; conspiracies
Been planned, assassinations dire, and all
Were waiting but the favored time. The plots
Now ripe, and he so far away, and in
Contempt for failures won, a rush was made ;
And Hell was in a blaze. The chiefs were out.
The tocsin sounded from the towers in peals
Of awful tone. The masses gathered like
A sea ; and, frantic, swayed resistless through
The wide campaign. Conservatives grew pale ;
And direst licence raged, and hate and lust.

And Satan's strongest holds fell one be one
By force or treach'ry overcome. A few
Were faithful ; not for love to him, but for
The fare they had, and scope for every lust.

The strictest watch was kept ; none dared escape
To earth and bear the news. But Satan soon
Surmised the whole. Suspicious ever, and
Forever on his guard, as tyrants must

Needs be, he read the whole from one small fact,
'Twas this : he'd telegraphed to Hell for aid.
The telegram was short and clear : " The priest
" Is ours—the work, begun—the prisons, full.—
" One martyr's dead—a learned zealous Jew
" Is making havoc of the church.—They flee
" For life.—Send thousand thousand devils up
" To earth."—None came ! He saw his power was broke;
And rose with swiftest wing, and left for Hell.

Arrived upon her coasts, he scanned the scene,
Unviewed, aloft, in middle air, above
The clouds ; perceived his holds, or most of them
In other hands, and wildest anarchy
Afloat.   The object first, had been attained,
To crush the ruling power ; 'twas next, to build
Another up.   Herculean task ! 'mid chiefs
Corrupt.   A thousand devils claimed the right
To rule ; and each his faction had, and sought
By plots of darkest dye, the others to
O'erthrow ; and bound to him by ties as strong
As ties among such can be, whomso'er
He could, by bribes then given ; and promises
Of good to come, (though never to be kept.)
Each slandered every other chief ; and spread
The vilest falsehoods.   Needless this, for all
Were bad enough.   The simple truth was all
The slander they deserved.   The pit of Hell
Has politicians not unlike to those
On earth.   The good can cast off tyranny,
And settle government with ease, but not
The bad.   Ambition foils their every plan ;
And envy blocks the course of every good.
'Twas so with these.   Each faction grew in strength,

And spirit fierce, from week to week, from day
To day.—'Twas clear, that soon the clash of arms
Would ring through Hell. Not one could dare decline.
But all must take some part, or be the prey
Of all. State sad of Hell, and oftimes so
On earth. The work went on, and all took sides,
For " *Blue*," or " *Red*." Disputes ran high ; and all
Was ripening for a bloody field, now near.

And Satan held himself aloof ; and saw
With high delight the drift of things, most sure
In progress for himself. The like is found
On earth. The tyrant, once dethroned, retires,
And bides his time ; while discords reign, and wear
The masses down, till weak ; then strikes the blow,
And takes the crown again, an easy prize ;
Or else, corrupts, and stealthily slips in,
And gains his end.

Thus Satan from his seat,
Among the clouds, looks down, with joy, and sees,
At length, what he'd expected and desired,
The Red, and Blue, with rancor fierce, long drawn
In battle-show, and eager stand. He sees,
At last, the fight begin ; and carnage reign ;
And spirits fall. And noise and dust ascend,
And stun his ear, and choke his vision up.

The solid ground gives way ; and trembles like
An aspen leaf, beneath such deadly strife.
What engines pour amain their globes of death,
On either side ! Shaft answers shaft, lance lance.
And bolt replies to bolt. The day wears out,
A day forever to be marked. What heaps
Of spirits lie, as far as eye can reach,
Bestunned, and maimed, and rent, and torn, and stabbed !

The battle scale is turned.   The Red prevails ;
The Blue is worsted ; and, in broken ranks,
Escape the field ; nor stop till far away
From fierce avenging foe.   The Red is all
In all.   Now Hell will be content, and rest
Forever on a stable base.—Ah, no !
The Red divides again on White and Green ;
And battles rage again ; as Albion drenched
Her soil for years about the color of
A rose.   'Tis sure.   The waste of war fast wears
·Them out.   And now, the foiled, in hot revenge
Look out for Satan to espouse their cause,
And wreak their malice on their victor foes
Thus much for oaths in Hell, for all had sworn,
From freest choice, and hearty will, whate'er
Betide, forever to oppose his claims ;
That tyrant's, who had trod them down, and drawn
Their blood, and wrenched their very vitals out.
But spite, not faith, is paramount in Hell.

   There is a desert, far away, among
The wilds of Hell ; in length and breadth
Beyond the vision keen of spirit eyes ;
A barren of the barrens of that world.
Dread solitude ! infested with disease,
And direst ills.   The plague is there, such plague
As spirits dread ; and fiery serpents, clad
With wings, which stealthy glide in midnight shade,
Or noonday's murky hour, and dart upon
The unsuspecting spirit, wand'ring, or
At rest, and leave the deadliest stings behind
Then slip, ere apprehended, from his reach,
And seek another soul, and thrust their sting ;
A region ever dreaded by the damned ;

Untrod by them, except from outward cause
Of force or fear. 'Twas here the vanquished hosts
Had sought retreat, in desperate flight from foes ;
And, day by day, the numbers thicken, till
That tract contains its billions, scattered far
And near, of every grade, from chief of rank
To low plebeian caste ; begashed with wounds,
And broken with despair. They wander here,
Their only safe retreat. For on the bounds
Of that Sahara tract are outposts of
Their foes, whose sentinels keep watch, to seize
And crucify whatever spirit has
The madness to adventure out. Thus hemmed,
And galled with inward ills, and pressed
By outward foes, their minds are ready for
Some master-chief, who could combine their strength,
And lead them forth to glut their vengeance on
Their haughty foes. But who ? A multitude
Of broken chiefs they had, within their midst ;
But none pre-eminent in might and skill,
To whom the rest would yield. And now, e'en here,
The curse of faction is at work again ;
And plots are rife, and war will range ere long
Among this vanquished crew. In truth, *that* is
Indigenous in Hell. And from that world
Was first imported into earth. And men
Whose taste is war, are mostly little else
Than devils clothed in flesh. You ask me " who,
" Or where?" Come, walk with me to regions of
The West. Behold that simple tribe, with wives
And babes, encamped upon an eminence.
They hear the tramp of civil feet, and see
The deadly gun and glittering steel :

And woman's cheek grows pale, and infants
Seek their mothers' breast, with bursting hearts.
A " talk " is asked, and granted. O the faith !
The civil villain is but gaining time ;
And falls upon their unsuspecting rear,
And, treacherous, pours their blood like water on
The earth, their wild barbarian blood ; yet, in
The sight of God, as precious as the blood
Of civil man. And he has answered not,
(O shame! O   shame to Christian name,) for his
Misdeeds ; but e'en is high at court among
The powers that be. He lives, he breaths,
As yet, the brave unhung !   The time desired
By Satan now is ripe. He lights unseen
Upon the Death-waste tract ; and cautious views ;
Then slips within a cave ; and waits what more,
Or chance or tact may bring to light. He walks
Abroad, disguised ; and hears what may be heard,
And sees what may be seen ; and in his walks
Finds Ashtaroth, and sounds his mind ; and fain
Would know, " what could be done to 'scape that tract
" Of death, and end their exile ; far more dread
" And ignominious than the hateful reign
:" Of Satan.   Better far to have a brave
" And mighty chief, a king, an emperor,
" If e'en severe, and with him live, and rule,
" Than die, forever die, out cast from all,
" In this curst tract of Hell."   (The bruise upon
His head, which must needs show, he feigned he had
Received in recent fight.)   He vowed, " he wished
" That Satan, hated as he was, might soon
" Appear, and take command, and lead them 'gainst
" Their foes ; for he was brave, though wicked. and.

" Whatever else, would make Hell great ; and that
" Would sure atone for his despotic sway.
" What great deplore, that he can not be called!"
  He said no more ; but Ashtaroth was won.
A time was set when they should meet again ;
And both should go, and make what proselytes
They could, and bring report.   " But first, how could
" They reach the ear of Satan should the plan
" Succeed ?   To telegraph to earth could not
" Be done, as all was in the hands of foes,
" Whose watch was sleepless, and the slightest hint
" Would bring an avalanche of death upon
" Them all.   And O that fate!" (not Providence,
But fate,) " would bring him on."   They separate.
And both have now a work on hand ; and each
Pursues his course alone.   And Satan soon
Alights on Sciva, savage god, whose tastes
Were war, yet stealthy war, and, with his crew
Of like, most hideous in their yells when joined
In fight ; but, faced by firm battalion, quick
Dismayed and put to rout.   Him Satan won,
As Ashtaroth, before ; and sent to find
His savage warriors, scattered far and wide.
  Another and another still he wins.
And these win others ; and the infection spreads
For Satan like the plague.   They soon begin
To cast inquiring looks to earth, and wish
Some lucky chance might bring him near.
  He comes not ; and their days hang heavy on
Their hands.   They hope 'gainst hope. that he will yet
Appear, and lead them thence.   At length, surprised,
They hear a noise in upper air ; and feel
A whirlwind, as of force of multitude of

Of wings ; and cast their eyes aloft, and spy
A cloud of spirits, hovering o'er ; and in
Their midst, with unmistaken sign, the wide
Spread wings of Satan. These he'd mustered from
The earth ; and left that field to try his chance
Again in Hell. The churches then had rest
Through all the land ; and walking in the fear
Of God, and comfort of the Holy Ghost,
Were multiplied, and built up strong in grace.
    O ! happy for the church, when devils fight
Among themselves, and draw their forces off
From earth, to other fields of strife. These all
Descend, and near the center of this waste
Erect the standard of their chief, that waved,
A meteor broad, and swept the clouds ; but not
Descried at farthest bounds ; or else the alarm
Would spread that he had come ; and battle might
Ensue too soon. A handful now, and yet,
The largest hosts of earth were handfulls to
This few. A long and streaming pennon waved,
And signified the want of men as used
By shipmen here on earth ; which, seen afar,
Was heeded by the wandering lost, who turn
Their footsteps to that beacon-goal. And soon
They reach the camp, and swell the tide
Of spirit life ; a crowd, a sea at length ;
A multitude, that human thought could ne'er
Conceive. These join the ranks, as urged of late
By emissaries, sent to bring them o'er
To Satan's part ; and make a host to dread
With any leader, but, with Satan at
Their head, the great Napoleon of Hell,
It seemed invincible. And yet the strength

Of Hell was on the other side ; and, but
For discords, sprung from envy, hate, and lust
Of rule, impairing wisest councils, and
Bedamping zeal, he must needs fail ; nor reach
Again, forever, his imperial throne.

Meantime the rumor got afloat, by spies,
Or traitors borne, that Satan had arrived ;
And was in force upon the Death-waste, and
Would soon emerge, and strike for empire lost.

They knew his power, his arts, his tact in war.
The wildest agitation reigned throughout
That world.   O ! could the scattered elements
Combine, and each seditious chief but yield
To one ; and all, in unison of heart
And hand, receive the foe, then Satan's hopes
Were vain ; and they were safe.   But no ! the *will*.
The stubborn *will* of each unholy soul,
Forbade.   The common danger drove them to
Adhere awhile, and Jupiter was made
Their chief.   And each swore 'legiance with a dire
Terrific oath : and took commission from
His hand ; and all seemed safe.   The deadliest arms
Were made forthwith ; and awful thunderbolts
Were forged ; and fortresses of old repaired,
And manned with strength ; and new defences raised ;
And troops were under drill, from morn to night ;
Or on review ; and new recruits arrive,
Each hour ; and swell the fearful tide of war ;
And take their arms.   Their camps, in vast expanse,
Are spread.   Their standards, raised, and each estate
Have rank assigned to take in line when e'er
The call of battle shall require.   They wait
The foe from day to day.   The foe comes not ;

But, far within the Death-waste, bides his time.
"He fears," say they, "nor dares to cope with us,
"So vast." And hence their watch declines, and they
Betake themselves to revelry and lust;
Such revelry and lust as Hell can give,
Which wakes a burning thirst for more,
An inward Hell, and damns anew the damned.
O sad relief from pain! which brings but pain
The more. Yet such is Hell. They chose it, and
They have their choice; and must forever feel
Its woe. Forever! O, forever!! dread,
Appalling word! Let men beware; nor choose
The self-same wretched lot, the fate of all
Who live, and die in sin. *Let men beware!*
"Their watch declined." This Jupiter perceived,
But could not mend. The chiefs had factious grown
Again, and spurned his rule. 'Twas only fear
Could give him sway one hour. That hour soon came.
For, in the depth of night, amidst their dire
Debauch, and brawls, and fights, a sound was heard,
A tramp of feet, and beat of wings, that shook
The ground, and tortured all the air. And lo!
The cry, "They come! they come!" They flew to arms.
It was their only hope: and Jupiter
At once gains sway; and gives the word of war;
And all obey; obey as far as each
One could, amidst the uproar, and the rush
For arms and place. But scarce the line was formed,
Before the shock of battle struck. It reeled,
The line, but broke not, and regained its ground,
And stood like mount of adamant before
A volley fierce of thunderbolts; and hand
To hand the battle raged, 'midst darkness, and

The shouts and yells of foe, in deadly gripe
With foe.   The direst blows were giv'n ; and thrusts,
That told too well on spirit forms, and thinned
Their ranks.   The deadly carnage reigns till morn,
Till noon, til! murky twilight's hour : and both
Draw off for rest and what repairs a night
Could make.
                    What day had passed ! The annals of
The damned knew no such day before ; not e'en
The day the " Colors " met. The morrow ! O !
What scene the morrow will evolve ! Their blood
Was up ; and vengeance sworn on either side.
  They sleep upon their arms, to ward surprise.
But others sleep not, where they lay upon
The field of strife, the wounded, waking night
With groans, unknown on earth; and pierced through soul
With lance or dart in venom dipped : and writhe
And welter there upon the barbed shaft
Infixed : or hold for ease their gaping wounds
And mangled limbs ; and wait the coming morn,
O vain ! to give relief. Ah, what relief
Can devils find, and wounded devils too ?
Their wounds for ages shall endure ; the flesh
Of devils heals so slow, corrupt, and filled
With humors vile. And, healed at last,
The wounds shall break afresh, again, and yet
Again ! O Hell ! I would avoid thy ills,
Thy deadly ills, the cost be what it may,
A hand, an arm, an eye, *it would be wise.*
  " They sleep upon their arms," such sleep as can
Be had by spirits lost. " Yet some sleep not."
But spend the night in preparation for
The day ; procuring, or repairing arms,

Or sent for observation on the foe, or spies
Within his very camp, on either side.
　But Jupiter, and Satan, each within
His tent, alone, amid their hosts, prepare
With utmost skill their plans of battle for
The coming day. 'Twas done on charts demarked
With rule and line ; and showed the first assault,
Retreat, and ambush where ; the phalanx, where
To press ; and lighter legion, where ; and where
The lancers, and the heavy guns ; and where
The savage bow and battle-ax. For Hell
Combines all modes of fight in every age
And clime : and thence they found their way to earth,
To curse the human race.
　　　　　　　　　　　The morning dawns,
And with it brings the mustering to arms,
In either host ; and fierce desire for fight.
The lines are stretched immense, and eager stand ;
But waiting still the word of leader, not
Yet come from out his tent. 　Each soon appears,
With plume, and belt, and dazzling armor bright.
And mounts at once his daring fiery steed,
An equine thunderbolt in battle's hour,
And curbed with golden bit and diamond reins,
And full caparisoned for chiefs thus high.
Scarce held, they bear their riders to their fronts
And burn impatient for the coming fray.
　Here Satan shows in stature vast, and seems
A worthy god ; a god deserving all
Command. His lineaments of face bespeak
All firmness, and his low'ring brow denotes
Impenetrable thought : and hope, so rare
In Hell, displays a twilight in his eye.

And Jupiter, scarce less in stature and
In mien, and gorgeous sheen of armor, moves
Before his lines, and views their vast extent.
A god he seems as well, and worthy of
The trust assigned, to save them from the grasp
Of Satan's deadly rule. He spoke in brief,
And pointing to the foe on yonder plain,
Reminded them of " that perfidious chief,
" Who, bland, and promising a world of good,
" Had ever failed. He promised them in Heaven,
" The throne of God, and brought them down to Hell.
" And then reduced them to the merest slaves,
" To crawl beneath his feet, O faith ! and crushed
" Them ever with his iron heel. And now's
" The day of vengeance. Now shall he atone
" For all his nameless wrongs and perfidy,
" Imposed, displayed, that have for ages chafed,
" And broken down the spirits of the sons
" Of Heaven. And now shall he commence a life
" Of endless days in deepest, darkest pit
" That Hell can boast, a dungeon drear ;
" Or chained forever on some lonely rock
" In Hell's dread ocean, there shall waste his years,
" And feel the beat upon his naked soul,
" Of her tempestuous and eternal waves."
He ceased ; and fiery ardor filled each breast,
And blazed in fury from each devilish eye.
The dogs of war are straining on the leash,
Impatient for the slip.   What Satan spoke
To his, the muse recordeth not ; but scarce
They kept their lines, from vengeance raging in
Their hellish breasts.   The columns move full soon,
With steady pace, and that with martial strains,

So full, heroic, rich, that ears in Heaven
Might linger long to hear.　Thought sad !　It was
The prelude to a work of death.　　The lines,
In near array, an awful front disclose.—
A flash is seen—a sheet of sulph'rous flame—
A thunder bolt is hurled ; and flash on flash,
And sheet on sheet, and bolt on bolt, begin
The fray, from side to side.　And smaller arms
Respond.　Like hail the deadly missiles fly,
'Mid flame, and deafening roar : as if the stores
Of Hell had all been yielded up, at once,
For that one single day.　Terrific scene !
The very ground recoils, and groans beneath
The strife.　The air is tortured ; and a smoke
Ascends, and overspreads the wide campaign
With direful pall.　The massy orbs besweep
The ranks ; and plow the ground, and rend the rocks,
And glance, and bound upon the far-off hills.
　　Here chariots rage with fiery steeds, and, armed
With scythes, invade the ranks, and cut, and gash,
And sweep the thousands down.　The phalanx, there,
A solid mass of life, but bent on death,
Assays the line, and presses from the rear
Its front upon a battlement of spears ;
Which braced resist as rock of ocean all
The fury of her waves.　The legion there,
Light armed, makes hasty onset, and retires
Pursued ; in ambush lies ; then closes on
The rear, and gives the rash pursuers all
To death, 'midst yells and piteous wailings of
Despair : while yonder, 'neath the farthest verge
Of sky, the savage tomahawk, and bow,
And battle ax are piled amain, from side

To side ; and spread a slaughter never known
On earth.
      The awful day rides up to noon,
And all in doubt ; and fearfully declines,
And doubtful still : and Satan fears ; for here
And there his lines are seen to bend.　His last
Reserves are brought to save the fight ; and fierce,
And fiercer still the battle raves each hour.
And Satan's presence is a host along
His lines : while eager driving to and fro,
Upon his curbed and stormy charger borne,
With dauntless bosom bare, and naked head,
And rowels buried deep.　　He orders all,
And fires their souls with praise, or stern rebuke,
And raises higher still the mercury
Of Hell.　　Nor Jupiter an idler there,
But drives along his ranks, supports, and fires
Their souls to seven-fold rage.　　This is the last
Great struggle Hell shall know, at least for years
And ages yet to come, (unless the God
Of Heaven shall send them war.)　The scale will soon
Be turned, the die be cast, which cycles great
Shall not reverse.　　What deeds were done that day,
Of reckless daring and of hellish spite !
They stormed each other's batteries ; and looked
Adown the throats of devilish guns surcharged
With death.　They rushed with madness on the point
Of spear and lance ; they fought 'gainst direst odds ;
Nor ceased till overrun by wheels, or trod
Beneath the mire with iron hoofs.　Where fights
Were equal, there the deadliest gripes were seen.
In fury devil throttled devil with
Relentless grasp, and wild exultant shriek.
  12

They ride the air inlocked, or roll upon
The bloody plain, as famished tiger on
The heifer's chest with teeth infixed and jaws
Besmeared with blood. In vain the suff'ring brute
Essays to shake the monster off. She roars,
And rears, and plunges till her life is spent.
So devil hangs on devil fierce and long.

Ye heroes here of earth, ye amateurs
Of battles, ye who make a pastime of
A day of blood, you'll never see a fight,
A perfect fight till you arrive in Hell.
For *here*, the most abandoned heart, corrupt,
Depraved, has still some spark of grace, some shred
Of human sympathy, that interfere
And mar the whole. But *there*, no grace intrudes
No better nature spoils that work of taste.
God's spirit never broods upon that world,
But deadly passions there hold perfect sway;
Revenge, and hate, and spite, and selfishness supreme.

The day and devils fast are wearing out.
And neither side can claim the field,
So even hath the scale of battle hung.
And Satan fears again, that some mischance
Of war, or stratagem of foe might turn
The poise to his defeat. A desperate case
A desperate course demands. His mind is made;
He'd stake the whole upon a single throw.
It was a charge, a simultaneous charge
Throughout his lines. A quicker speed he takes
And omnipresent seems from right to left.
His charger foams and feels the deadly spur.

Now every god subaltern is informed,
And hath the secret word. The centre now

He holds.   At one great signal given, a shout,
A thunder rush ! and foe is closed with foe.
    The lines of Jupiter, amazed, receive
The shock —And reel —And rally —And then reel.—
And rally yet anew, with desp'rate force.—
But reel again,   pressed hard and harder still.
    And Jupiter, with fiery haste and loud
And clarion voice, reminds them, that " their hope,
" Their last, last hope is come ; that now, their weal,
" Or never, must be won.   Hell's dungeons will
" Be glutted ; or the Death-waste be their home,
" A living death, throughout all future time ;
" Or crucifixions torture without end.
·" O shame ! that that inferior strength should so
" Prevail."   He said.   With heart revived, and shout
That tore the very hills, and shook the globe,
They gain a fraction of the ground they'd lost.—
Then pause.—And dwell.—And reel again.—Then hold
Their own with desp'rate surge and deadly thrusts.—
But yield again, though inch by inch.   Alas !
Now hope is dying out : while Satan and
The lesser gods apply their blades, which, like
The scythe of death, are sweeping thousands down.
    Now Satan's thunder voice is heard.   " One blow,
" One surge ! and all is o'er ; and Hell is ours."
    Like ocean billows, mustering all their strength,
To sweep some barrier down, that surge, with shout
Terrific, now is given.—They yield again—
The lines of Jupiter.—They dwell.—They dwell.—
They bend.—They break.—Their ranks are pierced, alas !
At every point, though fighting still.   They see
The ruin ; and they feel the force of steel,
And shafts and bullets winged with death.   They fain

Would rally, and renew the fight ; but such
Disorder can not be retrieved. The foe
With hellish fury sweeps them down in heaps
And windrows.   Jupiter beholds the wreck,
And, turning deadly pale, gives all for lost.
The foe like fire volcanic rolls along,
In tide resistless, and o'erwhelming all.—
Now hope is dead, the hope of all ; save what
Remains in flight. They flee. And now begins
A work of death, to which the slaughter of
The day seemed but a work of love. They flee
In wild disorder ; hot pursued by foe
With victory flushed, and unrelenting hate ;
Who reap them like the harvest of the field.
    The butchery drives on amain, nor stops
Till devils have bedrained their iron strength,
And cease for respite and repose.
                                    And now
What scene the eye beholds ! a scene to make
A neutral devil weep ; and pray that Hell
Might be reformed. What spirit forms bestrow
The bloody field ! Like autumn leaves they lie
On every spot, and everywhere in heaps ;
Be crushed with hoofs and godless feet, and trod
And trampled to the earth like mire.   What cries,
What wailings rise ! as far as ear can reach.
Such cries earth never heard !
                              This day shall be
Recorded in the books of Hell. This field,
The armageddon of the damned, shall be
Forever kept in mind. The wine-press here
Was trod ; and blood flowed out that day, and reached
The horses' bridles, ichor this, the blood

Of Gods.   The tumult of that desperate fray
Was awful to the ear.   In far off Hell,
A lonely devil here and there astray,
Affrighted heard ; and felt the sullen jar ;
And thought the day of judgment had arrived.
    The day is closed, and devils seek for rest,
Fatigued and jaded to the last of strength.
The fleeing sleep not, but for days and nights
Pursue their weary, mournful flight ; nor cease
Till far within the direful Death-waste, lodged ;
Their only hope, their only safe retreat.
    And here they rest from flight and outward foe.
Alas ! but how despoiled ! how thinned in rank !
How broken down in soul !   The ruin they
Perceive, but hope is fled.   They scatter, and
Betake themselves to caves and lonely depths,
And there unseen bewail their wretched lot.
" Bewail." Ah, who can tell what sighs were sighed,
What groans were groaned, what tears were wept, what
        pangs
Were felt by these lost ones ?   Ah ! lost by choice
Of theirs.   " Farewell," said one, that lonely sat
Within a cave, and crazed with anguish put
His thoughts in words.   " Farewell to hope, to hope
" That once was mine !   Those blissful fields where dwell
" The sons of light, were fair within my reach.
" I saw the hand of God, that beckoned me to come,
" And live and reign in everlasting bliss.
" He called and I refused ; reproofs I scorned,
" But chose my way, and now, alas, 'tis o'er,
" The harvest past, the summer ended, and
" My soul not saved !   Eternity shall tell
" My fault !   Eternity, that fearful word,

" Shall ever pierce my ear, and as her sands
" Shall waste away, her dreadful cycles roll
" Of endless years, my longing eyes shall fail,
" My dying hope shall ever, ever die!
" Farewell! Farewell! It is my weary lot,
" And none to give relief! Alone! Alone!
" Though thousands me surround, alone! alone!"
    Now Jupiter, the god of fairest part
Of Earth, of polished Greece, and conqu'ring Rome,
No longer sway shall hold ; but be deposed,
('Tis so decreed by Satan, ruling now supreme
Again), for his defect. His temples may
Remain for little time, and altars smoke,
But he shall not be there ; but pent in Hell
To expiate his crime. Another shall
His state possess, in time, called Man-of-Sin ;
The most corrupt, and bold, blaspheming god
That Hell has ever sent ; and he shall war
With God's elect, and wear his people out,
And bathe himself in blood. And he shall sit
As God within God's temple ; and shall show
Himself *that he is God*. But God shall him
At length destroy, with breath from out his mouth
And with the brightness of his coming ; and
The kingdom take, and reign to end of time.
    Now Satan takes his holds again, his forts
And fortresses throughout, and garrisons
With legions strong ; and adds munitions for
Long time to come ; and finds himself more firm
In power than e'er in times gone by. Affairs
Of State demand his instant care.—His men,
His ministers are named, and have their posts
Assigned ; and each his duties shown in short.

What duties ? bearing rule with righteous sway ?
Ah ! no. The sword has conquered, and the sword
Must reign. 'Tis nought what promises were giv'n,
What oaths were made if ever on the throne
Again, to rule with gentle sway. Both those
Who favored him, and who opposed, shall
Feel his faithless foot upon their necks alike,
When e'er his pride or malice shall incite.
    At length, the Death-waste has his care. He sends
Them terms of peace ; and sends out Janus to
Announce the same : a diplomate indeed ;
For he could say, and then unsay, and say
Again ; and make the most incredulous
Believe. He told them " Satan had been harsh,
" 'Tis true, but since this last revolt, he'd learned
" More wisdom ; and be sure he'll be a kind
" And gentle prince, if prince at all ; for he
" Has serious thoughts of abdicating power,
" To make his realm a self-controlling state,
" A fair republic, where the rights of all
" Shall be secure ; and each, the humblest one,
" Shall have a vote to choose the ruler for
" A term of years, and house of commons to
" Withstand the power of senatorial lords :
" Indeed, you scarcely can conceive the change
" Of temper that our lord has found ; in fact,
" He's been converted." Here a gracious smile
Spread o'er his face, that gave his words more force.
How sweet, how fair ! and they could half believe.
He pledged his honor, " if they would submit,
" And march from out the Death-waste, and depose
" Their arms, that all the past should be forgot :
" So Satan had decreed."   They asked for time

To think.—They called a convocation to
Decide.—The conclave met. What scene! how wan,
How haggard they! how withered up in hope!
They meet, but not like men, and chiefs
Who feel, though vanquished, they have strength yet left!
And can demand some fair and equal terms,
That should instate them somewhat as before:
But like rebellious city drained and starved
Till no conditions could be asked; but all
Their hope is from the mercy of the foe:
And he be trusted for the boon of life.

    'Twas so with these; but Satan knew it not.
Nor once e'en dreamed how wrecked in spirit, and
Demoralized they were: or he had sent
More haughty word; and made more stern demand.

    The day arrived, and Janus came to hear
The grand result. " We yield," said they, " but in
" The fullest confidence, that all his words
" Will be fulfilled; our rights be all secure."

    The writing signed and sealed, a day was set
When they should stand upon the Death-waste verge,
And wait their sovereign's will. It came. With pomp
The haughty chief awaits the hour assigned,
With all his hosts in full array; himself
Upborne sublime, in gorgeous chariot, seen;
His lords on either side, on magic steeds,
Caparison'd with gems and burnish'd gold.
They champ the fiery bit, and paw the plain,
And restless snuff the air with nostril wide,
As if from smell of battle from afar:
And press the curb, impatient to be gone.

    Now in the verge of sky the dust of feet
Beclouds the air. It was the vanquish'd host

In doleful march, to meet the hour assign'd.
But 'twas their best. To stay, was death ; and then
Be hunted down, from year to year, by scouts
Of armed bands, from Satan   sent ; and scourged
And flayed alive.—They near the scene like ox
To slaughter led, and form in line immense ;
But wan, and pale, and starved.   At signal given,
With tearful eye, and soul bereft of hope,
They ground their arms, and march to yonder plain,
A helpless crew : and shrink to see the arms
Of steel, in hostile hands, that them surround.
　　Ask not their after fate. The muse declines
The bloody record ; save to say, that all
The promises that Satan made were broke :
And thousands disappeared, and none their fate
Could tell. The rest, alas! forever groaned
And bled beneath his fierce despotic will
And everliving malice.
　　　　　　　　Hell ere long
Was hushed ; no clamors loud, no murmurs rose ;
No " shriek for freedom " heard : but all, throughout,
Is silent as the house of death. The sword,
The tyrant's sword, is all in all ; his foot,
On every neck : And *order reigns in Hell.*

END OF BOOK SIXTH.

BOOK VII.

THE muse ascends with willing wing, and 'scapes
The direful world of spirits lost, where wars
And deadly passions reign, and sins,
That shock the eye or ear, and pain the heart.
" Escapes," and fain would breathe a fresher air,
And range o'er fairer fields.
       'Twas day in Heav'n,
If day can be distinguished there where all
Is day, where light but flows and ebbs like tide
Of ocean, giving now a fuller, now a slacker sea,
But ocean still.—No sun is needed there,
Nor moon.—But God himself gives light, the Son,
The Father, and the Spirit, one. It rolls
From off God's mountain, not in dazz'ling beams,
To pain the sense, and darken every eye :
But down in soft effulgence, spreading wide
O'er all the vast domain of Heav'n, its slopes,
And hills, its copses sweet, and luscious groves,
And plains immense. There dwell the sons of God,
Those faithful found, who stood their time, mayhap,
In distant worlds ; who kept unbroke God's law ;
Or, breaking it, returned to him in time
With penitential tears ; and pardon found
Through grace vouchsafed. These now forever dwell
Before his face, arrayed in white, and reap

The harvest rich, that once they sowed.   " 'Twas day
In Heav'n."   A mustering of hosts appear.
In ranks the shining armies stand, in length
Unreached by spirit eyes.   And waving high
In air the common flag is seen.   It rolls
Its folds of gold and richest dyes, embossed
With figures, that declare full plain, it is
The standard of the King of Heaven.   Each corps
Its banner had, to signify the world
From which they came.—What worlds were there! how vast
The field from which God gathers home his own,
His faithful ones!   They march,   led on
By high archangel, to the heav'nly sound
Of instrumental notes.   They march to meet
The Son of God ascending up from earth,
From world redeemed.——He comes.   The banners wave;
A shout rolls round the hills ; and songs proclaim
Him victor o'er his foes.——" Lift up your heads,
" Ye gates, and be ye lifted up, ye doors,
" Ye everlasting doors, and let the King
" Of glory come.   The Lord, the Lord his name,
" And mighty to redeem."   Thus sang the host
As they received him, come, incarnate God
Of late, but " risen " now, with body of
The resurrection type.   Triumphal day !
    They pass the broad and golden streets, bestrewn
With palms and amaranthine flowers ;
And he receives again the glory that
He had before the world was made :
And which he left, becoming poor, that he
Might make poor mortals rich.   How rich !   He takes
His throne, and all the angelic hosts before
Him bend : and he is Lord of all, and called

The Lamb. Now God is seen in *form*, no more
In *light alone*, and from his mount ; but face
To face. He leads them out, and walks and talks
With his.——" The mount of God !" It rises high,
Beyond all ken of sight, and radiant
With glories uncreate, inspires an awe
That none can dare approach ; but nathless, is
The fount of every good. From this, flows out
That wond'rous stream, the riv'r of life. It rolls,
And rolls its ever brimming tide throughout,
And freshens all the vales of Heaven ; and laves
The trees upon its banks, that bear the fruits,
And yield them ripened every month.—" None dare
" Approach," except the Lamb, the Son. He talks
With God the Father ; passes up the mount,
And there holds close communion, wrapped in light,
And sometimes cloud, as with his fellow ; then,
Resplendent with the glory of the scene,
Descends, as Moses from the cloud and fire
With face illumed that Israel could not well
Behold ; " descends," and holds communion with
His own again.
    At stated times in Heav'n
Are festivals. They meet from every point
Of compass ; from the vales, and flow'ry dells,
And hills, and mountain tops ; as shade, or sweet
Repose, or landscape rich, or friendly talk,
Or contemplation staid, had moved their choice.
 The season lasts for days. What multitudes
Partake ! What fare is found ! The richest fruits
Are ripe ; such fruits as only grow in Heaven,
And most luxurient near the throne of God.
 The bread of life is served beyond all bound ;

And nectar, pressed from clusters of the vine,
The living vine, the tropic grape of Heaven.
   Repast is o'er ; and friendship now ensues.
What greetings then ! what long embrace of pure
Angelic love!   Old friends of ages gone,
Are joined again ; and talk their hist'ry o'er ;
Recount the scars by which their bliss was won ;
Their hairbreadth 'scapes reveal ; and then extol
That grace that long forbore, that Providence
That cleared their path, and led them on ; that love
That brought them home at last, and crowned them kings
And priests forever unto God.   "The voy'ge
" Was rough," say they, " at times, the tempest high ;
" And dark the clouds ; and wide the billows yawned.
" Our barks shipped seas, that threatened to engulph ;
" And faith was nigh to fail ; but God was in
" The ship, and that when least we thought.
" And, better than our fears, he brought us safe
" To land, the haven of our rest.   Our ship
" Is moored ; our anchor firmly cast ; and all
" Is o'er.   Eternal ages now shall roll,
" And we are safe.   No billows more to cross,
" No storms to meet ; no fights to win.
   " We hear the roar afar as mariner
" Arrived and housed upon the beach with all
" His joyous friends.—But where are they that voy'ged
" With us at first ?   They left the pole star of
" Their faith ; their compass threw aside ; and veered
" From out their course, and now are wreck'd and lost."
A tear now falls.—A tear ?   What ! tears in Heav'n ?
Yes, tears in Heav'n.   Have angels lost their love ?
If Christ himself could weep at Salem's fate,
Or at the tomb, then why not spirits saved,

For fellow spirits lost?   Ah, tears shall fall
In Heav'n for loved ones missed!   The father weep
The son ; the son, the sire ; the daughter, or
The mother weep, as one is not ; the wife,
The husband ; or reverse ; and friend, for friend.
Oh sin! oh sin pursued!   It wrecks the soul,
And checks the bliss of Heaven.   O Heav'n save!
   But men must have their choice.   God gives enough.
" Choose life, choose death, and bide the great result."
   But will not God " wipe tears from every eye ?"
Yes, these he'll wipe as well as those of earth.
For, of that feast, the last great day is come,
And near its close.   Th' assembly soon will break.
   And now the call is given, " *draw near to God*,"
In voice distinct from off the mount, a voice
Of love.—And Heav'nly influence begins
To fall.   The shining armies gather round,
And thicken from afar ; and stand with eyes
Upraised, expectant, towards the throne of God,
That topless hill, involved in clouds, and seas
Of ever living light.—The show'r descends,
And waters every soul, a show'r of love.
The soul is filled ;—they prostrate fall, subdued,
And scarce a pulse of life is left, from bliss,
From ecstacy of bliss.—" I charge you wake
" Me not ; but here forever let me lie,
" Entranced with love Divine."   God's hand is on
Them ; and their cup is full, and running o'er.
They pause, enwraped ; and silence reigns in Heaven.
   At length the tide abates ; and God withholds
His hand.   They rise ; in blissful stillness stand ;
For none would speak, and none would be disturbed.
   The hour is passed ; they soft retire, in smiles,

In whispers mild ; still more and more impressed
With God's unbounded love, and with the worth
Of that great Heav'n they've won.   Ah ! what in such
A world as this could wicked spirits do,
Who formed on earth no taste for such delights?
The vile shall never enter there, lest they
Disturb that lovely Heav'n they never could
Enjoy.   Let men remember ; let them full
Beware, it is " the pure in heart shall see
" Their God."   Then seek that fountain that alone
Can cleanse ; nor risk one moment by delay.

   The festal days are o'er.   The last great day
Of that great feast is closed.   They separate,
But not to solitude, and lonely life.
But friend with friend of old or lately found,
Allied, and families, rejoined from earth,
And safe arrived, though one by one, betake
Themselves to everlasting homes, prepared
And fitted up for them by God's own hand.

   They meet, they greet, they rest, they part no more !
Yes, " families," for ties on earth are ties
In Heav'n.   Though husband and the wife, as such,
Are not, the tie no less remains.   They meet
As friends, as dearest friends.   The mother clasps
With frantic joy her precious, lovely babe,
Of whom bereft on earth ; the brother and
The sister long embrace ; the hoary sire
That was, his long lost son ; the son, the sire
So long reposed in dust ; and mansions ring,
And grots and dells resound, with bursts of joy,
With shouts, that cannot be repressed, at loved
Ones safe conducted home.   'Tis joy to meet
On earth, though parting soon may come ; but what

The joy in Heav'n, where union shall revive,
And be as lasting as the throne of God?
O Heav'n! 'Tis worth the toil, 'tis worth the cross.
'Tis worth the conflict here.   They fled for life,
And dwelt in dens, and mountain caves ; were clad
In skins, and roamed o'er desert wastes ; were deemed
The filth of earth ; were buffeted, and vexed ;
Were starved, and parched with thirst : but they endure,
As seeing him who was invisible.
And now a harvest of eternal life
Is theirs.   'Tis true, tho sickle scarred the hand ;
Nay, gashed down deep at times ; but what care now?
The grain is all secure ; the harvest home ;
And garnered up forever for their use.
    Ah! this the REST that did " remain " for God's
Obedient ones ; the Rest prefigured by
The Rests on earth.   The sun lights on them not,
Nor any heat.   They hunger now no more ;
Nor thirst ; and never, never say, " I'm sick."
The fruits of Heav'n are theirs ; the tree of life ;
And waters gushing fresh from living springs ;
Or dipped from that great flood, the riv'r of life.
    But intellectual joys are theirs.   They scan
The works of God ; and pry with ease ; and stand
Amazed at wonders now revealed.   Nor on
The plains of Heav'n alone ; but far through space
On happy wing conveyed, they calculate
The laws of distant worlds ; weigh every force ;
And balance suns and spheres.   They guage the size
Of masses vast, and rate their speed, and trace
Their intricate librations as the effects of all ;
And problems solve, that ne'er were solved before.
    Nor always on the vast employed ; but e'en
13

Descend to most minute, and there descry
The simple atoms God has made ; descern
Their evanescent size, their shape, their weight ;
And note them still unworn and fresh as when
They first came weighed and measured from his hand,
Though fused and cooled, combined and decombined,
And ground, and crushed, for ages vast.—And then
Ascend, and note with vision keen the nice,
And endless combinations of these *few,*
To make the vast variety of all
God's works ; and then again ascend, and mark
The *work of life,* in building up the forms
Of living things,—from small to great ; the grass
Of microscopic size, to giant oaks
And pines ; from animalcules scarcely reached
By searching glass, to monsters huge of land
And sea ; the inner work of life ; a sight
Desired by men, but not revealed ; revealed
To spirit eyes alone :   While some their thoughts
To metaphysics give ; and all the deep
And dark phenomena of mind, explore ;
And find a field of rarest, richest thought.
And then descend to deep theology ;
And scan the government and laws of God.
And now find difficulties cleared, that once
Perplexed the greatest minds on earth.—'Tis plain
God acts from reason.   Now 'tis seen why some
Such thorny footsteps trod ; and suffered loss,
On earth, of all ; and wasted out, mayhap,
The flower of all their days, to hoary years,
In dungeons ; why the wicked and the strong
Had power to prey upon the innocent
And weak ; and rob of right ; and, darker still,

Why pain should be coeval with our birth ;
And infants, innocent of crime, should wake
To life in pangs, should live a day, and then
In pangs expire. Perplexing thought ! Why one
Should sow the seed, and then another reap ;
Why this to savage, that to civil life
Were born ; why some, and wicked too, should have
A surfeit of the things of life, scarce sought,
But flowing in like ocean tide ; while *want*
Beset the path of others from the hour
Of birth, through all their weary course of life,
Till death vouchsafed for them a welcome grave :
And why the son of living sire was spared,
While death, relentless, took the widow's hope,
Her only son, and left her helpless to
A selfish world.   These doubts, and thousands more,
That harrowed once on earth, are solved with ease ;
And God is cleared when he is judged.   The range
Is wide, and spirit minds forever search,
With keen delight, and never, never tire.

   O Heaven ! 'tis not to " sit upon a cloud,
And sing," as infidels have scornful said ;
But to receive a scope of social joys,
And intellectual feasts, that never cloy ;
And pleasures, ever more, through every sense ;
From sights, from sounds, from tastes, and odors sweet.

   Ah ! Heav'n is rich.—'Tis worthy of a God
To give, and worth our while to see
That we receive. We fain would have its bliss,
Its endless joys : Then let our lives and faith
Accord with this desire. Then all is sure.

   But some, on messages of mercy sent,
Are spread through earth, and mayhap other worlds,

As spirits "minist'ring" to those who need
Their aid, the ignorant, the weak ; but who
At length, if kept, may win salvation.—Swift
As thought they fly ; and snatch their charge, or turn
Aside, with gentle hand, unseen, from deaths
Or pitfals of the moral world.   The wing
Of angel mother hovers o'er her babe,
Late left an orphan in a friendless world :
A thousand arrows turns aside, and, as
His years advance, and snares of youth beset,
And courage fails, and principle gives way,
And all is near a wreck ;—infuses life
Afresh ; in midnight slumbers oft, or in
The hour of silent thought, in lonely walk ;
Or close retirement from the outward world.
    He feels his strength revived ; but knows not whence
It came. He battles on anew, nor falls
Thus far ; and mayhap yet will win the race
Of virtue here, thus saved ; and find, at length,
His guardian mother in the better land.
Who knows ?   Then, orphan, grieve not over much,
That in your tender years, your mother laid
Her trembling hand upon your head, and looked
To God, and prayed, and died. She may be near
Thee, keeping ceaseless watch with mingled hope
And fear ; and clearing up thy path, as God
Ordains.—Then gird thy loins, be strong, and see,
Thou disappoint her not.   Not this alone ;
The babe, late snatched away, the mother left,
The babe may come, to win the mother home ;
A youthful spirit now ; and borne away
To break her hold on earth ; and bind her to
The skies.—It fans her feverish brow, and soothes

Her aching head, and softly whispers peace
And comfort to her bleeding heart. *Yes, God*
Has uses for us in the other world.
And greatest joy will spring from greatest good
By us achieved, as spirits, in that world.

  Come soar from earth, and rise to heav'n again,
And note the angels of the first of time,
A patriarchal throng, retired upon
A mount, in conclave met, the SAVANS of
The skies ; discussing nicest points in all
God's works ; or weighing probabilities
Of things to come, the birth of worlds, mayhap,
Or end of those now made —These faithful stood,
With myriads more, in that defection great
When Satan faithless fell. And prominent
Among them all, sits Abdiel ; the first
Of all God's works ; a hoary headed youth :
How vast his age ! Eternity of years
Has almost run its course since he was made.
He woke to life, and found himself alone.
Not long. His fellows then were made, and since,
Forever since, angelic beings have been
Brought to life. (But late, they're clothed in flesh,
And stand their trial in terestrial worlds.)

  How rich in learned lore ! What worlds of
Facts they've garnered up ! for memory in Heav'n,
Unlike the same on earth, forever holds
When once impressed. These facts are sorted and
Compared ; and thence conclusions drawn, of worth
Unspeakable ; the most inspiring truths,
Of startling import, and profound, deduced
In physics, and the deep theology
Of God ; far deeper than the younger sons

Of Heav'n have reached : and yet forever when
They meet, new depths are sounded and new truths
Deduced.   These saw when God went forth to make
The worlds.   At first, he spake to being, through
All space diffused, the simple elements,
(Or mayhap, *one*, one element alone
From which, all others should in time be formed,)
Yet uncombined , a vapor thin and fine,
Scarce visible to spirit eyes.   They called
It matter.   'Twas distinct from spirit ; and
It took them by surprise.   They'd never dreamed
Of such a thing before ; for spirit, they
Had thought, was all that could be made.

   The spirit now of God moves on the face
Of this great deep ; and finished out the laws
Of matter then in full.   These laws were few
And simple ; but with God to give them force,
Were capable of working out in time
The problem great of worlds.   Now first begins
To act that all-coherent power, through space,
Called gravitation.   Matter moves and tends
To matter.   Centres form at length throughout
Illimitable space.   This ocean vast
Of vapor, wide beyond all reach of thought,
And deep as wide, and high as deep, now breaks
In spheres or cubes of vast periphery ;
And each department tow'rds its centre moves :
At first, with slow pro.rression, balanced nigh
By neighboring spheres or cubes, that draw adverse,
And tend, themselves, the other way.   But as
The spaces widen, and the outward forces wane,
And inward forces gain new strength, (as time
Rolls on,) from distance less immense of parts,

The atoms move more lively ; and with swift
And swifter speed, rush inward tow'rds the goal,
The centre far of their amazing mass.
The elements, condensing thus, become
More tangible. They still approach, approach
And thicken, pressing hard and harder still
Upon each other, till the pressure, and
Momentum checked by force opposing, and
The friction, bring forth fire. The atoms in
Dissociation long from heat, at length
Combine, some silently, (with fervent heat,)
While others with explosive force unite,
And sheets of flame, that shoot far out to space,
(Amazing sight! and awful sound as heard
Afar ;) and startle angels as they lean
And look from Heaven.   The war of elements
Has now begun ; and oxygen, the great
Right hand of God, performs its destined work.
The simples burn, fit fuel now become ;
And substances of diverse kinds are formed,
But vapor still, and still condense   as heat
Escapes through boundless space : they form at length
One globe immense of boist'rous fire.   One globe?
Nay, ev'ry block of matter, through all space,
Has been condensed, and burned, and thus become
A sphere of boist'rous fire, condensing still,
And still tremendous in its heat.   These globes
Are flaming suns, of amplitude immense,
The whole beyond all thought.   Stupendous scene!
And scattered through infinitude of space.
" Let there be light ;" and this the light that shone.
    These suns all wheel upon their centres ; and,
Condensing still by gravity still more

And more increased as parts approximate,
Revolve with higher speed, and throw off worlds,
(Or rings mayhap, which break to worlds,) and these
Again throw rings, which break and bring forth moons.
These worlds move round their central suns, and moons
Round them, in orbits more or less remote,
With speed immense, and blazing as they fly .
Which, cooled still more for ages vast, present
A hardened rocky crust, but waved and torn
By inward fires, and smashed by thunderbolts :
Not cold as yet, but hot and hissing to
The falling rains, which crack their substance as
The show'rs descend.

            Our globe,—(thus rent, and torn,
And worn, by act of heat, and rains, and floods,
And hurricanes, that waged incessant war,
To break, and grind the heavy rocks, and drive
The lighter to unstable banks and shoals ;
Thus pulverizing fine and finer still,)
Now calmer grown, and covered deep and wide
With the detritus of a billion years,
And clouds and noxous gases cleared away—
At last is ready for the work of life,
Another wonder soon to be revealed.

   God intervenes and makes the germs of trees,
And grass, and shrubs. These spring from earth,
And clothe with living green.   First, round the poles
The work of vegetable life is seen.
For there the genial climes begin. · And as
Each age revolves, and inward fires subside
From radient heat ; terrestrial verdure moves
To other zones. And when the earth is stocked
With food ; and noxious gases still more cleared,

(By minerals, and vegetable life,)
And air is safe to breathe, God intervenes
Again ; and animals are made. And first,
The lower ranks are formed ; then higher come ;
The reptiles, and the fishes : and with them,
Aquatic birds ; some small, and some of size
Gigantic. Lo! the saurians appear ; and sweep
The bays and marshes ; and with head erect
Display such length of body prone behind
As human eyes have never seen, and birds
That stalked the fens like moving towers, and frogs
Of elephantine size. These had their day,
And then were swept away by changes wide
And ruinous upon the crust of earth.

Then others took their place, of later type,
And higher order still. And these are lost
Again in turn ; and others then succeed :
While ages long elapse, and wars assuage,
Of elemental strife ; and earth is smoothed
And settling down ; and rip'ning for its last,
And highest ranks of life.

     At length appear,
(How vast the ages gone !) in myriad force,
The brutes of modern type ; the ox, the horse,
The stag, the boar, the mastodon, the dog,
The wolf, the bear, the elephant, the fox,
The lion, tiger, and the antelope ;
And all the rest, that now inhabit land,
And sea, and air. The earth is all their own.
They roam at will, o'er plains and hills, or in
The floods ; and crop the fields unhedged,
Or take a surfeit of their prey at will ;
And swarm the seas and bays unsought, and lash

To foam the shore-ward surf, unscared ; and wing
The air in fearless flight.   The noble steed
Besports himself upon the plain, untamed ;
The tigress roams secure with whelps
From out her jungle ; and the lion, now
So stealthy and secrete, then chose his lair
In open face of day.
                       But ere the full
Completion of God's works, there was an age
Of ice, which more perplexes man than all
The other ages earth has known. They saw,
These savans saw its reign ; amazement filled
Their souls, a strange phenomenon for earth,
From snows perpetual from age to age :
Till she was wrapped about the poles, and far
Toward torrid climes, with half of ocean piled
In shining masses up to Heaven. For though
The earth was glowing hot within, and heat,
In slow progression passing through her crust
Incessant, thawed the mass below ; yet still
It grew from greater increment above.
And age on age rolled on, and still the snows
Forever fell ; and hails, and sometimes rains,
That beat them down and glacified the whole ,
Till both the polar spheres, thus burdened, groaned
Beneath the load.   At length,—how vast the time !
The time, as time is reckoned now, with man,
(And yet 'twas but a day, compared with earth's
Whole time : nay, less, far less ; 'twas but an hour,
So vast the mighty sum of earth's full years.)
—The age of snow is o'er, and genial suns
Have now the work on hand, (how long the task !)
In summer days to disencumber earth

Of this vast weight, and send the waters back
To ocean bed again.   And yet it will
Be done, for God has time enough for work
Of every kind how slow soe'er the work
Goes on.   'Twas done at last : and temp'rate climes
Regain at length their lost estate ; and feel
Once more the touch of life. But oh how changed
The face of earth is now. This icy mass
So piled and piled about the poles, had slipped
(Like Alpine glaciers at the present day)
And slipped with force amazing, but with slow
And steady move, from its abutments far
Away ; had slipped for all the ages gone !
This mass immense, piled high above the hills
And e'en the mountain tops, had urged its way
Among the peaks and crags, and rent their tops,
And torn and worn their sides ; and ground the hills,
And plowed the vales and ravines deep ; and rolled
The looser rocks, and borne them off to other parts.
And floods subglacial during all this time,
Had bored their hidden way among the rocks ;
And wrought out channels, in the end, which still
Remain, where now our busy commerce floats.
At length, reduced in thickness and in power,
This mighty engine of the hand of God
Stood still ; and left its burden of debris,
Its polish, and its groves, upon the rocks,
To tell that it had been.   These savans of
The skies beheld this wond'rous age that drove
Its plowshare over earth to fit it more
And more for man's abode.

                          Thus years roll on,
And centuries of years ; and earth still waits,

And ripens still ; still waits the coming of
Her lord. " *Let* us *make man,*" at length went forth,
A work that called forth thought, a work that had
Full counsel ; and was marked as other acts
Of God's creating hand were never marked.
  Lo! man appears ; then female by his side :
The last great act of God's creative power
On earth.
              'Twas finished. And God rested from
His work. Creation was achieved. An age
Is now allotted to the human race,
Called seventh day ; and, that complete, the eighth
Day then will come, and God will work again,
Mayhap. And what that work will be, nor man
Nor angel can divine. Perhaps the trump,
The judgment trump shall wake the eighth day morn ;
When all of Adam's race shall hear the call,
And leave their beds ; and stand, to meet the "THRONE,"
And take the wages of their acts on earth.
Who knows ?
              The savans of the skies beheld
The work, from first to last, (howe'er 'twas done,)
Beheld the whole achieved, through all the vast,
Vast ages called the " SIX " great "DAYS." They saw ;
And with amazement traced each step, and were
Forever taken by surprise, and most,
That spirits could be clothed in flesh, and walk
Abroad in image of their God. They saw,
Not earth alone, but all that God achieved
On suns and worlds, that were produced
Throughout illimitable space. And they
Shall see yet more. And *we,* if but among
The blest, shall see new wonders springing forth

From God's prolific hand ; shall see when all
The worlds and suns that now inhabit space
Shall be extinct ; and God repeat again
And yet again, with variations, true,
 The problem great of making worlds.
Fear not, eternity has ample time.
And you and I shall sure be there to see
And wonder, (if we keep his law while here,
Or seek, and find forgiveness of our sins,
And walk with him obedient to his will.)
 What hopes are ours ! How bright the prospects rise !
What ages vast of knowledge we shall have !
What excellence attain ! and stand,—the time
Shall come,—where high archangels now are found,
And they, as much advanced from us as now,
And mayhap more. How kind that God that made
Us, and hath called us to such high estate !
The feast is ready, and we all are bid.
Let none delay ; lest he should rise and "shut
The door ;" and then, ah ! who shall open then ?

END OF BOOK SEVEN.

BOOK VIII.

THE while, the Church of God was taking root,
Full deep. The converts had been scattered, ere
The day that Satan left the field to save
His realm below from power usurped.
   They fled to every part, and preached the word.
And thus the seed was sown in every soil ;
Which sprang up, watered by the dews of Heaven.
A Saul had ceased to persecute, and now
Was building up with master-hand the cause
Which late he had essayed to overthrow.
The Holy Ghost was there ; and waited on
The word, by prophet and apostle preached,
Or by the simple child of God without
A name or office in the church.   But oh !
How foolish ! 'Twas the cross they preached, the cross,
The story of the cross ; and yet it cut
The heathen down ; and pierced the Jewish heart ;
And even made a multitude of priests,
With all their legal pride, "obedient to
The faith." The power was seen ; the heart was changed ;
And bloody men became as gentle lambs.
'Twas new, 'twas wonderful. The haughty Jew
With envy saw ; the wise beheld amazed.
   What hope for earth ! An element is now
At work,—how needful this ! that shall in time

Remould the face of things ; shall renovate
The human heart ; and wake the dormant mind
To intellectual effort ; and at length,
Though long the time, shall work the glory of
Our race ; a world converted ; and our earth,
Our desert earth, shall make a paradise,
A garden of the Lord. *That day shall come.*
    But ere that time, what storms, what tempests fierce
Shall sweep o'er earth ! what battle rage 'twixt truth
And error ! Yes, be sure, that Michael and
The dragon shall contend ; and age on age
Elapse, and still the battle high : but in
The end,—O haste the time !—th' opposing powers
Shall cease. O glorious thought ! and earth shall feel
The thrilling touch of life.   Then empires built
Upon despotic rule, shall totter to
Their fall ; and thrones shall crumble 'neath the feet
Of kings. The masses then, enlightened, and
Refined, and Scripture-read, and christianized
In heart, shall bear the rule ; and emperors,
And kings, and presidents, shall be installed
But servants of their will. Oppressions then
Shall cease ; the slave be free ; O blessed hope !
And our humanity all eager stand,
Equipped and ready for its glorious race.
    A century is gone, and lo the change !
The Nazarene is rising. Every land
Has heard his name ; and his disciples stand
In ev'ry clime, an earnest of his reign,
His kingdom yet to come ; not thickly sown,
But sparse 'tis true, and yet like wheat among
Abundant tares.   Among the low they're found,
The middle, and the high, and e'en in courts,

And palaces of kings.   A kingdom this
Within a kingdom ; silent working like
The leaven, till the lump shall own its power.

The Scriptures now are full, an ample rule
Of faith and life, with that great vision, closed,
Upon the isle of Patmos, seen.   And pens,
In eager haste, are throwing out the word,
The priceless word, to be the salt of earth.

The time seems long.   Yet what is time with God?
With him a thousand years are but a day.
Be patient, and the work shall yet be done.

But Satan took alarm, recovered now
From that stupendous war, that crushed his foes,
And seated him again in power.   He took
Alarm, and felt withal a deep chagrin,
That pierced his soul ; alarm, that still the cause
Of truth and righteousness was living on
The earth ; and deep chagrin, that nothing had
Availed, of all his plans ; that all his boasts
And promises had failed ; and this was known
And read of all ; was whispered round, and was,
Among his foes, where all were foes of his,
A never-ending source of fiendish mirth.

It stung him to the quick.   But what, what could
Be done.   Still greater pangs await him ; for
He must confess his weakness ; and must call
For aid on some more likely to succeed
Than he.   He called up Man-of-Sin ; and spoke
In humbler terms than wont ; and questioned him
If he was equal to the task ; if he
Could venture up on earth, and there could dare
Th' attempt to block the wheels and stop the car
Of Christ.   " I know your cunning and your craft ;
14

" I know your sanctimonious face, and lust
" Of power. I know you can assume a garb
" Of saintly mein, while daggers still lie hid
" Beneath. Can aught be done ? If so, you shall
" Be seated high, and next to me, your king ;
" And shall be deemed the benefactor of
" Our realm."   Then Man-of-sin, with brazen front,
Replied, " I dare the thing ; I dare to tread
" Where God has trod, to sit upon his seat,
" And in his temple take his name, and show
" That I am God. Your Holiness shall see "—
" No ! no !" said Satan, " not that title now
" For me. It shall be yours in time if you
" Succeed. ' Your Holiness ' shall be the term,
" The title sure of Man-of-sin.   But how
" Will you proceed ?"   " As stealthy as the foot
" Of time ; or death upon the sinner's track.
" I'll slip unseen and unsuspected up
" To earth.   I'll show a zeal for God and Christ ;
" A zeal no true apostle ever showed ;
" A flaming zeal, that shall the passions raise.
" And one shall be of Paul, another of
" Apollos, and a third of Cephas be.
" A little error then I'll sow, and men
" Shall differ in some points of faith. And hence
" Contentions shall arise, not fierce, at first,
" Nor threat'ning, but a cloud the bigness of
" A hand, a harmless thing, but which in time
" Shall bring the wildest storm ; with rage unchecked
" Shall cause the elements to reel, and shake
" The pillars of the church of Christ. And then
" From being brethren, *one* shall claim to rule.
" And bishop shall be *master* of each flock.

" And bishop then with bishop shall contend,
" And claim to be the ruler of the whole.
" The pagan also shall be roused with zeal
" Anew, to save his temples and his gods ;
" And with excessive rage, like famished wolves
" Insatiate, shall fall upon the weak
" And trembling flock. The land shall run with blood ;
' The shepherds, be a prey ; and thinned, if not
" Extinct, the fold of Christ. What more I'll do,
" Shall be revealed when next we meet."   He said.
And Satan smiled ; the first for ages past ;
So sure at last that his selection was
With wisdom made.
                    Now Man-of-sin prepares
To take his leave. He puts on saintly show.
And as he passed he startled all the damned.
They thought a saint had strayed to Hell,
So like he was. They rushed with daggers drawn,
To strike him to the heart. But Satan stayed
Their hands, and gave assurance he was one
Of them ; he was their fellow, Man-of-sin,
Was thus prepared to act the part of saint
On earth.—Oh ! he shall there deceive, deceive
The elect of God.   He went to earth ; and what
He promised quite too well performed. He stirred
Up foes within, and foes without ; the love
Of many waxing cold ; and many, faint
Returning back to earth. But still a seed
Remained ; a church within a church ; a seed,
That lived and grew. And yet how fierce the storm
To beat it down ! The plain disciples of
The Lord, are haled to prison more than erst,
And made to answer for the worst of crimes.

E'en infant blood was laid to Christian doors.
How false! and pestilence and adverse storms,
Were placed to their account, and ev'ry ill
With which God scourged a guilty world. They, they
Must answer for them all, and must atone
With tears, and blood.

      Alas! behold yon games,
An amphitheater with thousands choked,
The polished savages of pagan Rome!
They stamp and clamor for the coming sport,
And in the dread arena stands or kneels,
With eyes uplift in prayer, but pale, the child,
The death-doomed child of God, to die outright,
Or battle for an inch of life. A sword
Is giv'n, but not for him, but simply to
Prolong the sport : while on the shrinking ear,
Rolls awful from his den, the lion's roar,
Ferocious, late from scorched Numidian plains ;
Now chafed with hunger and the keeper's scourge.

 The bars at length are slipped, and with a bound
And thunder voice, appears the fiery brute.
Appalled, he gazes for a moment on
The crowd. Then spies the Christian near. With awe
He pauses at the human form and face. Then curbs
And sidelong moves half crouched, with mane erect,
And glaring, fiery eye and naked teeth,
And curling tongue, and chilling guttural growl,—
And roars and springs — But meets the opposing lance.
The victim slips aside. Again he springs.
Again he meets the lance. His prey escapes,
Though bruised and gashed with deadly teeth and claws,
And blood replies to blood, and mingles on the sands,
The blood of Christian and the blood of brute.

The while the frenzied throng bestun the ear
With wild tumultuous shouts.—Oh! Rome! this blood
Shall be required a thousand thousand fold!
Your sons shall bleed, your daughters fair be led
Away to shame ; your mould'ring ruins shall
Attest your sin throughout all future time!
  The fight proceeds, with doubtful scale. And teeth
And claws besmeared with blood, and lance contend.
Now strength is ebbing out. At length one spring,
One dire convulsive spring, and thrust, and both
Are locked in death !   The spirit of the brute,
The soul and spirit of the man now ooze
From out those wounds. The flesh lies quivering with
The last of life ; now less and less till all
Is still.   The heartless crowd retire refreshed,
Unmindful of the debt they yet shall pay.
  Thus died the martyr in the days of Rome.
But not by beasts alone, but tortures worse ;
By dungeons drear, by hunger, and by fire.
  See yonder garden planned by nicest skill,
With groves, and walks, and terraces, of green,
Of living green, and fringed with richest flowers :
And fruits of every clime on bending trees ;
And birds of every plume and every song,
And bursting fountains, sparkling in the sun ;
While fish of gold and silver scale besport
Below. The vine is there, the olive and
The palm ; and every wish that every sense
Could crave. And near, a princely palace heaves
Its massy walls, with pillars high, and frieze,
And porticoes, adorn'd. The chisel there
Has done its work, and art has spent its skill.
The pile majestic stands, and like a prince

With brow serene and grave, o'erlooks the whole.
How rich! a kind of paradise let down
From Heaven,   The shadows fall; the sultry day
Is gone; and lo! the gates are choked with throngs
Of coming guests, to catch the breeze, regale
The eye, and breathe the Eden-fragrance of
The hour. A thousand lights now blaze around.
And here and there a cone of flame is seen.
The sight is magic. Doubly decked and rich
Each tree, and vine, and flower appears. The fish
Renews his gold, and Iris there spreads out
Her gorgeous wings; and gems of every hue
The fountain showers.   Now friend meets friend;
The laugh is heard; the shout goes up; and all
Is merry as a bridal scene.—Alas!
Within each cone of flame a Christian dies!
There,—chained, and staked, and smeared, and fuel-girt
And gagged,—he burns; and lights the garden of
His king.—*Thus Rome filled up the measure of*
Her sin.
            And yet the word stayed not, but grew,
A power within, that could not be repressed;
And outward worked, and promise gave, in time
To oversweep the world. "In time." How long!
  Yes, Man-of-sin must have his day; and teach
A lesson to a sinning world.   Time sweeps
Along; and still the contest fiercely reigns.
The shepherds now must fall, and one by one
They feel the hand of power. They bleed, or lie
In chains, or flee to savage wilds, to let
The storm go by; nor guard from grievous wolves
The trembling fold.—Ah! why such suff'ring for
The flock of Christ? God knows! Was it for us?

A lesson to all future time ?   Did they
For us thus sow the seed ? and now we reap
The harvest of their toils, their tears, their blood ?
" *But be thou faithful unto death, and thou*
" *Shall have a crown of life.*"
                  The storm at length
Is o'er.   The pagan temples fall, and all
Is safe, and Cæsar takes the side of Christ.
The church now reigns ; the world is at her feet,
And homage pays.   " Is safe."   No, no ! not safe ;
For now another trial waits her course ;
The favor and the flattery of men.
And Man-of-sin did not forget to seize
On this, his chance, to work her fall.   She now
Is wedded to the state : and offices
Of wealth, and trust, must come through her.—And will
She hold her simple faith, and life, her trust
In God, and readiness to do his will ?
Or be seduced away from him, and turn
To earth, and seek her good therein ; and thus
Forget her STRENGTH, and be like Samson when
His hair was shorn ?   Alas, for her ! She went
The downward road, though step by step, till all
Was lost.—She should have been a city set
Upon a hill ; a light to light the world.
But all was dark.   A darkness that that could
Be felt.   The hope of earth was gone again !
And moral midnight reigned from pole to pole.
Appalling, starless ; and no hope of dawn !
   Ah, no ! there was a spot, now here, now there,
Where light was not extinct, a feeble star,
That glimmered, and that shot a scanty ray
Across the dark and dread horizon, that

But served to show the gloom, the blackness of
The hour.—The word of life was closed, and Christ
Dethroned ; and priests ascend his seat ; and men
Were made to seek salvation at the hands
Of men. They bought it at a price ; the rich
Obtained, the poor were sent away ; and men
From men—O shame!—bought licence for themselves
To sin.
   'Twas done. She could no lower fall.
But oh! to trace her downward course, the muse
Declines the task ; save but to say, 'twas not
Achieved at once. The strife was long and fierce.
The choicest spirits earth could boast withstood
Her growing sins. They preached, they watched, they
  prayed ;
And then for this poured out their precious lives.
But wolves were there ; they lodged within the fold,
And preyed, by night, by day, upon the sheep.
 Now Man-of-Sin had reached his hopes ; the field
Was all his own. He sat upon a throne
With mitre on his head and staff in hand,
And Latin on his tongue, and cross upon
His breast ; and at his feet the nations bowed,
O blasphemy! and called him "Lord our God."
 His mark must be on all ; none dared to buy,
None sell, except in virtue of his name.
He made the faith of all ; and ruled the words
Of men, and e'en their thoughts. What he allowed
They thought ; what he forbade they uttered not.
He cast out knowledge from the face of earth ;
And bound the human mind in chains, in chains
Of adamant, and loud proclaimed abroad,
That " ignorance the mother was of true

Devotion ;" bade the world believe, believe
Not in the Lord, nor in his word, but in
The church ; and worship saints and images,
And bow before a cross of wood or stone,
And homage pay to relics, *made for sale ;*
And rate their virtues—not by faith in God,
And in his holy word sent forth to man,
And in the living of a blameless life,
And deeds of love—but by the prayers they said.

And when they sinned, e'en sins of deepest dye,
The priest stepped in, and made all clean again.
And thus spake peace where God had spoken none.

The heart was left untouched, unquickened, dead
In sin ; the sinners, still in guilt ; and yet
Deceived : for who but God can pardon sin,
And that from faith in Christ, with penitence
Of heart ; and not from faith in priest or church,
With penance done ?

Now years on years revolve ;
And Man-of-Sin holds grasp upon the world ;
Nay, holds the keys of Heaven, the keys of Hell.
He locks, and who can ope ? He opes, and who
Can shut ? His nod is law ; his frown, the wrath
Of God ; and kings obey, and peoples fall
In prostrate worship at his feet. His throne
Is firm, an everlasting rule ; and Hell
Is now triumphant in the earth.   What more
Could Satan wish, except that he himself
Had done the deed direct, direct instead
Of indirect by Man-of-Sin ? But this concerned
Himself alone, for all the rest preferred
It as it was, lest Satan's pride should gain
Its former height, and they be galled anew

By prestige won.

 Now Man-of-Sin returns,
And makes report. A saint in mein he's still.
All devils start again as he appears ;
(For devils hate all saints with perfect hate :)
And now can scarcely keep their seats. They ache
To rush and rend him into shreds : till they
Descry his hands, his hands to elbows red
With human blood. They rest. They knew 'twas he ;
'Twas Man-of-Sin, and not a saint of God.

 " All's well on earth," said he. " We hold the whole.
" We're safe. We've won the priesthood, cast out Christ
" From rule, and yet they see it not : but think
" He governs yet. They battle strong for him ;
" But 'tis in fact for me. 'Twas done so still
" They knew it not. Ah, yes ! a few ; but what
" Were they ? We crushed them as the worm
" Beneath the foot, or drove them from the haunts
" Of men ; and seized their lands, and flocks, and herds,
" And gave them to our pious ones : bewhile,
" They starved, and froze, in deserts lone, and wilds
" Of mountain tracts. We call them heretics,
" And brand them all. The parents and the babes
" We slay alike ; and make men think 'tis work
" Achieved for God. 'Tis thus we cheat them in
" The ' holy church.' We slip the ' saints of God '
" (So called on earth, but what they are we know)
" Like dogs of war, and keep the race, the race
" Heretic few and far between. And yet
" 'Tis toil. They spring up ev'rywhere where e'er
" The ashes of a martyr fall, like teeth
" Of dragons sown ; and faggots, and the rack,
" Can scarcely keep them down ; and nothing saves

" Us but the Scriptures hid. O! that we could
" Destroy that book. But, ah! we lack the power.
" We can conceal for most ; 'tis all that we
" Can do. We make it penal to possess
" The Word, and yet it is possessed. We make
" It heresy to read, and yet 'tis read.
" And, what alarms us more than all the rest,
" A way has been devised to give it wide
" And wider range. No more the *pen* is used,
" But *types*, to bring it forth. And hence, where one
" Was made, now thousands spring to light."
A shiv'ring came o'er Man-of-Sin ; his teeth
Then chattered, and his knees together smote.
And paleness sat upon his face, which ran
The round of Hell. For nought so dreaded there
As types, instinctive dread!——" But still," said he,
" We hold, and with due care shall ever hold
" The reins of power on earth. The son of man
" Shall never gain a foot-hold there again.
" If types must come, we'll use them for ourselves.
" We'll publish fables ; we'll corrupt the Word
" In text, and make it null and void. At least
" We'll break its force by commentaries giv'n ;
" Besides, the masses shall not have its use.
" We'll give it disrepute ; and write it down
" A dang'rous book ; and safe for priests, and priests
" Alone, whose holiness cannot be marred
" Thereby. And, then, traditions, we'll invoke
" Their aid, and set them off against the Word
" Of God. We'll get up miracles, to prove
" Us true. The lame shall walk, the blind shall see,
" And relics shall perform the whole, a bone,
" Or ashes of a saint, declared. O fools!

" We'll thus secure them, and befool them out
' Of Heav'n."—And here a laugh went round, that men
With reason blest, and far enthroned above
The brute, should be thus caught, thus caught with chaff.
  " The MORALS of the church are ours.   No more
" She draws them from the hated word, but from
" The ' schools.'   We even *make them new,* to suit
" The time.   ' No faith with heretics ' is in
" The code.   She promises—her promise breaks.
" She swears, swears solemn, swears upon the Word
" Of God, the evangelists, then breaks her oaths.
" Unbinding as a rope of sand ; and all
" Is right, because 'tis for the church's good.
" In fine, the *end* there justifies the means."
—And here another laugh went round again.
" Yes, all on earth is safe.   We search their hearts,
" The secrets of their very souls   And thus
" We root out heresy ere it begins.
" 'Tis called auricular confession, and
" It binds in chains of adamant ; deceives
" The soul ; corrupts the priest ; and opes the gate
" For ev'ry open, ev'ry secret sin.
  " We thus are sure.   Our eyes are ev'rywhere.
" We search out all.   Whate'er we wish to know
" We know ; what wish to hide, we hide ; for mouth
" Of all is dumb at our command.   We have
" ' Forbid to marry.' "   " This affords our cause
" Uncounted good."——And here a blush o'erspread.
The throng.   Yes, devils blushed at thought of deeds
Of shameless deeds produced thereby.   O sin !
O sin thus caused, unknown to man save those
In crime, but which the judgment shall in full
Reveal!   What mean those massy walls ?   What mean

Those gates and bars   if all is right within ?
And why should females there be kept for life ?
   " But I must tell," continued Man-of-Sin,
" A triumph now.   You've heard of Huss, John Huss."
All devils nod assent.   " His heresy
" Was rank ; his face was flint ; he feared nor man
" Nor Hell.   He laughed us all to scorn.   From him,
" Alas ! contagion spread on ev'ry side ;
" A very death-spot where his face was seen ;
" And he must die ; must die, or we must fall.
" We sought his life ; but he eludes, now here,
" Now there.   At length we summon to appear,
" And show his cause.   But he declines, unless
" He's safe.   He is assured of that.   And hence,
" Appears.   But, in our hands, he's ours.   We scorn
" The promise made.   'Tis for the church.   We seize,
" We judge, and we condemn, and lead him to
" The stake.   The faggots make short work, and he's
" No more ; and we are safe again.   We should
" Have joy untold, did not a terror hold
" Our souls, and cause misgivings day by day.
" Alas ! at midnight's hour, indeed 'tis said,
" We even know, that lights are seen about
" That spot ; and voices heard ; and e'en the fire
" Is yet unquenched.   The rains have come, the snows
" Have pressed, and lo ! the embers smoulder still."
—Here Satan paled, and Man-of-Sin grew faint
And sank to earth.——The ashes of John Huss!
The fire that smoulders there, shall never be
Extinct ; but shall in time be raised to flame,
And start a burning that shall sweep the world.
O, hope ! shall burn up all the chaff, the works
Of Man-of-Sin, his crosses, altars, racks,

His temples, relics, images, and e'en
His throne itself, his awful seat where erst
He sat, the dread of all the earth, and ruled
The nations with an iron rod. His smoke,
Like that of Sodom shall ascend and cloud
The Heavens. *That day shall come.* Another Huss
Shall rise, and God-sustained shall baffle all
His plans, shall lay his wickedness abare
To earth, shall show him up to men, the scoff
Of all the world ; and he shall gnash his teeth,
And call on kings for aid ; but all in vain ;
Shall feel the sceptre shake within his hand ;
And hear dismayed the moaning of the ground
Beneath his feet ; and see the lurid heavens
Portending coming storm, the day of wrath!
And he be impotent to shun the hour.

　　O Babylon! that hold'st the church in thrall,
The pious ones that have not bowed the knee;
Ah! thou shalt fall as Babylon of old,
That held the ancient church in bondage drear.
Thy palaces, like hers, become a waste ;
Thy halls, like hers, untrod ; **and silence brood**
O'er all thy wide domain. The owl shall **build**
Her nest within thy walls, the bittern woo
Her mate, and dragon reptiles lodge where song
And dance went round.

END OF BOOK EIGHTH.

BOOK IX.

TIME sweeps from midnight's hour.
And day is drawing near. A flush is seen
In eastean sky ; but doubtful if 'tis day,
Or cheat of sense. The eye is strained, and strained,
To make it sure. A streak at length is seen ;
And hope is born. The day is broken which
Shall never close, though darkness linger long.
  Within a cloistered cell a monk is seen,
Bewildered, pale, and trembling, not from fear
Of man, but from unquiet mind. He'd found
The Word of God, the priceless Word, there chained
Lest some should take it thence. He turns its leaves
And reads, now here now there ; and startles at
The truths he finds revealed.—He knows no rest
By day, by night. The priest steps in to give
Relief by pard'ning sin. But no avail.
Nor priest, nor all the moral lumber Rome
Can bring, can cast a sunshine on that dark,
Benighted soul. He finds at length a friend,
Instructed in the Word, who knows the way
Of life, salvation gained by *faith*, and not
By *works*. And he believes, believes and finds
Remission of his sins.—The shadows flee.
And light springs up ; and he is saved, is saved

By faith in the atoning Lamb ; and not
By penances performed.—How simple was
The way! He went to God direct, and not
Through pope or priest. What he had found must now
Be spread abroad. The WORD is now his book ;
And built up strong therein he publishes
Abroad its gracious truths : which fall upon
The hungry crowds like manna from the heavens.
   He spake as of authority, and not
As modern priest or ancient scribe. The Word
Had life, and caused the dead to live. The priest
With rage perceived his mass neglected, and
His gains decreased ; and more, e'en ridicule
Upon him heaped ; his blessing scorned ; his keys
All useless by his side, with which he erst
Could open Heaven or shut. His licenses
To sin, like shopworn wares upon the shelves,
Lay by, and none poured coin upon his lap
Therefor.   " This must be stayed, or all is lost.
" The giant heretic must be o'erthrown :
" Nor left to draw the world to him. He must
" Be brought within our reach, and we must deal
" With him, as erst with Huss.   He came at call,
Nor stood alone as Huss. His friends were there,
And, brave, deserted not as those of Huss ;
And he immortal till his work was done.
The conclave met. He answers from the Word
Of God. But what care they? the Word of God
Is naught to them, to men corrupt ; who seek
Not truth, but would their own iniquitous
Designs achieve. Their dogmas old must be
The test. But, right or wrong, the man must fall.
The church demands it, make then no delay.

The church! the church, then, makes this bloody call!
O tell it not in Gath! let not the streets
Of Askalon receive the sound! The church
Calls loudly for the blood of men.   By day,
By night they plot to seize their prey. But seemed
Withheld, as those were curbed who seized and led
The fearless Jesus to the hill-brow, there
To cast him down. But passing from them, he
Escaped. So our young heretic eludes
Their grasp. His time had not yet come.   He preached
The Word ; he gave it to the masses in
Their tongue, and thereby gave to Man-of-Sin
A wound that never, never shall be healed.
The flame, now kindled, spreads from land to land,
And light and warmth imparts to earth. The long,
Long shadows flee, the frosts of ages melt,
And earth gives promise of an Eden new.—
    He died ; and left his glorious work a boon
To future times.   But Man-of-Sin still lived,
Nor quit the field ; but battle joined with hope,
How vain! with hope, to overcome. His eyes
Were held. He saw not on the wall the hand
That wrote, nor read the lines so plainly traced
Thereon. Yes, he must fall, but fall not he
Without a struggle fierce. The ground shall all
Be faught, and inch by inch. And he will still
Deceive. Like Proteus of old will change
His form ; assume all shapes to suit the times.
    In monarchies he'll be for monarchies,
The one-man pow'r, as suited best for his
Designs, to rule the consciences of men,
And check defections, and impatience of
His sway. But in republics, and the hope
15

Of change extinct, he'll be for them ; and plead
Their cause.   But still the church should be above
The whole,   should shut out public light, and keep
The Word of God concealed ; nor suffer it
In learning's halls to raise its voice, and be
The guide of men.   And ruling she must sit
In state, and glitter in the trappings of the world.
    Ah ! how unlike to him, who, meek and low
Of heart, taught humbleness to all mankind.
    O muse, declare how martyrs bled in this
Great war ; this last convulsive death-throw made
By Man-of-Sin.   The years were long, the field
Was red,   the masses had the Word, and this,
The hope of earth, must seal his fate.   He felt
His time was short ; and full of rage, like the
Apocalyptic dragon, came down fierce
To be avenged on men.   His sword and torch
Saught ev'ry land, and Gaul gave hecatombs
To his demands ; and Albion scourged poured out
Her richest blood.   The blade, the faggot, and
The rack, and flood, performed their work, upheld
By bloody power : till hearts grow sick, and foes
Relent.   What land where Christ was named, felt not
The scourge where Man-of-Sin could reach ?   The Isles
Were smitten, and Europa groaned.   Renowned,
O Smithfield, for the death of saints ! thy soil
Has drunk their blood.   And thou shalt yield it at
The judgment day ; and thou, O Rhone ! whose wave
Has born the martyr's dust and shed it in
The sea, shalt be a witness swift when God
Shall square accounts ; and ev'ry prison-house,
And cave, and rack, and chain, shall have a tongue
In that disastrous day.

But time moves on ;
And truth gains ground, though still the battle high.
Th' opposing pow'rs give way ; and Man-of-sin
Is pressed on every side ; and ere aware
Is shorn of half his strength.   Whole lands reject
His sway, and hold him in contempt ; and bid
Defiance to the thunder of his power.
   Brittania casts him out, and Gaul o'ersweeps
His realm, and fills his seat with darkness ; **and**
Displays to all the world that he is sure
Not God, and his Anathemas but wind.
And when his sacred person was immured
In prison walls, he lacked the power to move
The bars, much less to open Heav'n or Hell.
The conqu'ring Gaul, presumptuous, laid his hands
Upon him and still lived !   The charm was broke ;
The world then, laughed.   His prestige waned from that
Sad day ; and now at length his hour has come ;
And like a child chastised and full subdued,
In this our year of eighteen sixty-two,
He whines, and looks up piteously for aid.
Yes, he whose awful word was law, who ope'd
His mouth to curse, and none could bless ; who blessed,
And none could curse ; who put up thrones, and cast
Them down ; who trod upon the necks of kings,
And made them prostrate bow, and kiss his feet ;
—Now calls out piteously for aid, with sighs
And abject tears.   O fallen Babylon !
Remembrance of thy ways has come before
The throne ; thy yoke is broken, and thyself
Despoiled ; and soon thy desolation shall
Be full, and thou shalt be of things that were.
And then a shout shall rend the skies, a shout

And Alleluia ring from pole to pole ;
And those that loved thee and grew rich within
Thy walls, shall stand aloof and weep, to see
Thy smoke, thy burning reach to heaven ; alas !
Such riches, come to naught, such power, despoiled !
    Yes, let her fall. Let her who took the sword
Now feel its power ; let her who captive led
Be captive now ; and deal her double as
The portion of her cup.

END OF BOOK NINTH.

BOOK X.

BUT Satan had
Been ill at ease while Man-of-Sin held sway
On earth. At first, and thence for centuries,
He'd had but little doubt of his success.
But since the deadly wound that Man-of-Sin
Had felt from recent heretic ; and from
The Word of life, unhid, and broad-cast thrown
O'er many a land, he read, sagacious more
Than wont, that Man-of-Sin might yet be spoiled
Of sway, and driven back in shame to Hell.
Lest that should hap, and he be caught, he planned
In time to ward the blow. He made a call
Imperious for the states to meet. They met,
In multitude beyond all thought of man.
  And Satan took his seat, and sat sublime
As wont above the rest. His starry crown
Flashed living light. His robes resplendent shone ;
And on his thigh reposed his trusty sword,
That awed the millions down, and stifled all
Complaint.
        The noble peers of his vast realm
Were ranked on either hand, on seats less high,
But eminent above the crowd ; while these
The lesser gods fill all the space below,
Immense, a wondrous throng.—All silent wait
The council to begin. The cause was hid,

But shrewd conjecture pointed up to earth.
    Then Satan rose and spoke. " My lords upon
" My right, and left, and you, my firm supports,
" That fill this mighty space," (in voice so clear,
That all to utmost verge distinctly heard,
And shrunk aghast at its imperious tones.
Instinctive horror! as is felt when climbed
To some high tower, one casts his eye beneath,
And shudders at the appalling depth below,)
" Our cause on earth is not beyond a doubt,
" Though Man-of-Sin has wonders wrought, and ground,
" For centuries gone by, beneath his heel,
" His glorious iron heel, the real church,
" The hated church of God. But she's not dead.
" She yet may rise, to our dismay ; and push
" Us from the earth. What mirth would be in Heaven,
" If, after all our toil and hopes on earth,
" We should be found to fail! It must not, can
" Not be ; and yet it will, I fear, unless
" Some new device is planned, some scheme to check
" The light or neutralize its power : which, else,
" Shall shine and over-sweep the world.
" The church, the church of God, (no other church
" I mean) must be o'erthrown. But how? Some new
" Deceit. if aught avails, must be our hope.
" Our former wiles she knows, and ne'er will fall
" By them again. But let us move in time ;
" And make assurance doubly sure. So, if
" Our Man-of-Sin should fail, we shall be in
" The field, all ready to sustain our cause.
    " But what shall we attempt? Let all be free
" To speak."
            Then Nisroch rose, and " deemed it best

" To try return to idol worship once
" Again ; perhaps the church could be seduced
" By this." But Satan mild reminded him,
" That Man-of-Sin had that already in
" The field ; that in *his* church men bowed to wood
" And stone in shape of Virgin, babe or cross ;
" And homage paid to relics as to God.
" What could be done with that, be sure he'd do ;
" But something more efficient must be tried.
" Toils old will hardly take a second time."
    Then rose Anammelech, and he would give
Her, surely give her fame. " But Man-of-Sin
" Has tried that too : with good success thus far ;
" But she might learn to shun that snare, if laid
" A second time. Some new, some new device,
" Be sure, must be our care ; and take her off
" Her guard." Adrammelech then thought
The lust of worldly power would draw her off
From God. " But Man-of-Sin has that," was then
Replied. " The way to worldly power is through
" The church ; and kings and emperors but reign
" By her high leave. They bow submissive at
" Her feet ; and own her sovereign sway."
    Then Mammon rose, a god of wide repute,
If not of high respect. He stood in view,
With sharp and piercing eye, but shop-worn in
His mein, and thin and hungry ; with his hands
In clutching mood, as if to make a grasp
At something in his reach ; and those near by
Removed, instinctive care! lest something should
Be missed before the session closed. His brow
Was creased with thought, and in his face, her lines
Arithmetic had furrowed deep. He spoke

With slow and well selected words, as if
From caution in the choice of means.   He spoke :
" Your Holiness," said he, to Satan on
The throne.——The throne! ah! who can full reveal
The splendors of the throne of Hell?   For there
The artist had bestowed his utmost hand,
Great Vulcan, once, in purer days, well known
In Heav'n by wondrous works of skill and taste,
Bewildering to the sense whenever scanned
By spirit eyes ; but now the architect
Of Hell ; his goodness gone, but still his taste
And skill not lost.   He wrought the whole.   The mines
Were searched and spoiled of gold and richest gems,
And rainbows quarried from the living rock.
    From such he raised the structure, firm, but light
In mould.   The architraves, the pillars, base,
And caps, and frieze, were in proportion due.
The pavements were mosaics, such as earth
Knows not ; the seat, of burnished gold ; the front,
Of silver and of rainbow stone, relieved
By drapery of tyrian dye, and stiff
With ev'ry stone and pearl of gorgeous hue.
    Nor less in richest taste the canopy
Above ; which hung festooned with skill
Untold.   Here Satan sat, as kings are wont
To sit ; all lovely to the sight ; but vile
Within, and rotten to the core.——Said he,
Said Mammon, with his usual choice of words,
" Your Holiness well knows that one, one trait
" Marks man distinct from other living things,
" The love of gain.   He loves to see his stores
" Increase, his lands enlarge, and feel that he
" Has goods laid up for years to come.   And hence

" He sits up late, and wakes betimes, and toils
" His body down to very bones ; and this,
" Not simply for his meat, and drink, and wear ;
" But from the love, unsated love of *more,*
" For more than he can use ; and hence he scours
" The world ; he braves the flood, the tropic fires,
" And arctic frosts ; and dives beneath, and digs
" The bowels of the earth ; and tramples on
" The laws of God and man ; and sells his soul,
" And all his hopes of Heav'n for worldly gain.
    " Can we not reach her here ?   I mean the church ;
" And set a snare for her unwary feet ?
" But how, how shall the thing be done ?   Methinks
" 'Tis in the scope of Hell, to lay the plan
" To draw her off from God by worldly gain.
Let some more shrewd devise and state his views."
He sat ; and none the silence broke ; though all
Were pleased, yet none could see the way to reach
The end.   All eyes were fixed on Satan ; and
They saw a twilight in his face, as if
Some new and happy thought had struck his mind.
    He rose.   " I think," said he, " I see the way
" To reach the end by means just now proposed.
" The love of gain has, true, been tried before,
" And with success.   But now I see a plan
" To cheat her with the love of gain anew,
" And make her think 'tis love of God and man.
" And this has always been, as well you know,
" A keen delight to us, to see her do
" Our work, when she was sure, the while, that 'twas
" The work of God.   My plan is this.   You know
" A world, a western world has late been found
" On earth by daring Genoese ; and that

" It promises to be the home of man,
" Of millions of the race of man ; and there,
" Methinks, our deadly foe in Heav'n intends
" To plant his church, and set her free from us,
" And all the snares we spread in older lands.
" Yes, he intends to make her there mayhap
" A City on a hill, far, far removed
" From Man-of-Sin. Now we will see to dim
" Her light, and make her good to evil turn.
" A horde of Bible fools have crossed the main,
" Called Pilgrims, and have taken foot-hold there,
" And cavaliers in sunny-south ; and both
" Are spreading wide ; and promise give of large
" And larger growth. Before their wave the beasts,
" The savage beasts retire, the forests fall,
" And goodly fields, with harvests crowned, delight
" The eye. A kind of Eden there may grow
" In time. But let us mar it as we marred
" The first ; and let us seize their piety
" To do the deed ; and harness it, and make
" It draw our car."—And here a smile went round
On all, though devils doubted if the thing
Could be. " You know," said he, " across the flood
" From where they dwell, the Afric shores extend.
" The people there are simple, weak, and some
" Say wicked. They are heathen ; and my plan
" Is this : to make an effort to convert
" Their souls."—All devils started to their feet,
And thought that he was mad.—"Be cool," said he,
" You have not heard the whole. We shall not send
" The Gospel out to them, and leave them in
" Their native vales, and spicy groves, and 'mid
" Their friends, and homes, and brothers, sisters, wives,

" And fathers, mothers, loves, and children dear.
" O no! 'twould cost too much, and Mammon thinks,
" Forever thinks of cost. But I intend
" To have them brought to Western shores, where light,
" And life can be acquired, and Gospel truth
" Be learned ; and give them pious masters, who
" Shall care for them, since they've been purchased with
" A price. These masters dear shall teach them love,
" And lash the lesson through their heathen skins ;
" Shall teach them honesty by taking all
" Their toil unpaid. Shall teach them truthfulness
" By telling them that they were made to serve ;
" In fine, shall give them lessons in the rule,
" The golden rule, by doing unto them
" As they would *not* that men should do to them
" In turn."   The devils laughed ; and saw that he,
That Satan, had outdone himself in this
His shrewd concocted plan. They voted it
At once ; and voted Mammon master of
The field ; a missionary, sent to earth ;
The first that ever went from Hell, to care
For souls.
                  O Africa! what griefs await
Thee now. 'Twas done.—What direful ills were hers!
Such ills! What wars, what deaths, what plund'rings and
What pangs of fathers, mothers, brothers, for
Their loved ones lost, torn ruthless from their arms
By Christian hands, and scourged, and manacled,
And packed in pestilential holds, and swept
Across the main in pirate ships ; and chafed
And sickened by the rolling waves! What deaths
Among thy simple children in their path
Of midway ocean! down whose awful depths

Their wasted limbs have sunk ; and whose broad floor
Is thick o'erspread from land to land, with their
Unsevered bones! an army of the dead!
Unseen ; a vast subaqueous Golgotha ;
In multitude beyond what earth e'er saw ;
Composed and waiting for the judgment day :
The giant frame that battled strong, and scorned
To be a slave, then leaped the deck ; the maid
And stripling slumber there ; the brother and
The sister side by side, ejected when
Their life was done ; and on her bony chest
The mother's arms still clasp her fleshless babe,
Forgetful of those tiny hands, those eyes,
Those sable lips, that once gave such delight :
Yes, " waiting for the judgment day," for they
Have tales to tell.   *Their time shall surely come.*
    The living far from home bemoan their lot.
The whip is heard from day to day, the sigh
Suppressed, the stifled groan ; the soil is wet
With tears, enriched with blood, and hope is dead,
And manhood crushed from out their very souls.
    The years roll on, and Afric's shores still bleed.
The burdened ocean groans ; the winds lament,
And all, but man, has sympathy for man.
    The sable race is thronging in the West ;
And marts are full, and trade is brisk.   Their toil
Brings wealth to many a sumptuous lord, and in
The market they are sold, as beasts, to swell
His store.—O Mammon, direful child of Hell!
    'Twas wonderful ; the true philosophy
Had come at last, to make a nation rich,
And save a heathen race.   All scrambled for
The prize.   All felt unheard-of zeal for souls.

They bought, they sold, they bred for sale, they drove
Afield for daily toil ; they catechised, they prayed,
And mingled sweetly things of earth and Heav'n.
And when the ship arrived, or coffle-gang
Had come, their zeal was then renewed, they felt
A yearning for these precious ones. The saint
Then bought, the sinner bought, the matron from
Her prayers, and e'en the preacher from his desk,—
'Till none remained. Such thrift must not be lost,
And hence another ship or coffle comes,
Another scramble, and another heap
Of pelf ; till angels sicken at the sight ;
And turn away and weep. The Church,—now veered
From out her course,—had left the love of God
For love of man, and that of sable skin.
And whom each loved he chastened oft, and hence
Among his household gods the whip was found,
And manacles and Bibles rested on
The self same shelf. And when the saint kneeled down
To pray, the dagger gleamed beneath his vest,
Or pistol rattled by his side, all primed
Or capped, with deadly bullet charged. What prayers !
New laws now sprung to light, unheard of in
The Draco code. Laws partial, made to meet
The bondman's case. His wife was now no more
His own, nor babes, nor aught he held most dear.
The law of Heav'n was not a law to him,
But law of man. Thus man with impious foot
Stepped in between his God and him. The book
Of knowledge, in this land of light, was still
No book to him. 'Twas locked by law. His lips
Were sealed in courts of right ; and midst a world
Of wrongs, of keenest, fiercest wrongs, no scales

The hand of justice held for him.   His sons
Were manacled and sold ; his daughters, dragged
From out his hut by lustful hands, his wife
Was scourged before his eyes,—but no redress.
Now mark you, if he did but raise his hand
To save the shame, or ward the blow, then he
Must die. His wrongs were heaped on wrongs. What years,
What dreary years were his !   What decades of
Despair !   His soul grew weary, and he prayed
For death.—O hark ! what sound is that ?   A shot,
A pistol shot, and groan !   A manly form
Of sable hue lies prostrate on the ground.
His hands are clenched; his eyes glare fire; his teeth
In frenzy grind;—at thought of what for years
He'd patient borne ; and now, for some offence
Of trivial moment, lies there bleeding out
His life, by law-protected despot slain.

His brawny chest is heaving hard for breath ;
His mouth, begushed with blood.—And death-hue now
Shows ghastly on his form.—At length his nerves
Relax.—His eye is glazed.—Convulsions tear
His frame.—A moment more—and step by step
Death's shade in full steals o'er—and all is still.—

A dog is dead ; a man for whom Christ died.
What shrieks in yonder hut !   What stifled cries !
What half-concealed despair !   The father and
The husband's dead ; but ah ! there's no redress.
The land will clear its skirts ; they'll call a fast,
And rend their garments all to tatters soon,
And pray, and long abstain, and wipe it out.

No funeral sermon preached, no decent rites
Of burial giv'n.—The worthless carcass, thrown
Within some pit, with rubbish covered o'er,

Lies there uncared for and unknown. But ah !
It waits the dreadful reckoning yet to come !
  Years still drag on, and decades wear away ;
And still the millions groan beneath their load.
The public heart is more and more corrupt,
The conscience seared, and all is rip'ning for
The wrath of God.   What crimes are wrought, unheard,
From year to year ! What villanies are brought
To life, and walk the land ! What states receive
Their wealth from sale of—not of flocks, and herds,
And golden grain, and thousand fruits of earth,
And wares and fabrics from the hand of toil
And skill,   O no, but from the sale,—O shame !—
Of their own sons and daughters. Yes, the men
Who rate themselves as Chivalry, and claim
A rank above the level of the world,
Who scornfully look down on laboring thrift,—
Live shameless on the plunder of the poor,
Or means derived from setting them to sale !
O Chivalry ! was ever wickedness,
Was meanness ever, ever seen like thine ?
  But crimes increase. The whip, the rifle-shot,
The knife, producing death, and deadly hunt
With dogs upon the track of victim fled,
—Grow stale at length, and now are quite too tame
For public taste ; and, as a warning to
Each sinning wretch, the stake and chain must come
In aid.   Behold it grimly stand, and bound
Thereto the sable victim doomed to death,
And breathless from despair. He gazes round.
Alone he stands 'mid hearts of steel, and none
To plead his cause and beg the sparing of
His life. The sable crew aloof like sheep

From lion in the fold, with breathless awe
Shrink back till forced to nearer view. They stand
Amazed, while wicked hands pile deep the food
Of fire. The torch is plied, the smoke ascends ;
The flame shoots forth : he shudders at
The sight, and shrinks aghast at its approach.
   It crackles and devours, and nearer draws.
He backward strains, and strains to utmost strength.
   And now a shriek, and clank of chain !   His flesh
Is reached ; and then his shrieks are heard afar !
He begs, he prays, he tries his utmost might,
Again, again, again ; he begs, he prays,
He calls for water ! water ! water ! grasps
The hissing links, then casts them down ; then grasps
Again, and lets them fall ; then grasps and lets
Them fall again ; and tries again his strength,
Again in vain.—His quiv'ring flesh, beset
With flames, is roasting while alive ; his shrieks
Now turn to groans; his eyeballs stare; his mouth,
Distended wide; his features, scorched, are fixed
In agony.   The while, the jeering crowd
Stand mocking at his pain ; and his poor kin
Bleed silent at the heart.   *Dost thou believe*
In God?   Will He not be avenged on such
A land as this ?   The wretch expires ! the groups
Retire ; the one, alas ! in blackness of
Despair ; the other, jocund and refreshed.
   And where's the Church ?   Does she not raise her voice
Against such sin ?   O ! no.   She holds her peace,
Nor suffers those to speak who would.   Yes, when
A few fanatics rise to show the sin,
And lay its hideous features bare, and call
On her to rise and sweep it out, she falls

On them, and hunts them from her fold, and says
" 'Tis politics, and that the Church must not
" Be found therein ; that she must care for souls,
" And eschew, always eschew worldly strife.
   " Besides, 'tis law, and she must always heed
" The law."—And yet she *made* the law, or helped
To make it such, herself.   The word of God
She half forsook.   She fasted, but she broke
No yoke ; she rent her garments, but she left
The burden still unbound ; she put forth tracts
And came out strong against a thousand sins,
—E'en some that hardly could be noted sins,—
But this great sin, this sin of sins, this breach,
This wholesale breach of God's whole law, that placed
Its impious foot upon the decalogue
And law of love at once, she left untouched.
She labored hard for heathen, far beyond
The sea.   But O! the heathen in her midst,
She left unlettered, and unread in God's
Great word.——Ah ! yes, there were a few, and sparce,
Indeed, that raised their voice with trumpet-sound
Against that Heav'n defying sin.   But they,
Ah ! they were sure to be proscribed, and shunned,
And written down disturbers of the peace.
They prophesied, but prophesied in vain ;
Declared the judgments of the Lord to come ;
But who believed ?   The ruthless rabble rose
In arms, and sought their life, despoiled their goods,
And led them through the streets with ropes about
Their necks ; and lo ! the Church looks on serene
And calmly smiled ; so sure it was a work
All done for God ; and almost said " their blood
" On us, and on our children fall."   Ah ! yes,
16

It shall upon their children fall, if not
On them.   For this great sin shall breed the clash
Of war ; impatient grown and arrogant
From long unbridled sway.   The deadly strife
Shall come, and she, the Church, shall give her sons,
Her stay, her hope, on thousand battle fields
To bleed.
   Now Mammon, satisfied to full
Desire, repairs to Hell ; and makes report.
 The concourse was immense ; and devils thronged
With eager ear to hear what word he brought ;
To know how Satan's plan had gone above ;
For they had had some inklings of the good
Success.
   They wait for Mammon to begin.
He rose, and bowed to Satan, and with words
Of measured time rehearsed the whole from first
To last.   He told them of the pious care
And labors of the Church, " That she had sent
" Him missionary to the Congo coast,
" And there that he had kidnapped souls, and sent
" Them o'er the flood to be baptized and saved ;
" Yes, saved by ship-loads in a Christian land.
 " Here truth requires," he fault'ring said, " that some
" Had doubts, and said, in case they did not *know*
" 'Twas pious work, that they should surely think
" 'Twas stealing men ; a thing forbid in God's
" Great word.   But I was sure on hand to soothe
" Their minds, and reconcile them to what half
" Appeared a sin.   Yes, I could always calm
" Them down, by quoting largely from the word
" Of God.   I showed them Abraham, but sure
" I never hinted at the golden rule ;

" And always wielded strong Onesimus
" And Paul." The devils laughed. " No matter if
" It was unsound, if they but took the bait,
" And thus were caught, 'twas all that we could wish.
   " Yes, yes, I have on Earth whole conferences
" And synods, and conventions, and the mass
" Of membership. And these I harness in
" At will, and make them draw my car.
" Don't laugh ; 'tis true. But I have something worse,
" Or rather better still. I have on Earth
" A D. D. pampered to the full, who spends
" His time in writing 'South Side Views' of that
" Most patriarchal state, to set in bold
" Relief its beauties to a doubting world.
" I left him at the quill, on taking leave."
The devils laughed again, and shook their sides,
To see a D. D. caught, thus nicely caught,
And made to do their work.—Here Satan checked
Their glee, and begged them be more soft, for fear
They might be heard on earth ; and 'twould be learned
That Mammon was at bottom of the whole.
For that must not be told, but must be kept
A secret, deep and dark ; while we befool
The Church, and set her up a laughing stock
Throughout all time to come.—
                              What's this ? A pause—
Here Mammon faultered in his speech, and blushed ;
And Satan rapped ; but Mammon still delayed ;
And Satan rapped again, and bade him to
Proceed and tell the whole. For sure there could
Be nothing that should wake up shame, and cause
A blush in Hell. But Mammon still delayed ;
And Satan rapped, to wake the dead, and showed

A fire of eye that none could dare gainsay.
　What could it mean ?　There must be something done
On earth that devils blushed to tell.—'Tis out
At last, for he proceeds at Satan's stern
Command.　" We have a law on earth," said he,
" Called Slave-law-fugitive."　The devils start,
And half of them involuntary hiss.
For they had fierce remembrance of that law
In Hell.　'Twas once enacted there, to bring
To service due, the fleeing devil, to
His bloody lord.　　This law was Satan's pet,
'Twas more like Hell than any other law
That devils ever felt.　But 'twas repealed
At length ; though not that devils better grew,
Or Hell was on reform ; but very shame,
For shame they wiped it out.　The angels laughed,
They thought, and mocked them for the choice they made,
Of such a rule, when they seceded from
The rule of God.　　But while it lasted, O ! ´
What scenes were witnessed in that dreadful world !
　For they had slav'ry there, in olden time.
The powerful overcame the weak, and brought
Them into bondage.　Then they made them serve.
Yes, devil weak was made to serve, and cower
To devil strong.　He went, he came at his
Command, and did his menial toils ; and kneeled,
Or prostrate fell before him, as to power
Of higher grade, and of superior worth.
O ! shame, and constant laugh of Heav'n, when all
Were devils there upon the self-same plane,
And that exceeding low : and yet, laid claim
To worth ; and talked of better blood, ha ! ha !
The chivalry, the aristocracy of Hell.

He trembled at his word, and perished at
His frown ; and died ten thousand deaths beneath
The daily lash, bestowed on him through mere ·
Caprice, or malice of the devilish heart.
And when to phrenzy driv'n, then he escaped,
And shelter sought in other parts of Hell.
Then Satan made a law, at once, that all
Good devils should be on their guard, and watch,
And apprehend whatever wretch might flee
From lash and toil, and safe return him to
His death again.   It took at first, a kind
Of pastime.   And the scenes that then ensued
Made thoughtful devils even weep.   The wretch
Escaped no less ; but O! pursued by all
The vulgar, all the elite of Hell,—half dead,
And shrieking,—through her wide campaigns, beset
With yells, and hell-hounds foaming on his track.
When caught, the marshalls judged the case, and sent
Him back as Satan had desired.   For there,
His will, not justice, holds the scale.   " It took "
At first, and devils of some fair repute
Took office to enforce the law.   But shame
At length compelled them to retire.   And how
The pale and trembling wretch besought them to
Release their hold, and let him flee !   What pleas
He used !   What tears he shed ! that fell in drops
Of blood, and wet the ground.   But no, the will
Of Satan must be done, his laws enforced,
Whate'er injustice shall accrue thereby.
They took a second thought, and said, " It marred
" The reputation of the land ;" though that
Was small indeed.   And here instanter all
The marshalls, bailiffs, and the lesser packs

Resigned ; and none were left to run the cursed
Machine.   It fell of course.   And Satan, in
A rage, swore loud, swore loud and long with oaths
That frightened Hell, that he *would have* this law
Revived again ; " and if too bad for Hell
" It will not be too bad for earth.   For there
" A race will yet be born that will enact
" This law at my desire, and run it for
" Some years at least, and that without the shame
" That you have here."   That day arrived in time.
'Twas done, and Mammon blushed to tell it down
In Hell.

        The devils, though displeased at this
Last fact, yet, on the whole, felt high delight
At his success ; but blamed him not for what
He did at Satan's stern command ; for he,
For Satan, when he speaks, must be obeyed ;
Though 'twere the direst ills to be endured,
The " harri-carri " e'en of half the damned,
Inflicted by their own unwilling hands.

   O Hell ! yet this, yes, this was that dread rule
They chose instead of that of Heaven ; where God,
Though he supreme, yet rules forever for
The good of all.   They chose it ; yes, they chose
It.   Such the blindness, nay, the madness of
The wicked heart.   And men will do the same,
And share their fate.——The devils were full pleased,
And toasted Mammon high, and voted him
The only hope of Hell that now was left,
(For hope in Man-of-Sin was long since dead,)
To work corruption in the church, and bring
Her final fall.   'Twas but a gleam of hope,
Yet shouted they, and made the welkin ring

Be not too sure. It is indeed a shoal,
A dangerous rock, and she may ground thereon,
And may be wrecked ; but God may interpose,
And save her in her hour of need ; and warned
She may be proof in time against the snares,
The strong allurements of the golden god,
And take more thought than e'er in times gone by,
To place her treasure where no thief, nor moth,
Nor rust, can ever come.   O haste the day
When she shall have her last, sad lesson learned ;
And rise and shine, a bright and burning light,
Throughout the world, to light the darksome sea
Of life, the stormy wave, and guide the mariner
With precious freight and shattered bark through reefs
And quicksands safe to port.   Thus Mammon told
The whole, and Satan saw that he had not
Misjudged ; that Mammon had accomplished all
He wished, and that, beside, this care was just,
To have a burden new upon the church,
Lest Man-of-Sin should fail at length, and she
Should rise and thrust him from the earth :
And then, unfettered, should be free to spread
Throughout the world.——But will this always weigh
Her down ?   Ah no !   She shall repent ere long,
When wars shall spring through this great sin, and death
And carnage sweep o'er all the land, and steel
Of brother drip with brother's blood ; and path
Of foe be traced by day by corpses strown,
And lurid flames by night, of harvests fired
And happy homes of men.   Yes, she shall then
Repent and cry to God.   And in His might
Shall shake forever from her soul this sin,
This blackest, deadliest sin.

                              The time is near
For her reform.   Delay it not.   If come
It must, then let it come, the deadly strife.—
'Tis here.—The trumpet sounds ; the roar of war
Is heard ; and armies rush to combat dread
Upon the crimson field ; and engines sweep
Them down like grass before the scythe.   Our friends
Are there, our fathers, brothers, sons.   The church
Is bleeding now at every pore ; and sees
Her sin as never seen before.   She heard
The bond-man cry ; she saw his tears,
And heard the clanking of his chains ; she saw
His babes torn ruthless from the mother's breast,
And sold for gain ; his daughters forced away
To toil or shame.   She saw him fainting in
The burning sun ; and quickened by the lash ;—
Till death vouchsafed relief.   She saw, she heard
It all ; and closed her eyes and ears, and bade
Him hush lest her own peace should be disturbed.
    'Tis now disturbed !   There's wailing heard within
Her walls ; her "first-born" sons are slain.   Ah, she
Had long forgot, "*first* pure, *then* peaceable."
Her peace has gone ; and mayhap yet will come
Her purity to bless the world.——Rejoice   .
Not then, too much, ye powers below.   She may
Escape, as Isr'el, after years of pain
The dire Babylonian thrall.   For God intends
To set her on a hill, all pure and white,
The grand attraction of a sinning world
"In time."   Be patient, Earth, that day is yet
To come ; and wait, ye islands of the sea,
And Ethiopia, still, still stretch your hands.—
The time is hastening on.   The signs are clear.

The captive millions feel the loosing of
Their chains, which soon shall fall, and be of things
That were. And Man-of-Sin is at his last,
Last gasp, no more a power on earth, to bind
And loose, and pale the millions with a word,
And make the monarch tremble on his throne.

The bars are giving way, and pagan doors
Are opening wide, and God's great gospel finds
A lodgment there. Be patient, wait, the work
Shall yet be done.

END OF BOOK TEN.

BOOK XI.

CHRONOLOGY, A.D., 11,862.

As at Bethesda's pool,
The comers waited for the angel's wing,
That swept the flood, and gave it healing power,
So I await, not out of hope, the breath
Of inspiration, that shall ope to view
The onward flow of time, that bears upon
Its tide the works of earth 'till all at last
Shall be out-swept to that great sea that all
Ingulfs.
       Ten thousand years have gone. Behold
What change! The stream is to the loins, the stream
The prophet saw, the stream that flowed from out
The threshold eastward. First 'twas scant, and reached
But to the ankles, then, in onward flow,
The knees, the loins, and did at length a flood
Become, a river deep and wide, that none
Could pass ; a river giving life to all
Within its wave.   Roll on, thou precious stream.
O ! haste the time.
        "The stream is to the loins.
Behold what change on earth ! The din of war
Has ceased, and nations settled down in peace.
   The sword, the gun, the bayonet's glittering steel,

Are now no more, save each in archives kept,
As relics of the past, to show the things
That were.   The ship is freighted deep to lands
Afar, but not with thunder armed.
Her canvas wings   or whirlwind steam, the work
Of later art, bear goodly merchandize,
And messages of love, and greetings kind
Of land to land.   The fortresses of earth
Have crumbled down, and orchards bend with fruit
And harvests wave, with golden sheen where erst
The soil was vexed with martial feet ; and war
Was learned by military drill.   The trade
Is gone, the trade of war ; and all have quit
The scene for works of peace.   The Cup
Is gone that maddened half the world, and led
To poverty and crime ; the drug and weed
That stupified and sapped with slow but sure
Approach, the citadel of life,—are now
Extinct, or growing wild like brambles in
The hedge, or kept for mere botanic show,
Or medicines for such ills as poisons cure.
And pris'ns now are things unknown, and locks
And bars on household doors.   The armies of
The world, that watched with jealous eyes the rights
Of nations, and with arms of steel beset
Their long frontiers ; the thick police that ranged
Through cities day and night to keep the peace,
And save from violence, and give repose,
Are now disbanded, and have long been sent
To till the soil, or bless mankind in works
Of art.   The waste of war nor draining wealth,
Nor tearing down what peace builds up, the works
Of man remain ; and children reap the toil

Their fathers made ; and theirs in turn their own.
The world grows rich ; the wastes are all reclaimed.
And science guides the plow, and tills the crops ;
And triples all the harvests of the field ;
And half relieves the strain of human toil.
The world moves on.   God's problem of our race
Is working out, and highest promise gives
Of glory greater still to be achieved.

   All this is done   And yet the highest reign
Of righteousness has not full come.   But men
Are still who sin, but most in secret sin ;
Nor dare to come to light lest public shame
Should crush them down.   Such sentiment there is
'Gainst evil deeds.   And these will be reclaimed
In whole or part, so strong the leaven is
Within the lump.

           The breath of God has passed
O'er Afric's wilds.   Her forests now are gone,
And beasts of prey.   A polished Christian race
Now till her soil, or ply the arts that bless
And ornament the world.   And sages there
Are found,—of Ethiop skin, no longer now
Despised,—of deepest lore in things germane
To matter and to mind ; who scan with eye
Severe the mysteries of air and earth ;
Or mark with nicest skill the moving spheres ;
And calculate the footsteps of the whole
A thousand years to come.   And India too,
And far Japan, and Russ barbaric, these
And all the tracts of earth that erst were dark,
The habitations dread of cruelty
And death, have felt the touch of life ; and like
The man among the tombs, are clothed and sit

Regenerate among the families
Of God. But O! the struggle to attain
This height of excellence on earth! The war
Was long, the waves of battle high. But truth
And righteousness at last prevailed.——The strife
In Western world for human bondage, long
Had ceased. The slave was free, the despots were
Subdued. The temple they had reared, and hoped
To make eternal, and to stand on wrong,
⹀ The bondage of a race, in madness as
The " gods decreed," like Samson in his rage
And blindness, they had pulled upon themselves,
And found a grave beneath.   America
Was purged ; her sin was gone ; a better race
Then took the southern field. Where once the slave
With trembling footsteps trod, and writhed beneath
The lash, and poured his tears and blood,—he stands
A man ; his wife is his, his babes are his,
And his oppressors, like th' Egyptian host,
O glorious change! were heard and seen no more.
The church was cleansed from this great sin, that weighed
Her down, and clogged salvation's car. Yes, cleansed
By fire and blood. Her wealth was spoiled, her sons
Were slain, and she, in sack-cloth and in tears,
Turned back to God. Another lesson she
Had learned, and had it graved upon her soul,
As with a diamond point.   Thus, God instructs
By lessons ; seldom by command direct ;
And may the teaching never, never be
Effaced. It shall be so. And never shall
A slave clank chains again within the church.
   And Satan had perceived with much dismay
That Truth and Righteousness were gaining more,

And still more strength on earth, in spite of ιll
His efforts to withstand their course ; and felt
With all, a deep chagrin, that all his foes,
(And who were not, e'en in that lower world ?)
Had proof anew, that he, alas! was not
Almighty ; but though strong, was less, far less,
In strength than he would have them think. They loved
His cause, though hated him, and feared ; and so
Were ever ready to perform his will ;
And that to utmost strength. Besides, all place
Of honor and of trust, was from his hand,
Th' appointing power. And whom he would he raised,
And whom he would he cast degraded down
To dust.   Thus policy, and hate of good
To man, enchained them to his will.   He called
A council of his highest chiefs, to see
What could be done to gain the foothold he
Had lost on earth. But first he would require
His last embassadors to make report.
And Man-of-Sin and Mammon answered to
The call ; but shamed and scalded to the quick,
That their great works had tapered down to naught.
    First Man-of-Sin was ordered to the floor
To make report.—He came with front of brass
And names of blasphemy upon his brow,
But old, and crippled, and effete. He paused,
Then staggered to the stand, a beggar clothed
In rags. Ah! how unlike to him that went
To earth to rule the nations there, and set
His throne above the throne of God! Yet he
It was. So rich and strong in times gone by,
And now so poor, so weak! And he must tell
The whole, and tell the truth ; for Satan would

Have truth *to him*, though lies were otherwheres
Their stock in trade.

     " Your holiness," said he,
To Satan,—Satan bowed assent,—" I did
" On earth whate'er I could, to make, and keep,
" The church corrupt. At first the struggle was
" Severe, but after weary centuries
" Of toil, as all who hear me know, I cast
" Her down, and made her do my bidding through
" A length of years. I placed my seat on high,
" And ruled the world. And when I seemed secure
" And saw the kings of earth before me bend,
" And felt assurance of eternal sway,
" The Word of God escaped from out my grasp,
" Which I had kept to rule the nations with
" By misinterpreting its simple text.

 " I strove to call it back, and chain it up
" Anew. But all in vain. My stern decrees
" Were set at naught. My bulls roared thunder round
" The land ; but still in vain. The Word, once free,
" Was like a bird uncaged. She scorns the bars
" Again. From land to land th' infection ran ;
" Aud men defied my power, and cast contempt
" Upon my throne, and tore my idols down.—
" Not all ; but still enough to give alarm,
" And bring the direst fears of final fall.

 " I plied the torch, and axe, and dungeon drear ;
" And interdicted knowledge to the world ;
" I expurgated books ; and chained the press ;
" And took all measures of severest kind,
" To hold the ground I had ; but all in vain.
" I even changed with times, and took now this,
" And now the other side, with hope still long

" And longer to extend my sway.   And this,

" In part, availed ; and lengthened out, a space

" Of years, my stay on earth.   But time wears all

" Away ; and changes e'en the very face

' Of earth ; and so it was with me.   My creed

" Was spurned, my relics, laughed to scorn.   Alas !

" And all my miracles,—that once so chained

" And stupified the crowd ; as knowledge filled

" The land,—were one by one exposed ; and I

" At length became the laughing stock of all.

　　" It seemed the angels laughed from Heaven ; nor could

" I brook a longer stay.   But in the still

" Of night, took wing, reluctant wing, with face

" Bedewed with tears, and heart full wrung with sense

" Of disappointed hope, and sped myself

" To Hell.—I've told the whole, the whole in short,

" At your command.   Your Holiness has heard.—

　　" Now let me hide within some rock or cave,

" And never, never more be seen again."

　　Vain, vain desire, there is no rest in Hell :

For devil envies devil when he seeks

Repose ; and chafes his soul, and wars upon

Him without end, vindictive most to those

Who kill their hopes.　　And so it was with him.

He slipped from out the council, and betook

Himself to flight, not unobserved ; and hence,

Was followed by a pack of fiends, that yelled,

And hot pursued with fierce malicious wing ;

Nor suffered him to rest, but searched him out

From rock or cave, or desert lone, where'er

He sought repose ; and with the keenest scoffs

And satire, such as only devils know,

Bescalled and blistered him through every pore,

17

Till chafed to madness he would fain resist.
But what could he ; but one against the whole ?
  He fled again ; and yet again ; again
And yet again pursued. Remonstrance was
In vain, or scalding tears, that coursed adown
His cheeks.——No rest to him, nor day nor night
While sands shall run, or cycles shall be told
Of the eternal year. He cursed on earth,
He cursed the saints of God, now curses God
Himself, and groans, and writhes, and gnaws his tongue
For pain.—'Twas thus with Man-of-Sin. *No hope!*
        And next must Mammon make report ; and tell
The whole, without once flinching from the truth.
And, this, in open conclave called, where gods,
Where envious gods were seated round in scores ;
And inward joyed at every devils fall.
  He looked somewhat decayed, but not extinct
Like Man-of-Sin, for he had still some hold
Above ; for Mammon is the last, last god
That shall be driven out from earth.——He stood.
" Your Holiness,"—and then proceeded to
The task ; a task indeed : for he had failed,
Had failed in his last, greatest mission up
To earth,—" I spread corruption in the church,
" That part that Man-of-Sin had long since lost ;
" That had with wondrous zeal opposed his sway,
" And washed her hands of all connection with
" His sins. And yet I caught her with my guile,
" And made her draw my car, the pain of Heav'n,
" The laugh of Hell. She stoop'd to deeds that e'en
" Our Hell could never dream. Such sophistries
" She used to prove them right, that almost made
" Me blush. The taint spread right and left, and all

" Were struck, from stripling member to the head
" Of hoary theologian.   All went strong
" For making bondmen of a race entire.
  " But mark you, 'twas from care of souls, their long
" Benighted heathen souls, as in my last
" Report, was full set forth.   Not all, as said
" Before, but those that dared oppose were few
" And weak ; and soon apparently crushed out.
" But strange to tell, when stricken down, they rose
" Again and stood erect and prophesied ;
As did the " witnesses " in 'Pocalypse.
  " At length, it must be told, we overshot
" Ourselves.   We boldly claimed that bondage was
" A blessing sent from God ; and should be spread
" Throughout the world.   We raised sedition to
" Attain the end ; and took the sword ; and bade
" Defiance to the nation's laws.   The strife
" Was fierce ; we silenced every tongue ; the truth
" We falsified ; and bathed the land in blood.
" And, this, to make eternal, human bonds.
  " And, while the strife was high, the chains fell off ;
" And all were free.   But not till penitence
" Had reached the Church ; and she had full confessed
" Her sin ; and turned away from me to God.
  " And now what hope is left ?   She will not be
" Thus thralled again.   Ten thousand years have full
" Elapsed since that sad day ; to them 'tis long ;
" But not to us, who have eternal years
" Upon our hands."—And here a sadness fell
On every face, at thought of that long, long
And weary course that never, never should
Be run !—Eternal years ! Appalling thought ! and that
Without one distant ray of hope !   " To me

" It seems but yesterday since I was foiled.
" But since that time, I've tried my hand, and not
" Without success, at least in part, to hold
" The Church with love of gain ; such over-love
" As would her ardor cool, and make her less
" Efficient than she surely would have been.
" And here again I half o'ershot myself ;
" For when the Church grew rich ; indeed grew rich
" In part for riches sake,—with lavish hand
" She gave, to my dismay, to spread the Word
" Of God, and send the Gospel through the earth.
" HE overruled, and I could not resist.
" Yes, God compelled me to undo myself.

   " My feet, once firm, are slipping on the earth,
" And soon my reign will be unknown to men.
" It must, it must inevitably come."
Yes, *Mammon, Mammon soon will cease to be*
A god of earth, so long, long worshiped there.

   " If we succeed, methinks, some other god
" Must take the field, more sly or potent than
" The rest, a god as yet untried ; and take
" Her unawares again if that can be.
" For, she has had so many warnings now,
" 'Twill be no easy task to bring her down
" Again.   She's rising, rising, rising, and
" Ere long, if we remit, will be a light,
" A sun, a heav'nly sun in blazing sheen,
" A wonder to the world, the pride of Heav'n,
" The everlasting shame of Hell."   And here
A dire sensation ran through all.   The whole
Assembly, pale and flushed by turns, showed rage
And inward spite,—unknown save in that world,—
That could not be suppressed.   But some grew sick

At heart and fell to earth.——Here Mammon sat.—
Now Satan called on Juggernaut to make
Report. For he, and hosts of other gods, had long
Held ample sway in Indian climes, and chained
The nations to their direful, bloody cars.
  The night was long ; a starless night. The bars
Of that dark prison-house seemed never to
Be broke.   At length a gleam appeared, that streaked
The sky, and day unhoped for did appear ;
The shadows fled, the long, long gloom of death ;
And tardy sunshine burst upon those lands.
  The cumbrous god stood up, of savage ear
And beastly sense ; whose tastes were crash of bones,
And dust besmeared with human gore. His face,
Of hideous form, that shocked the sight, and brought
A shudder through each devilish breast. He stood ;
The representative of all the gods
Of Ind.   " Your Holiness,"—and Satan bowed
Assent again,—and devils kept, as wont,
Their face. But each cast glance on other, that
Too plainly told their inward thoughts ; and that—
Though reverential to their spiritual head,
As each was duty bound,—they felt no less
The deep and murd'rous irony that lay
Beneath. Yet Satan saw it not ; but half
Believed 'twas title he deserved ; such " spots "
Of " weakness " are in holy heads.—" 'Tis done.
" Our reign in eastern lands is o'er, and long
" Since passed away as men count length of time.
" But you will give us praise : for sure no gods
" Of earth e'er kept the field so long as we.
" From tower of Babel through an age of years
" We held those lands in undisputed sway ;

" Defied Jehovah's power, and barred him out
" From that vast field of earth. He had a nook
" Or two, 'tis true, in Western lands, and we,
" The world beside. Our altars half were served
" With offerings rich of human hind. We heard
" The lovely wail of infants cast to us
" In Ganges' stream ; and snuffed with grateful sense
" The odors of the widow's pile ; and heard
" Enrapped the shriek, and crash of bones beneath
" My ponderous wheels, and saw, more smiling than
" The rosy lawn, the blood-stained path of my
" Triumphal car. We revelled there from year
" To year, from age to age, and thought, like him,
" Like Man-of-Sin, our reign eternal ; but
" Observe, a ship came by, and dropped a man,
" A man of cool demean, and purpose firm,
" But nothing dang'rous to the eye ; and with
" Him left the Word of God,"—here all grew pale,
And bit their lips with rage,—" the Word of God,
" That love of Heav'n, that hate of Hell, that seed
" That should in time bear bitter fruit to us,
" Like apples near that flood where Sodom stood.
　　　" 'Twas slow in taking root ; and we began
" To hope the soil was adverse to its growth,
" And that, full soon, like seed on stony ground,
" 'Twould wither up and die. But no. The root
" Struck down at length, the trunk arose on high,
" The branches spread abroad ; the leaves were green,
" The flowers, though gall to us, in truth were like
" The garden of the Lord ; and angels snuffed
" Them from the hill of Heaven : and, O ! the fruit—
" And must I tell the whole ?—the fruit, alas !
" A harvest of despair to all the gods

" Of Ind.——The Bible, cursed, cursed book !
" The Bible drove us back to Hell. And here
" We shall forever stay. What hope to us
" Is left ? For God's great Word—I hate it from
" My soul,—will ever keep us from the realms
" Of earth.   No more shall victims bleed beneath
" My car ; nor mother cast her infant to
" The beast of Ganges' stream ; nor widow, in
" Her phrenzy, burn upon the pile !—Our day
" Is o'er. Alas, that hated Word hath done
" The whole."   He said : and lumbered from the stand,
The bulky, beastly god, and mingled with
The rest of that dire throng.
                  But what could now
Be done ? The gods had all been foiled. The Church
Was living still ; and living better far than e'er
Before. And shall the field be quit, and shame
Forever settle down upon that world ?
It must not, cannot be. Some way must be
Devised by which they may redeem their name,
And wreak their vengeance.on their mighty Foe.
   The gods were silent ; vent'ring not to hint
A plan that might with slightest ray of hope
Give ultimate success. For none appeared
In view. The best had all been tried, and tried
In vain at length. And now, they felt that hope
Had fled.   They sat in silence as of death ;
And might have learned how impotent they were.
   But some one must propose ; 'twould never do
To be thus stunned, and make a laugh in Heav'n
They felt, they keenly felt. And Satan felt
Still more.   But now begoaded to the quick
He rose, and silence broke. " Our hope is not

'Extinct, believe me we shall yet succeed."—
And then essayed to show a smile for their
Relief; but 'twas a ghastly smile, that shocked
While they beheld; which told too well his heart
Had sunk within.—" We'll send no special god
" To earth; but such as make the choice may go,
" And try their hand, and wander up and down,
" And tempt whene'er they can, and whom they can;
" And thus keep down the sum of God's great fold."
     And has it come to this? no longer sure
Of full success, to blot from earth the Church,
But ever thankful for the smallest boon,
To-wit, to keep her growing numbers down,
And make her somewhat less than she would be?
     O Satan! Where's thy boast, and where's the boast
Of all the gods, alas, so often made,
In days gone by? Th' assembly broke, they all
Retired; and each, in thoughtful mood, betook
Himself to some lone spot, where he could mourn
His lot; or mayhap plan some new design
Against the Church. But they had little hope.
For though they had their number still, their *will*
Unbroken by defeat, yet she was strong,
And stronger growing day by day. If they
Had failed when she was weak, how could they now
Succeed? And still they must not yield the point.
They were committed to her fall; had talked
So loud and long, had laughed at Heav'n, and mocked
At God himself; and filled his universe
With promises of his defeat, that if
They yielded and acknowledged " whipped," 'twould be
A sting within their souls, a worm, a death
That never dies. When they seceded from

The rule of God they laughed to scorn the dupes
That stayed behind : While they, the Chivalry,
Despised the reign of Heav'n, and sought a rule
More suited to their worth. They promised all
Who cast their lot with them, a future far
More glorious than Heav'n could give ; and dared
In boastful terms to give assurance that
Not God himself, with all his ancient claims,
Could hold in check their tide of full success.

They'd had, 'tis true, or seemed to have their way,
They'd held the world, or most of it ; and laughed
At angels as they stood amazed. But God
Was neither negligent nor weak ; but was
In wisdom working out a problem that
Should last forever in its grand results.

As years and centuries elapsed, the lines
Were drawing close and closer still, and now
They find themselves in thrall, and struggling in
The darkness of despair. And must they yield ?
O never, never that ! and yet they saw
The hand upon the wall, and read thereon
Their speedy, direful doom. O dreadful thought !
What shame, what burning shame they saw in store !

It fell on all ; and some were withered up,
And seemed extinct ; while others were awaked
To rage unknown before in Hell. They gnashed
Their teeth—they tore their hair—they stamped the
    ground—
They cursed—beyond all words to tell. They'd straight
To earth and see what could be done.——They went.
They first collected on an open plain ;
Then rose with rattling wings and fiery eyes,
And upward took their flight with fury driven,

And left the confines of their Hell, and launched
With direst venom on the bord'ring deep,—
The deep, out stretched beyond all reach of thought
'Twixt that, their home and God's creation fair.
    'Twas dark and dreadful, filled with direst sights ;
That wide, unfathomable solitude !
But what to them ?   Their nerves were fitted to
The task.   They'd seen such sights before ; for Hell
Has fearful regions of its own.   Besides,
The inward spite of their volcanic souls,
Would suffer no delay, no shrinking on
The brink whatever fear might rise to drain
Their strength, or chill and freeze their very blood.
    They drive amain ; a darkling host, and make
The darkness darker still.   Their wings wrought up
A tempest as they sped ; and Silence took
Alarm, and started from her seat, as this
Portentous cloud went hissing by.   They came
To earth, and spread upon her coasts like swarms
Of locusts in the days of Egypt's fall,
A sad, sad thing for her.   It was, alas !
Th' Apocalyptic "loosing of the power
"Of Satan" to assail the Church, and draw
Her through a trial once again.—Despair
Not, Earth, for first the Apocalypse must be
Fulfilled : And Satan loosed again, but for
" A little season ;" then his race be run,
And he forever far removed.—They plied
Their arts with all the skill that dev'lish wits
Could bring, and all the spite that dev'lish breasts
Could feel.   They tried for years, nay centuries,
And that, it must be said, with sad success.
    They started doubts in time about the word

Of God, that had such glorious wonders wrought.
That ancient book, "who knows but 'tis a lie,
"A cheat, by priestly heads conceived, and put
"Abroad by wicked hands? Its teachings, how
"Absurd! Its facts, impossibilities.
"And those who would be bound thereby, the fools,
"The veriest fools of earth." They thus seduced
Now this, now that and now another from
The fold. The dire infection ran at length;
And fearful inroads made upon the Church.

The host grew large, the men that set themselves
Against the word of God. They showed their faith
Or rather lack of faith with burning zeal.

From land to land, from isle to isle they grew
In power; and temples built and altars raised
To REASON; treading once again the track
That faithless Gaul once trod, in years long, long
Elapsed. The fallen lower, lower fell. At last
Touched bottom, downright Atheists grown;
Denied a God, and wrote the gospel down
The vilest thing on earth.——Then crimes grew rife
Again, and discords reigned, and wars were waged,
And violence returned anew; and blood,
With all its ancient horrors, now ran down
The earth.——But first, the love of many had
Grown cold; or they had never fallen from
Their high estate; and devils never could
Have drawn them off from God. Let all beware
And ever keep them from the first false step.

"Denied a God!"—The rains and summer suns
Beclothed the earth with green;—"And yet there was
"No God!" The fields in autumn waved with rich
And bounteous harvests for the life of man

And beast ;—" And yet there was no God."   The trees
Were strained on every bough with golden fruits
Of nectar juice, to tempt angelic taste,
And yielded them to man ;—" And yet there was
" No God."   The snows and frosts came down, and locked
The earth in death, and drave in winter storms ;—
" And yet there was no God."   The spring returned,
And winter bars gave way, and genial suns
And showers, like magic, bade an Eden rise,
Bedecked with flowers, and filled with odors as
Of Heav'n, that ravished quite the sense ;—" And yet
" There was no God."   The tempest hung on land
And sea, and swept the earth ; and heaved the waves
Of ocean to the clouds ;—" And yet there was
" No God."   The thunder's awful voice was heard,
And lightnings smote, and with their fiery swords
Fought battles in the clouds ;—" And yet there was
" No God."   The earthquake raved beneath, and split
The globe, and sent a fiery deluge to
Consume ;—" And yet there was no God."   And man
Had all, in fine, his soul desired, his heart
With food and gladness filled ;—" And yet there was
" No God."   And science pierced the heavens, in gaze
Of telescopic sight ; and found new scenes
Of wonder, that o'erwhelmed the soul, the field
Of view still more and more enlarged as age
On age had passed, and instruments of search
Were wrought with higher skill, and knowledge had
Been stored from sage to sage ; each building on
The knowledge thus bequeathed till men had reached
Far out in God's domain ; and settled points
Of wonder never dreamed before ; had solved
Such problems in far outward space as caused

The mightiest intellect to reel beneath
The thought ;—" And yet there was no God !"
And she, from vast, descended to the small ; and scanned
The world below, as worlds above ; and searched
New laws of matter, not surmised in days
Of yore, and thence, conclusions drew, of vast
And startling import, and that cried aloud
Of wisdom infinite ;—" And yet there was
" No God." She searched, beside, down to the first,
The lowest step of life, and gazed with awe
Upon the millions there, that sport within a drop,
And find full sea-room in their wide domain :
All organized, with parts essential to
A living thing ; and yet the whole, so small
That glass of highest skill could hardly reach,
In sunbeam light, their evanescent forms ;
She saw, he learned their ways, their food, their life,
Their death ; and with amazement viewed the whole :
The man thus taught in all these wondrous things,
Still blind, came back, and with his hardened heart,
In madness cried, " There is no God !" All proofs
Were thrown aside ; such proofs as should have made
A faith to move the very mountains from
Their seats ; yet all was lost on him,—and why ?
Because he lived in sin ; and feared : and then
The thing he wished, he would, he would believe.——

CHRONOLOGY A.D., 12,863.

A hundred decades now had passed, and found
The Church, though thinned, yet battling high against
Her atheist foes. The ground had been retrod,
Of ancient times when atheists swarmed on earth ;

The arguments of yore been urged again ;
And others new that then were quite unknown,—
By skilful hands ; and men began to see,
And feel, and turn to God.   The work went on
From year to year, from score to score of years,
And centuries of years.   Her victories
Were great.   The opposing powers gave way ; and she
Was seen once more a city on a hill.
O glorious sight ! and shall she fall again ?
No, never as her former lapse.

　　　　　　　　　　　　　　'Twas done.
She'd stood the test far better than in times
Gone by.   They'd tried, they'd tried in vain to cast
Her down, forever down, no more to lift
Her head, on earth again ; in vain !   They'd stirred
Up Gog and Magog, whom they had seduced
From out her fold.   They'd sought her fall, they'd cast
Their camp about her holy towers.   But God
Had interposed, and said, " It is enough ;"
And scattered all her foes, and swept them from
The earth.——Now Satan had been chained, and loosed
And Gog and Magog slain ; mere figures of
Those great events that should o'ertake the Church,
As shadowed forth in 'pocalyptic scene :
The *real* chaining him is yet to come.

CHRONOLOGY, A.D., 13,863.

The course is now nigh clear, the race her own,
A race all glorious, for all future time.

END OF BOOK ELEVENTH.

BOOK XII.

CHRONOLOGY, A.D., 23,863.

A THOUSAND decades now had passed, since she,
The Church, had shaken off her foes, as Paul
The serpent from his hand and in the end
Received no lasting harm ; her mighty foes
That swarmed in time long, long elapsed, her foes,
Called Gog and Magog in Apocalypse.
But since, she'd not been free from fierce assaults
From here and there a wicked few inspired
By Satan ; as he still had scope on earth ;
And with his legions marred in some degree
Her lovely outlines ; as th' undying surge
Of ocean, 'gainst the rocky cliff abrades
Its adamantive sides, abrades, but not
O'erthrows.   The rock stands firm, and laughs to scorn
The thunder of its power.   So she had stood,
And under God had bid defiance to
Her deadly foes.——But 'twas enough.   Her time
Is drawing nigh.   The signs are being full,
When God shall free her from her chiefest foes,
And set her still more clear " a city on
A hill," the New Jerusalem, whose gates
Shall be forever open wide,   whose sun
Is God himself, who hence shall have his rest,

His tabernacle here with men ; whose hand
Shall wipe all tears from every eye ; and lo !
Shall make ere long such glory on the earth
As if the heavens and the earth were made
Anew ; so full of righteousness of men.

What scene is yet to come ! when Satan's hosts
Shall leave our earth, and take themselves to Hell,
To fight among themselves, their chief enchained ;
To fight among themselves, through endless years.

There faction shall contend with faction, and
The bloody wars of that dread region, ah !
What tongue can tell ? For Satan kept them curbed,
While holding sway ; with iron arm suppressed
The longings of each would-be rebel chief.
But now, the great, great autocrat, that like
An Ætna sat upon the fires and kept
Them down, removed forever from their fear,
Each chief shall rise, and chief with chief contend,
And make that dread abode a double hell.

What wailings shall be heard, the wailings of
Despair, out-wrung from every bosom of
The common damned ! No rest for them by day,
By night. But ever dragged to take the side
Of some vile chief, shall spend their weary years
In pent-up forts or camps, or waste their strength
In marches and in contests without end.

What future is for Hell ! a future soon
To be commenced, which shall eternally
Endure.

But Satan was defiant as
Of old, nor heeded he the meaning of
The times ; but spent his days and nights, with chiefs
Surrounded or alone, in planning how

He might assail the hated Church, and bring her to
The dust again ; or make her quite extinct.
The task was great ; for she was strong ; and hence,
His spite was tenfold greater than in times
Gone by. His ill success had chafed him to
The soul ; and raised a phrenzy that, at times,
Boiled out in fierce volcanic fires.——Again,
He sat in moody silence, not resigned,
Though spirit-crushed in part, yet still resolved
To bid defiance to the God of Heaven ;
And wage eternal war against his Church.
His blasphemies must not be told, nor threats
Of vengeance that should yet ensue. Nor he
Alone, but thousands round him, heated to
The quick, looked upward, cursed, and were forthwith
To madness driven.   They planned an onset new
" To earth. " All Hell shall rise so strong that God
" Himself shall tremble on his throne."   'Tis thus
The wicked plan, and for the time forget
That God is greater than themselves. Vain ! vain !
A fate awaits them that they little dream.
For soon their chief shall be enchained ; and they,
The minor chiefs shall be in deadly strife
Among themselves.   And yet they might have known,
At least conjectured that some direful ill
Would soon befall. For signs there were in Hell
That frightened all that world. The air was filled
With battles, and the direful clash of arms
Was heard ; and blood fell dripping from the clouds ;
And ran in fearful streams along the ground.
And sights were seen in midnight hours that chilled
The blood, and withered up their souls.——Again,
From air and earth strange words were sounded forth,
18

From rock and cave in midnight's deepest gloom,
(As at Jerusalem befoie its fall,)
That drank the very marrow of their bones,—
In voice, in hollow awful voice pronounced,
"*Let us be gone; come let us haste away!*"
And caverns deep replied and echoed back,—
"Let us be gone ; come, let us haste away."
Alas! they were in Hell, and how escape?

Again, 'twas dark for days and days ; a pall,
A darkness *that* that could be felt. It hung
Like death on all that lower world. They grope
Their devious way with trembling and despair ;
And whisperings heard within the gloom, that drained
Their very life. They fain would flee to right,
To left, or back recoil ; but all in vain.
The whisperings whispered still, and nearer drew ;
And in their very ears hissed out their voice.

And yet they saw no shape, no form could touch ;
The voice, the voice was all ; in darkness wrapped,
Intangible, and yet forever heard.—

And then, the darkness gone, the ground was seized
With trembling, such as never known before.
The towers of Satan fell, and mountain tops
Leaped headlong to the vales ; and devils scarce
Could keep their feet. For days and weeks the strange
Vibrations lived ; unlike the earthquake shocks,
That ever and anon disturb that world.

The caverns groaned ; and from the desert came
Up fearful sighs ; that sighed and sighed again,
And wept and wept ; and never, never ceased.

These all were signs portentious of some great
Impending ill ; and so the common damned
Believed. But Satan and his chiefs, though half

Convinced, refused to give a feather's weight
To all these omens that the times produced.
   The while in Heaven were signs as well ; not signs
Of dread ; but such as filled with joy the souls
Of that blest world. The saints grew buoyant far
Beyond their wont ; and yet they knew not why.
They laughed out-right, and clasped each other in
Their arms.——Their dreams were of the sweetest kind.
They dreamed of earth, their native home ; and saw
An Eden there, a reign of righteousness
And peace. The thorns of earth were gone ; the wastes
Were now no more ; but were to fertile fields
Reduced, and flowery lawns. The Amaranth
Was there again, transplanted back from heaven to earth,
Whose clime, now changed, shall never blast it more.
It shone in bloom perpetual round the globe ;
And sent its grateful fragrance up to Heaven.
   Of mountains leveled, and of valleys raised
They dreamed ; and goodly harvests waving quite
From pole to pole. The savage beast was gone,
And man possessed his forest home, redeemed,
And tilled, and rich with food for man.—They dreamed
Of intellect displayed, and knowledge gained
Beyond what had been thought before ; and saw,
In clear and lovely vision, Adam's race,
Their brethren here below, so pure, so high
In every worth, that earth seemed but a step,
One single step from Heav'n.   Diseases were
No more, nor death. The tree of life they saw,
Sprung up again in ev'ry soil and clime ;
Whereof men eat and lived ; and never said
Again "I'm sick."
           The waters now were seen

Again ; the same that once the Prophet saw,
That issued from the temple eastward, and
Were now a sea, a sea that none could pass,
So deep, so wide they flowed. The waters these
Of life, Salvation's flood, which onward rolled
In silv'ry sheen, and caused the growth of food
And ev'ry healing tree upon its banks :
And onward sweeping, reached at length the sea,
And healed its wave ; and filled the same with life,
Abundant life. Oh ! glorious sight for earth !
They saw in vision, and with raptures thrilled,
Burst out in shouts—and then awoke ;—and lo !
It was a dream, but with a faith, a strong
Abiding faith, that earth would soon be blest
With some great act of God. And this, the more,
As God the Father and the Son seemed now
To hold more frequent council. Oft the Son
In human form still wrapped, though glorious and
Divine, went up the mount of God, and lost
Himself within the cloud, the glorious cloud,
That ever wraps that topless hill ; and is
The light of that vast world above.

Again descending he with Moses and
Elias talked. They cast sweet looks to earth ;
And seemed to smile beyond their wont.

Again, sweet music in the air was heard,
That stayed the footsteps of each spirit blest :
That sang of earth, of glory yet to come ;
And filled each listening soul with joy unknown
Before. These all were signs in Heav'n of some
Approaching good to earth. And so it was
Believed ; and daily looked for by the blest
With eager eye. But what or when was far

Beyond their reach, though some of shrewdest kind
Had half deciphered out the truth ; yet still
In doubt. They knew that God had promised great,
And lasting good to man ; and that his church
Should not forever be pursued with spite
Of Satan ; that the time should come when God
Would say, "It is enough. She now shall be
" Relieved from her most deadly foe ;" for she
Had stood the test ; had written for herself
A record fair, upon the whole ; and one
That shall endure throughout all time to come,
That she can stand the assaults of every foe ;
And,—though at times cast down, enfeebled by
Her own miscourse,—still can arise and stand
Upon her feet ; and battle strong again
For God and right ; and stronger still she stands
At every rise ; which shows a doubting world
That she has life, inherent life, that lives
And shall forever live. The world shall know
It, and shall see, and feel this living proof,
This overwhelming argument that she's
Of God. They knew that Satan should be chained,
A fixture somewhere in the realm of Hell,
No more to lead the world astray, and blast
The prospects of the race of man.—But when,
When shall the thing be done? Is that blest time
At hand ? or is it far, far distant in
The future cast ? This none could solve beyond
A doubt, but still they hoped 'twas near.—
                                        Meantime,
In Heav'n the signs were rip'ning fast, and cloud
On cloud, dispersed ; and doubts soon yielded up
To full belief. The hosts of God were warned ;

And mustered on the plains of Heav'n ; and at
Their head stood Michael, vet'ran chief, renowned
In times gone by, when Satan warred with God.
    Upon his face, though glorious, were scars
Of battle, and his weapons shone with gold,
And gems, and burnished steel. His form, erect,
And tall above the rest, and vig'rous frame,
Showed him no common foe to meet alone.
But with the hosts of God to back him up,
What prodigies of war might he not do !
    The hosts were all arrayed, and marshaled ; and
A grand review was held. They marched in long
Procession through the golden streets of that
Bright world, with banners flying, and with tunes
Of richest sound and all-inspiring in
Their martial strains. It ravished angels ; and
Infused an ardor to each breast that told
Full well what might be felt by any foe
That dared with them contend.——These are the hosts
Of God ; that ready stand to vindicate his cause ;
And now about to fight his battles down in Hell.
    They halt in long, long line upon the plain
Adjacent to the Mount of God ; and stand
Awaiting his behests.—The scene is changed ;
The light withdrawn, and darkness shrouds that hill.
And now is heard within, deep thunder, peal
On peal, in loud and awful voice : and fires,
In darkling flame, shoot forth ; and hide themselves
Anon—and then from that rent cloud glare out
Anew. Terrific scene ! appalling e'en
To angel ears and eyes.—'Tis God, about to pour
His wrath upon his unrelenting, fierce,
Blasphemous foes.   The darkness wanes away,

And light again returns ; and God vouchsafes
His smile anew throughout all Heaven.—The hosts
Break out in shouts ; and praise and magnify
That goodness that has saved them, and bestowed
On them that glorious Heav'n they hold ; that he,
Though swift, at length, against his foes, yet makes
Their Heav'n with his benignant smiles.—A voice
Is heard from out the cloud, as once was heard
On Sinai's Mount.— ' Go, Michael, smite the foes
" Of God, my fierce, incorrigible foes.
" And let them feel, again thy strength ; and take
" Thou Satan, whom for ages gone I've spared ;
" Nor on him poured the full infliction due
" His crimes.—Yet he has sinned, and sinned again ;
" Defied my power, blasphemed my name ; and fired
" His chiefs, and all the common damned to break,
" Forever break my law ; and dare my hosts
" To meet them in the field again.   Go, go,
" My faithful ones.   Go, Michael, let them feel
" Thy arm.   Make every knee to bow and tongue
" Confess ;—and take thou Satan, who has so
" Seduced my flock of angels and of men ;
" And filled my works with sin, and poured out blood
" Of saints like water ; who has prowled like beast
" Of prey throughout my universe to seek
" The ones he could devour ; but chief on earth ;
" Where he has ranged for ages past ; and sought
" The ultimate extinction of my church :
" Has crushed the innocent, the weak, and dragged
" Them down, and blasted hopes that never can
" Return.—He warred in Heav'n ; I sent him down
" To Hell to find a lesson there, nor dare
" My power.   But he could never learn to heed

" My law, though threat of future ill was sure
" To come. He wreaked his malice on my poor,
" And made them cry to Heav'n ; and caused whole lands
" To leave my rule and wander after him ;
" And practice crimes that shocked the world. Go thou,
" Take Satan, bind him hand and foot, and him
" Transport to some lone isle far out upon
" The barren face of Hell's wide sea ; and there
" With chains confine him. Go, and take the chain
" Provided for that very use ; whose links
" Shall hold him fast, unbrakeable, throughout
" Eternal years."——He said ; and darkness veiled
His throne again ; and lightnings flash anew,—
And thunders roll—and shake the region round.—
    There was no fear from God, and yet so dread,
So awful was the scene, that all the hosts
Grew pale, and trembled ; and e'en Michael said,
" I do exceeding quake and fear :" as said
By Moses when he stood before the Mount.
    Now Michael took the chain from where it hung,
And took the thunder of the living God ;
And with his hosts, full armed, and ready for
The task assigned, departs from Heav'n, and takes
His downward flight to regions of the damned.
    They crossed the wide abyss ; so wide that thought
Could scarcely span the whole. What barren wastes
Were in their track ! What fields of empty space,
Where sight nor sound was ever known before !
Yet naught they feared ; the good have naught to fear.
    For days, and days, with zeal, and utmost speed,
They voyaged downward through the whole in loose
Array.—They spy at length far, far beneath,
The dark and dreadful, yet stupendous globe of Hell ;

In size, compared to which, our solar orb,
Though vast in bulk, is but a single drop,
To ocean.—Here they halt, close up their lines,
And send forth scouts to make assurance sure ;
To guard against surprise : Lest having note
Of their approach, their wiley foe should steal
Unseen with all his hosts, and lie in wait,
And smite them unawares.'—They send forth scouts,
Who near with cautious wing the confines of
That world.   And soon they hear the murmuring
Of sounds, that rise in strange confusion to
Their ears,—from that lost world, that world of death
And woe, the dire, dire sodom of the damned.
 It filled their ears as never filled before ;
And checked their speed to listen.   Voices now
Distinct were heard ; and plaints out-wrung from breasts,
From breasts of spirits lost, who mourned their lot.
The debauchee was there ; and he that lent
Him aid in his designs ; and he that robbed
His neighbor of his wealth and hid behind
The technicalities of law ; and he
That did it without law at all, and swore
Him out of right, or set up witnesses
To do the same ; and he that lived upon
The earnings of the poor, outwrung from their
Unwilling hands ; and he that with his wealth,—
Not satisfied with lavish gains,—but broke
His humble brother down in trade ; and sent
Him out, with wife and babes, in poverty
To struggle on in life anew ; and she
Whose " steps took hold on hell," who caught the young
And thoughtless in her snare, and took them to
Her house, wherein their blood was shed ; and he

That slew the saints of God at bidding of
The holy church ; (yes, he was there. He went
All pardoned down to Hell ;) and judge unjust,
Who held the scales for gain, and robbed the poor
Of right, and set th' oppressor up on high ;
And had forgotten that a Judge would judge
The judges in the end ; and he that swore
For gain, or did the same to please his friend,
And thwarted thus a righteous cause.   'Twas sad.
But God is righteous in his ways ; and sure
All sins at last will find the sinner out.—
The drunkard and the man that furnished him
The cup that made him thus, were sadly there,—
And last they saw, far off in lone retreat,
The man, the man, that Jesus told, who erst
Had sumptuous fare, alas ! whose clothing was
Of linen fine and purple dye ; who sought
His good on earth, and not in Heav'n ;—
How wan and haggard now! and how forlorn !
'Twas sad and pitiful ; and yet his time,
His long eternity had scarce begun.—
All these and more, far more, the angels saw.
Their souls were pained, and tears rolled down their cheeks.
Yes, yes, the lost drew tears from angel eyes ;
E'en as the Saviour wept at Salem's fate.
    But time would fail to name the secrets of
The varied sins that were revealed to ears
Angelic as they hung o'er Hell. For there
Is ev'ry crime ; and ev'ry bosom lost,
By strange impulsion forced, declares
At times his sins, though loth, and feels the keen
Regrets, the pains untold their ceaseless stings
Inflict ;—and owns, reluctant, yet with voice

Distinct, his sentence just.——The angel scouts
Move on, and nearer draw to that lost world ;
And see, with view distinct, the doleful throngs
That there abide. They mark their haggard looks,
Their careworn sunken cheeks, and hollow eyes ;
And see the very picture of despair
In every face. They see, they pity, and
Their hearts within them sink. But 'twas the wrath
Of God, outpoured upon them for their sins,
Their sins they would not leave and keep God's law,
Would not seek pardon when God's mercy called.
They had their warnings, but they took no heed ;
No heed to Mercy's call, or plea, or tears.
Now MERCY is no more. The angels saw her not,
But JUSTICE there instead ; with steadfast eye ;
And blade unsheathed ; and, what amazed them more
Not here alone ; but omnipresent she
Is seen throughout that world ; and ev'ry eye
Beholds her ; and with painful vision shrinks
Before her features stern and glitt'ring sword.

They saw the contests that forever mark
The days and nights of that dire world, that world
Where hand of ev'ry one in violence
Is raised against his fellow.   And their ears
Were stunned with sound of brawls and fights,
That rose as sound of Sodom in the days
Of old.

Meantime the scouts of Satan met
Them on their way ; and instant sped and bore
The news to Satan's ears.—But he was on
The watch ; and had already felt surmise
That foe might be on hand. For he had seen
In far off sky a strange phenomenon ;

A nebulous streak unseen before. Ah! he
Was wary, and forever watched the heav'ns,
To see what foe might come from other worlds.
    This small contracted cloud he wondered what
Could be ; this infant milky-way.—It was
The host of Michael ; there in halt to close
Up ranks, and form in battle line ; and with
The light of Heav'n all glowing as the light
Of distant suns through our ethereal space.
    But when his scouts, returned, reported bands
Of armed foes from Heaven,—all doubt was gone.
A foe was on approach. He instant gave
Alarm. It swept through Hell,—by trumpet sound,
By bell, by beacon fires and telegraph.
    All Hell was moved. And minutemen
Like leaves of autumn flocked to every goal ;
But chief where Satan had his seat. They bring
Their arms along ; and engines are brought out,
Of newest, deadliest kind. The army swells
And lengthens till the keenest spirit eye
Can scarce discern its bounds.
                          Meanwhile the light
Of Michael's host, so small from distance seen,
Grows large and larger every hour.——At length
At close of day they light with all their arms
Upon a wide-spread plain of that vast orb ;
And there intrench themselves, throw out their guards,
And seek a night of rest.—At dawn of day
They're roused ; and what was left unorganized
Before, is finished now. And all are to
Their posts assigned ; and watch-words given ;
And ev'ry chief advised in his command.
And soon they move in march to find the foe.

Amazing sight! Phenomenon for Hell!
Their armor, bright and flashing to the skies,
Of newest make, and dreadful to the view,
And soon to be essayed on spirit forms ;
Supplies immense, and ev'ry needful store
That Heav'n, with its unbounded wealth, could yield.
   Their lines how vast in length! and yet compact ;
And all advancing with unfaultering step ;
And full of zeal for God and good.
   These are the armies of the skies, that fight
The battles of the Lord ; that tread his foes
Beneath their feet ; and at command chastise
Them even down to Hell. Ah! woe betide
The force that dares oppose.
                They march through wastes
Of fearful space ; and over Alps of height
Immense and rugged cliff ; and day by day
Draw near and nearer to the foe. At length
They make descent, and wide deploy their lines
Upon a vast, unbroken plain ; a plain
Not green and fertile as the plains of Heav'n ;
But barren and forbidding to the sight
From winds of Siroc breath, and deadly heats
And altern colds of that dire world : And there
Intrench themselves to ward surprise and seek
Repose again from weary march. The guards
Are posted, and the pickets set ; and all
Are buried soon in slumber sweet. Their dreams
Are of the richest kind ; of Heav'n, the joys
Of that bright world ; of converse with the just
Now perfect made ; of fruits, that hang on trees
Of Heav'nly growth ; of draughts from that great flood,
The everliving cool and sparkling stream

That flows forever from the hill of God.

    Behold them prone and slumber-locked within
Their tents, or open to the air ; with brow
Serene, and youthful glow.—Some hoary heads
Were there, that show them vet'rans in the cause
Of God. Yet still the bloom of youth is on
Their cheeks ; and youthful vigor, in their frame,
So healthful is the clime from which they came :
Each grasping in his hand his trusty steel.
They stretch immense ; in number, vast beyond
The power of human mind ; refreshing for
The day about to dawn. For who can say
What day that day may prove? Perhaps, a day
Historic,—in the books of Heaven and Hell,—
For matchless deeds achieved, for victory lost,
Mayhap, and victory won. The day will tell.

    But Satan, wiley chief, had had his spies
Within the very camp of Michael. They
Had traversed it from end to end ; had seen,
And noted down its strength, its minor arms,
Its batteries of awful power, supplies
For sustenance and ammunition to
The fullest wish. Why not? for Heav'n is rich,
And has exhaustless stores for years and years
To come.—These spies repair to Satan and
Report. " The host is vast, such host our Hell
" Has never known before, so vast, so well
" Equipped, with minor arms, and these sustained
" With engines of the deadliest kind ; besides,
" *We saw the engine of the living God !*
" That awful deadly instrument of war."

    At this his Holiness turned deadly pale :
For he had felt the fatal blows of that

Dire engine on the plains of Heaven what time
He made revolt, and battle joined to gain
The throne of God.—His spirit sank within,
And he was dumb ; but, roused, prepared to meet
The foe.—His hosts were large, and vet'ran most ;
Had followed him in all his num'rous wars ;
Were armed in latest style ; were drilled, and trained
In highest art ; and ready stood to do
His bidding ; to receive the stunning shock
Of battle when it fell, or at the word,
To hurl themselves like thunder-bolts upon
The foe. He knew their metal, and their hate
Of all that dwelt in Heav'n. He knew, if strength,
If utmost strength of theirs, with utmost hate,
Inspired, could overcome the foe, it would
Be done.——And yet an inward sentiment,
A strange foreboding held his soul, that he
Would fail of ultimate success. Though he
Had conquered on a thousand fields, and that
The mightiest chiefs that Hell could boast, each one
A host himself ; yet now 'twas Michael that
Would tax his might and skill. As Pompey on
Pharsalia's plains, though great himself,—yet felt
That Cæsar sure was greater still, with whom
He now must measure arms ;— so he now felt
Superior presence. This possessed his mind,
And in degree bereft him of his skill
And wonted fire. He, nathless, nerved him up.
To every effort to overcome his foe.

 For here his all was staked. The field must now
Be won or never. For 'twas plain, he saw,
That Michael had come down to square accounts
With him. He knew his crimes, yet loved them, and

But wished them more ; such hat'red wrankled in
His breast against the God of Heaven.   He knew
If now he failed he lost the throne of Hell ;
Must either flee,—Ah ! whither flee?—or win
A chain.——He'd marshalled all his hosts ; had called
His out-posts in from distant parts.
What need there might be there he heeded not.
The greatest need was here of all his power.
If here, he won, he won the whole ; if here,
He lost, he lost the whole.——But scouts return, and tell
Him, Michael is approaching near with firm
But cautious move.   And soon the tidings come
That he has halted ; and is making camp
Beyond that ridge of hills, no doubt, to spend
The night, from weary march of day
Just past.—Good news for Satan.   Here, he thinks,
He sees a hope for vict'ry o'er his foe.

His mind is made,—he'll wait no morning dawn,
But quick, and with impetuous force, assail
The foeman's lines, surprise him in his sleep,
And ere awake in full, make slaughter, and
With panic fill, till all in wild dismay,
Bewildered from the shout of sudden foe,
And senses drowsy still,—shall break, and flee,
Like antelopes before the lion's roar.

He marches all his host with stealthy pace,—
Drives Michael's pickets in,—who give th' alarm,—
But instant at a signal given and yell
That broke appalling on the ear, and roused
Those unwaked,—rushed fierce and devilish on
The Heavenly lines.——These yield, for scarcely had
They sprung to line before they felt the weight
Of numbers vast, and fearful blows of arms.

They yield, but not with panic filled as hoped
By Satan.—They retire, but slow, and firm,
And fighting. Satan crowds his masses on
Them, and begins to feel that vict'ry sure
Is his. They stand at length ; and take the shock
Of all his power. For Michael, skilled in war,
Had line on line, arranged in rear, to give
Support, whene'er superior force assailed.

The conflict now is dreadful. Satan hurls
His masses here, now there, and there again,
To pierce the lines of Michael, but in vain.
And after loss immense, retires, and yields
The struggle up. The time was short, but who
Can count the havoc that was made in that
Short, bloody hour ?—Hell fought for Hell, and **Heav'n**
For Heav'n. And fought as if the universe
Was staked upon that single field. And now
The foe of God and man is found again
Within his lines, and sees, dismayed, the loss
His force has met ; and burns with vengeance 'gainst
His stubborn foe. And vows revenge to come.—

The day just broke runs on ; and all is still :
Th' intent of Michael is, next day to storm
His works. And preparations are on foot
At once for that design, so hazardous
To even Heavenly arms. And every means
Was sought for full success. And Michael's tent
Is thronged till midnight watch with higher chiefs,
To know his plan ; and take the post assigned
Them in that bloody hour. Meantime the host
Had sought repose, and quieted lay prone
Refreshing for the struggle soon to come.
The minor chiefs were then informed ; and each
19

Departed to his post to rest and wait
The morning onset-signal.——Morn at length
Appears, and lo! the foe is not. He'd slipped
From out his works beneath the cover of
The night, and fled to parts unknown. But he
Will soon be found. For Michael is resolved
To search him out, and bring to battle at
The earliest day.
     His scouts return before
The close of second day, and give him word
Where he will find the foe.—-The next day dawns ;
And Michael is on early march for camp
Of Satan. All his engines and supplies
As well as host so vast, are on the move.
And yet no special haste ; for he was sure
Of vict'ry, when the trial came : For what
Had Satan to compare with him in arms
Or numbers of his host? Besides, the cause
Of Satan, though believed by him to be
At least as good as Michael's, yet 'twas bad ;
And had the frown of God upon it ; while
The cause of Michael was of Heav'n ;
A cause to bless the universe of God—
With liberty, and peace, and every good.
And hence God's favor and his blessing must
Be on his arms. For God regards the right ;
And though for reasons, known indeed alone
To him, he suffers right to languish while
The wrong prevails ; yet, in the end, the right
Will rise ; and, like God's witnesses as seen
In vision clear on Patmos-isle,—will stand
Erect, and see the overthrow of all
Its foes.—This faith had Michael and his host.

They moved in order due ; and not in haste,
Nor slow ; but with such pace as well became
Such host immense and multitude of train.
The way was rugged ; for the face of Hell
Is broken. Rocks forbidding choke his path ;
And chasmas yawn ; and here and there a stream
Of lava thwarts his course, still fiery hot
And hissing from the bowels of that globe.

But all impediments give way before
Superior skill. The Heavenly host moves on
From day to day, and soon draws near the plain,
On farthest verge of which was Satan's camp.

They halt ; and rest ; pitch tents ; and spend the night.
But Satan, humbled now, makes no attack.
The lesson, taught of late, he must needs heed.

He stays within his lines, behind his forts ;
(Not much defense, 'tis true, in haste thrown up,)
And waits th' attack of Michael, which be sure
Will not be long delayed.——But what will be
His course ? Will Michael rush in furious charge
Across the plain, and make assault in force
On Satan's works ? or will he flank his lines
And force him out to open fight, or swift
Retreat for other parts of Hell ; and then
At once pursue, and crush him in his flight?

These questions time, and that full soon, will solve.
For Michael came to make short work, and not
To drag the war for years ; to overcome
The foe of God and man ; to chain him, and
Return again without delay, to more
Congenial climes ; and there to rest his troops,
Instead of wearing out their strength in Hell,
That clime, that loathsome, unpropitious clime.—

What means this pause?   A day is passed, and all
Is still.—Another day :—And quiet reigns.—
And Satan and his host feel courage rise.
E'en hope is born in devilish breasts, that they
Shall stand the test, and wear out Michael with
Delay ; or else, by chance of war, and choice
Of ground, break down his forces when he makes
Assault ; or better far demolish him
In open fight ; and thus conclude the war.
 The third day dawns—and all is quiet still.
The hours run on—and no advance, or sign
Of war.——At length, a thunder-peal speaks out
From Michael's lines, that vexed the air, and shook
The steadfast globe of Hell.—From end to end
The livid sheets of fire shoot forth, half 'cross
The plain.   And missiles dire are hurled, that rend
The mounds, and smite the damned.   But Satan soon
Replies with awful pow'r, and sheets of flame
Terrific, that eject his thunder bolts
With deadly aim, and scarcely less in weight
And force than those of Michael ; and they smite
And smite amain upon the host of Heav'n.
 The battle rages, and the mercury
Of Heav'n and Hell still higher reigns.   No pause.
But batt'ries new are brought to bear ; and fires
In thicker blaze dart forth ; and havoc swells
On either side.
     From hour to hour the fight,
The dreadful conflict raves ; and Michael's hosts
Advance, and ply their smaller arms with aim
Of deadly line ; and Satan's quick reply
In kind ; and havoc wider still bespreads
The ground, to make an iron bosom weep.

Ah ! such is war ; a dreadful remedy ;
And yet the only cure for certain ills !
    At length a mine of sulph'rous flame explodes.
The air is shocked, the ear is stunned, the globe
Of Hell, so vast, down to its centre reels.
And Satan's works and ranks are swept like chaff
Before the blast. It was the engine of
The living God, just brought to bear upon
His lines. To this, all other engines seemed
But childish play, all other sounds but seemed
Mere whispers, and each shock of other arms,
But gentle jogs to wake a sleeper from
His dreams. The host of Satan stood appalled.
Though vet'rans they, and trained to every fear,
And battle shock, they felt their courage sink.
They slackened fire.—This Satan saw, and rushed,
Upon his charger borne, along his lines.
For he perceived that nothing but his words
And presence could preserve the day, if that
They could. His words were sharp or kindly as
It seemed him best. He kindled fires anew
In every breast, and roused them to the fight.
    " Alas !" said he, " the chivalry ! Shall they
" Give in ; and quail before the dastard sons
" Of Heav'n, this mean, corrupt and cowardly
" Affair lead on by Michael ? Cowards ! yes,
" Who dared, in truth, not meet our hosts in fight
" On equal terms ; but shrinking called on God
" For thunder ere they came ; while here we use
" No thunder but our own. And shall they hold
" The rule o'er you, the aristocracy ?
" Your blood !—such blood runs not in other veins—
" And shall such blood as yours be overcome

" By this plebeian race ; who'd rather cringe
" And crawl in Heav'n, and have her dainty fare,
" Than join our high-born ranks when we rebelled,
" And take secession as their noble lot,
" And have their freedom in our glorious Hell ?
" What right have they in Hell to bring us war ?
" Have we not right to build a kingdom for
" Ourselves, and rule as we shall please ?   Is this
" The justice of the Tyrant that holds sway
" In Heav'n ?   We ask but to be let alone."—
     Indeed ! " to be but let alone ?"   Had he
Been always just to " let alone " the ones
Who wished no call from him ?   Where is the world
He has not ransacked ?   Where the land, on our
Green earth he has not traversed like a beast,
A roaring lion, seeking whom he might
Devour ?   His inroads on the works of God
Have never ceased ; and never will till he
Is chained ;—and now, forsooth, because he finds
Himself pursued, and pressed by foe, beyond
All hope of victory, or e'en escape —
He whines ; and talks of justice ; and complains
That he's not let alone.   No, no, his feet,
His godless feet, with all his godless crew,
Have trod on every soil, his mischiefs filled
All worlds throughout the universe of God.
And now he shall no further go ; but shall
Be finished up, throughout eternal years.
So says the hand that writes upon the wall.—
" We ask no odds but to be let alone."

     These words and many more he scattered through
His host in passing on from corps to corps.
They saw him dauntless as they heard his voice ;

And took new life ; and made the welkin ring
With shouts ; then plied their arms and batteries
With fury never known before in Hell.
And Michael's ranks are swept, and hurled in heaps
And windrows by their awful power.——The while,
The direful engine of the living God
Was playing dreadful on his suffering lines ;
And shot forth globes of death and iron hail
And bursting thunder bolts, which so beswept
The works of Satan, and becrushed his ranks,
'Twas plain that all the valor and the might
That he and all could bring, would not suffice
To hold the battle till the close of day.
   But now two heavenly flags are seen behind
The left, and right, of Satan's lines. They were
Two flanking corps of Michael's, which had made
Detour, and just arrived to take them in
The rear.—A shout from heavenly lungs, that earth
Knows not!—a charge in front and flank upon
The hosts of Satan, now dismayed anew !
   His wings now pressed in front and rear, recoil
Disheartened ; and at length crowd in upon
The center, which awhile withstands the shock
Of Heav'nly arms, as adamantine rock
The billows' surge.   But what could they alone ?
They yield at length, o'erborne by crushing weight
Of columns, mass on mass thrown on them ; and—
They break—and—*all—is—lost ! !*
                  The Heavenly hosts
On every side close in upon them ; and
Escape is now beyond all hope. They see,
They comprehend the whole ; throw down their arms ;
And ask for quarter from the foe ; which giv'n,

They feel the war is at an end! And here
They rest. The chivalry submit, chagrined.
And make a virtue of this sad, this dire
Necessity. And they decide to put
The best face on the thing they can. The while,
Are inward stung, to ask for *quarter ;* and
Receive the boon of life from that same crew,
That " mean, corrupt, and cowardly affair
Led on by Michael ;" and to stand unarmed
And passive in their hands, and be disposed
Of as they shall decree.
      Alas! alas!
The Chivalry! *The better blood !* that talked
So loud ; that boasted erst so high!—And has
It come to this at last!——Now where's the boast
Of Satan, that at some not distant time
He would possess the throne of God? His hosts
Are captured, and himself has fled with scarce
A body-guard. The prospect for his hope
Seems now not most auspicious ; and the sky
For him looks rather like a storm. Yet let
Him boast and promise ; and let those believe
Who will. But time will verify, and that,
Perhaps, full soon.——But where is Satan? Fled —
With utmost speed —and nigh alone —and left
His host, his arms, and his supplies, and e'en
His hopes —behind ; and towards the Death-waste drives
His fleeing steps, with hope that Michael will
Not find him out.——He reached at length, far, far
Within, the direst tract that region dire
Could boast, untouched before by devilish foot.
Its ills were greater than a devil could
Endure. But he was in such strait as he

Before had never dreamed. He halted here,
A refuge now from greater ills, a treat,
A luxury, he scarce could hope to find.

He there concealed himself ; deep stung that he,
The ruler once, the autocrat of all
The Hells,—before whose feet the billions bowed—
That he,—great potentate, whose nod was law,
Whose wars and vict'ries never knew an end,—
Should fly a foe ; and, like a midnight thief
Escaped, should be compelled to hide himself
Like beast or reptile in a noisome cave ;
And there keep watch ; and dread th' approach of feet
Plebeian. Such is wickedness ; full sure
To bring disaster in the end, though long
Delayed.

But where is Michael ? Will he search
Him out, and bring him to the block or chain ;
The duty he had orders to perform ?
He will. His bands are out in every course ;
With charge to leave no nook unscanned, no rock,
No cave, no desert tract ; and bring him bound
Forthwith.——But days elapse and no return.

Meantime, the captive host are kept on guard ;
Nor suffered on parole to pass the bounds ;
For what parole can bind a devil fast ?
He'll swear, pledge honor, but he'll keep no faith.
His promises, his oaths, are ropes of sand.
Who trusts the wicked trusts to his dismay.

But *they*, shall *they* escape the justice due ?
Ah, no. Their punishment shall be the loss
Of Satan's power : no chief to keep them down.

Now civil wars of that dire realm shall rage,
And never, never cease. But earth shall gain

A profit in their curse ; for they shall find
No time to visit her, and mar as erst
The Eden growing there.——But days on days
Elapse. Still no report from scouts, sent out
To search for Satan's whereabouts. They scour
The globe of Hell in every compass point ;
But no avail. They sweep the arid plains,
They search the barren hills, climb unknown rocks
Of rugged cliff and Alpine height ; and grope
Through yawning caverns of forbidding depth :
But no avail.—The search continues still.
He's nowhere to be found in all the wilds
Of Hell.——At length they near the Death-waste. There
They halt upon its fearful edge ; and look
Abroad upon its doleful scenes, that bring
A shudder over every heart. Could he
Be there ? Would he, to shun ten thousand chains,
Betake himself to that abode ? He would.
His spirit proud will never, never yield.
He'll suffer,—but he will not bend. The search
Must, then, be made ; and they prepare themselves
Forthwith for perilous adventure through
That dang'rous waste.—They know the ills that there
Beset ; and ev'ry caution use to ward
Them off, or, met, to overcome them on
The spot. They clothe themselves in mail, and guard
Their limbs in every part ; the head, the face,
The feet ; and then, with weapons held in hand,
And, not without an inward shrinking at
The thought, launch forth upon that heath of death.
  The muse recoils to 'count the sights and sounds
That met their sense ; what serpents coiled, with eye
Of fire and brandished tongue, they scarcely shunned ;

What mammoth reptiles prone, they passed ; what asps
Of deadly sting, they brushed from off their forms !
What voices strange from every depth and cave
Came sighing forth ! what shrieks from empty air !
What groans from shadowy hills were heard ! All, all
Were such to make the boldest angel pause ;
And give the strictest heed to every step.
   They journey on, the angel band, and search
By day, by night, and scarcely stop for rest.
But no avail. No Satan or his trace
Can yet be found.——At length they near the edge
Of what appeared a plain, but frightful to
The eye as well as ear ; with ev'ry ill,
With every terror filled. Its breath upsteamed
Was charged with death—a Bohon-upas tract
Of Hell—a Death-waste in a Death-waste of
That world.——They pause again ; and though inured
Of late to fearful scenes, yet now their hearts
Within them sink. They feel a terror rise
Unfelt before through all the range of life
That they had passed. What can this be ? A Hell
Within a Hell ; to which all other parts
Of that dread world, seemed nigh a Paradise.
Must this be searched ? Must they adventure forth,
And scour such tract as that ? 'Twas more than they
Had thought, or ever dreamed. Yet duty called,
And they must strict obey. They launch at once
Upon this inner death ; with ten-fold care
Guard every step ; and search for days again.
   At last in utmost verge of murky sky,
With utmost strain of sight, they see, what seemed
A pile, a pile upthrown of rocks of rough
And daring cliff.——Who knows but Satan may

Be there, ensconced in some deep cavern in
The bowels of that mound ; or there intrenched
Behind some strong defence ; so strong to bid
Defiance to all coming foe ?—They urge
Their course that way ; and find as they had thought,
A massy heap, which seemed a mountain late,
Now shattered by some blast of God. They gaze
Upon the scene ; a scene sublime for Heaven
Itself. In bold relief the masses lay,
Piled high, with cliff on cliff immense, to reach
The clouds. And far within, beneath an arch,
A natural arch, they find what seemed a cave,
Or rather, entrance to a cave. The mouth,
Strong barred by pond'rous rocks, as if thus placed
By recent hands.—They pause.—" Is this the place,
" The refuge of our conquered, fleeing foe ?
" Poor Satan !" they ejaculate aloud ;
" If here, will he surrender when he finds
" Himself beset on every side ? Will he
" Be bold to answer when we call ; or whipped
" So sore, will he show less of daring than
" His wont ; and, cowering in the sides of this,
" His den, in silence tremble at our voice ?
" Poor Satan ! Fallen, fallen, fallen ! Once,
" I've heard it said, he stood in eminence
" In Heav'n. 'Twas Abdiel who consented kind
" To hold discourse with me. We talked of him,
" Of Satan. He had known him well, and had
" Distinct remembrance when he first came forth,
" A spirit young, from God's creative hand ;
" His person fair, his frame of wondrous might,
" His intellect betok'ning giant strength.
" He grew in greatness as he grew in age.

" In search of knowledge every barrier fell ;
" And in his upward flight of knowledge and
" Of excellence, he swept by all as e'en
" The comet in its upward flight outstrips
" The stars, and leaves them all behind. And yet
" None envied, but rejoiced in his success.
" 'Twas plain the time would come when he would stand
" Above all creatures else of God. That time
" Arrived. He gained the height, and looked abroad,
" And saw a vast expanse, where all beneath
" Him lay. He looked above, and nothing saw,—
" Save God alone, at awful distance, high
" And lifted up.——And then,—who could believe ?
" He sinned and fell !—Oh fool !—And lost him Heaven !
" Oh Lucifer, how fallen, fallen now !
" I've heard it said that sin, though sweet at first,
" Is sure to work out ruin in the end."
They said : and Satan heard within, and blazed
With passion that knew no control. He dared
Not venture out. They were too strong. But safe
Within, he bade defiance to them all.
And bade them enter if it seemed them best ;
And they should know full soon if Satan was
Himself or not. " 'Twas true, the chance of war
" Had brought him low, had 'reft him of his power,
" And 'hap his kingdom for all time to come.
" *Yet he was Satan still ;* that be assured."
Thus he :—The angels summoned him to yield,
And make surrender to their will, or that
Of Michael, for they came at his command.
" Surrender !" cried the haughty chief. " And is
" This Satan ? He surrender ! Never ! Tell
" Your chief, if he withdraws to Heaven again,

" And leaves us undisturbed, and leaves our soil,
" The sacred soil of Hell, the war shall cease.
" But nothing short will we accept. Go, tell
" Him. Let him then decide."—What madness! Here
Is Satan, pent within a cave ; too weak
T' encounter this small band ; and yet presumes
To dictate terms of peace to Michael, who
Has conquered him ; and brought him down thus low ;
And holds his host entire, now conquered, in
His grasp, with all his arms and requisites
Of war. " If Michael will retire and leave
The sacred soil of Hell, he'll grant him peace !"
How kind is Satan to the Host of Heaven !—
To grant them respite on such easy terms
And fair !
   The angels could not see it, nor
Could Michael when informed ; but ordered forth
A force to go with utmost speed, and take
The Rebel Chief without delay, and bring
Him bound, to him.
    And they obey at once.
And reach the hold of Satan, and demand
That he should quit his lair, and yield himself
Without reserve a captive to their hands ;
And yield his sword to them, no more to war.
 Now Satan could not see it ; and refused
With utmost scorn ; and " if they wished his sword,
" 'Twas there, and they had but to come and take
" It." Ah, no easy task to take that sword
That dire terrific blade, and wielded by
That arm of high archangel strength ; that sword,
That had achieved such high renown ; that had,
In battle's hour, in fearful fury raged,

And cloven down so many hostile chiefs.
Ah! woe betide the single arm that 'tempts
A deed so bold! No arm was equal to
The task, of all that came from Heav'n, save that
Of Michael; and he now is far away.

But Satan must be seized, and borne to him.
And how shall they succeed.——They ponder o'er
The various ways that promise most success.
But none seem so much better than the rest,
As to secure unanimous consent.
And yet, some plan must be devised, to give
The Rebel to their hands.—Now this, now that
They choose. But on review the same they cast
Aside. They fix their choice another way;
And then relinquish that again, till lost
In deep perplexity what means to use
To reach their end.

     At length, an engineer
Of that bright corps, proposed to lay a mine,
And blow that mountain fastness to the clouds.

It was agreed. And day by day, and week
By week they seemed in idleness to waste
Their time, unequal to the task they had
In hand. They set them down as guards around
That pent-up few; and there it seemed their hope
Must end. But they grew hopeful more and more,
As day on day elapsed; and Satan grew
Defiant more and more, at seeing their
Delay.—" 'Tis well," said he, " that they should be
" My guards, these angels, who so long have breathed
" The air of Heav'n. Yes, let them stay. 'Tis well
" That they should have a little taste of Hell;
" And here, pent up within our Death-waste, should

" Outwear their days, and never see their Heav'n
" Again. And Michael, waiting their success,
" May pass his years, if he shall choose, with all
" His host ; and breathe our blessed air, and feel
" The vigor of our clime ; and go, if hap
" The thing shall be, to Heaven again, with health
" Renewed, and even wisdom quite improved.

" Yes, let them stay in this our Hell, and spoil
" Themselves for Heav'nly fare again. 'Tis good ;
" It gives me joy at their enjoyment here.
" Hah, hah ! We welcome them to our sweet clime."

*Be—not—too—sure,—*yourself and godless few !—
Their stay *may, haply,* shorten e'er you are
Aware.——They were engaged in mining ; and
He knew it not. He heard the sound at times ;
But thought 'twas subterranean fires, in growl
Of strife, so common 'neath the crust of that
Unsettled globe. He heeded not, nor dreamed
The sure volcano rip'ning 'neath his feet.
They scooped a vista deep and long, and then
Spread out in chambers wide to right and left
Beneath the centre of that pile where lurked
The conquered, deadly foe, with few ensconced ;
Yet unsuspicious of the danger near ;
And each recess, with cautious hand, they filled
With dynamite, that should ere long disturb
The very globe of Hell. Retiring then,
They bar the entrance strong with massy rock ;
And chink with earth, till all seemed solid as
Before their toil. They then retire ; and stand
Aloof. Which Satan seeing, took new heart.
" I knew 'twould come to this at last," said he,
" Though overthrown, we're still too strong for our

" Malicious boastful foe. See now they leave
" Us though subdued. Yes, they're afraid that we
" Shall issue from our castle here, and sword
" In hand shall give them chastisement severe
" For their intrusion on our private hours.
" Yes, yes," said he, " though hard, yet *we must* part.
" We bid them then affectionate farewell ;
" And hope they'll tell the truth on reaching home."
    In like derisive mood, the others there
Joined in, and made a laugh that shook the cave,
And echoed back from the surrounding hills.
For once, they had facetious grown ; and seemed
A jolly few, as if in session o'er
Their cu ps.—
              At length, the long, long train is touched ;—
And all in breathless silence wait the grand
Result.—Another laugh within the cave,
At witticism given ; a long,—loud—laugh—
A thunder peal ; or rather earthquake! and
The globe of Hell is to its centre jarred ;
And that vast pile of cliffs immense, is shot
In wild confusion to the clouds. Alas !
And Satan and his few are mingled with
The wreck ; first upward hurled,—then downward dashed,
And whelmed by pouring masses of debris.
    They lay bestunned, and bruised in every part.
And now's the time,—and now 'tis full improved.
The foe of God and man, thus stupified,
Is seized, and ironed safe. He soon awakes,—
And finds himself undone ;—secure, beyond
All hope ; with fetters, locked, unbreakable.
Yes, he who has forever, since his fall,
Roamed forth at will ; and, though chastised severe,
20

Defied the power of God with impious tongue ;
And gloried in his never-ending crimes,—
Is now in fetters held ; the first time bound
In his eventful life.——Recovered now,
His frenzy none can tell. Like tiger fresh,
Or forest boar, he shook his fetters, foamed
And gnashed his teeth ; that awed his captors down,
Though bound both hand and foot.——The siege is closed.
At once they leave, and take their hasty march
For Michael ; and in time arrive ; and to
His presence bring the haughty captive chief ;
Bestung at soul, yet bold in outward mien.

He stood in silence and in scorn ; and heard
While Michael read the stern decree of God :
" That for his crimes, his oft-repeated crimes,
" His crimes against the God of Heav'n, his crimes
" On earth, and other worlds of God, his crimes
" In drawing after him the myriad hosts
" Of Heav'n, and, now, of earth, whose cries have reached
" To God ; his crimes, though dark and fearful, yet
" A pastime to his taste, the offspring of
" His fierce, malicious soul : for these, *his race*
" *Is run :* and, now, henceforth he shall be chained ;
" No more to rove through earth and skies ; and wreak
" His malice on the good ; and draw
" God's creatures off from him."——He heard ; nor deigned
Reply. But sullen, yielded to his fate.

Rejoice, oh Heav'ns ! And earth, hold jubilee !
For he that wasted you is now no more.
His arm is broke ; his rage is impotent.
Go on and prosper till your cup is full,
The cup of blessing, to the brim ; till all
Th' apocalypse shall be fulfilled ; the bride

Descend to meet her spouse, the church, the New
Jerusalem, the City of our God ;
The church ; in which he will forever dwell ;
And be the light thereof ; nor needing sun,
Nor moon ;—whose gates shall never, hence, be shut,
Inviting freely all ; to which the Kings
Of earth shall come ; and there their glory and
Their honor bring ; through which a living stream
Shall flow ; and nourish green the tree of life,
Whose leaves shall heal the nations through the world.
Rejoice ! thou church of God, expand, and fill,
And bless the earth a thousand thousand years !—
But Satan now must be transferred to that
Dire spot where he must ever, ever dwell ;
And that far out upon the face of Hell's
Wide sea.——And Michael now prepares to take
That voyage, lone and dang'rous, on that sea ;
Whose billows are the fear of all of Heav'n
Or Hell ; upon whose face the stormy winds
Forever rage ; and hurricanes, beyond
All thought of man ; upturning that dread deep
Of pestilential wave in madness to
The clouds. And yet that deep must be essayed ;
Its tempests, darkness, and its terrors, braved.
And no subaltern hand must have the charge,—
Lest he, their furious captive, should escape ;
Or, chained, the work should not be safely done.
The weal of worlds hangs on this last, great act.
It must be done, as never to be done
Again. And Michael goes himself, and takes
The charge of all, and risk of all.——But no
Delay, save that for preparation due.
And all are tasked to utmost skill and strength ;

And day and night, and night and day the work
Is urged, to fit the means to dare that sea.
 In time the day arrives ; and they embark.
They leave the shore ; and with them take the chief,
The sullen chief, reluctant, chafing to
The soul ; but high and haughty as before.
 They urge their way ; and soon are far beyond
The view of those they leave behind. The sea
And Heav'ns now meet on every side ; and dark,
And dreadful is the path they course, o'erhung
With tempest-clouds ; and far from line direct
By warring winds ; yet making headway towards
Their goal as days elapse. What shoals immense
They scarcely shun ! What sunken rocks they graze,
That broke the waves, and flung in wildest surge
And roar, the foam and breakers high in air.
 They're safe as yet ; and onward, onward is
Their course ; but never with a placid sea.
 At length, at mid-day-hour, the skies grow black.
" A storm, a storm," they cry. And all prepare
To meet its rage.—The darkling heav'ns now roll
With deepest thunder from afar ; and fires
Awaked play awfully behind the scene :
And with a flickering glance befringe the far
Off clouds. Nor tarry long concealed. But now
Forth dart in forked living streams ; and rend
The pall, and glare upon the stormy deep.—
 The onset soon will come ; the mad'ning winds
Are heard afar ; the billows swell.—They wait
With awe-struck hearts, the coming shock.—It strikes.
And heav'n and sea are mingled in one wild
Tumultuous roar. The voy'gers hold for life.—
Their bark is but a feather on the wave ;

And, driven like a bubble in the blast,
But, broken not.—Ah! what are storms on earth
That seamen tell, to these?—as far below
In wildness and in might, as earth is less
Than Hell's vast orb.—Each billow seemed itself
A sea in size ; and loudest thunder of
Our sphere were but electric sparks, to those
Dire claps that rent the heavens of Hell.
E'en angel ears were pained thereby ; and eyes
Were blinded by those sheets of living fire.—
Such tempests brood upon, and sweep that globe.

And yet, their way is onward ; but their path
Is awful still ; and now to right afar,
And now to left. For days and days, they ply
Their gloomy course. But not alone are shoals,
And sunken rocks, and storms within their path ;
But monsters of gigantic size ; that hide
Within the caves, and dark retreats of that
Dire sea. These ever and anon athwart
Their track. They spy them far ; with head on high
And winding trail of foam ; that tells the length
Of body prone.—The heart is sick, as now
They near the bark ; their jaws distended wide,
Their eyeballs glaring from their serpent heads.—
They dwell hard by ; and overlook the bark
With darting tongue, and hissing breath, and arch
Of scaly neck ;—and threaten imminent.—
Then slow subside ; and steer away to parts
Unknown ; and lash the brine till lost to sight ;—
And seek, mayhap, their darksome caves again.—
The seamen then take breath,—and feel untold
Relief.——No slack of speed! But faithful still ;
On, on they press, the ceaseless howling winds

Above, and yawning gulfs below! By day,
A black and threat'ning heav'n ; and oh! by night,
A starless sky! and billows high, to chill
The blood ; then sinking to a bottomless
Abyss ; down which the faithful voy'gers plunge
Amain, to make the bravest angel bosom shrink.

But God had called them to this fearful lot ;
And they obey. Yes, angels ever do
His will. 'Tis only men and devils disobey.

The days pass on ; and night succeeds to night ;
And onward still.
                          A storm again   more dread
Is near ; to which all other storms had been
But zephyrs in their evening play. It's wing
O'erspreads the deep. It's coming roar bestuns
The ear. A blackened whirlwind falls upon the sea ;
A dire tornado of that direful world.
And hurls its billows to the clouds again
With ten-fold fury. Where again's the bark
Of Michael? . Gone! Ah! gone from sight!—A blank
Is left on ocean face. And has it sunk,
To rise no more?—O no! Behold it rise,
And ride the dizzy wave, and sweep the clouds
Again—God guards.—The mission shall succeed ;
The work be done.—But Satan prayed that all
Might sink ; but not to God, he prayed to fate.
For naught he dreaded, as the rock and chain ;
Nor cared he aught, what other ills might come,
If these, his destined fate, could but be shunned.
His prayer shall not be heard ; his fate is sealed.—

All day the fearful tempest hung, and had
Not eased when night set in. Ah! who can tell
The terrors of that night? The thunder pealed

Its voice, and lightnings crossed the heav'ns from pole
To pole, and streamed from heav'n to sea, from sea
To heav'n; bestunned the sight,—then shut the scene
With pall impenetrably dark;—then burst
Again with awful splendor bright;—then closed
Again in darkness that could e'en be felt.—
   The storm-god raved; and shapes were seen, that walked
The midnight wave, and froze the blood. Thus raged
The storm till dawn of day; and yet the bark,
Though strained in every part and shattered sore,
Still lived, with all her crew; and promise gave
That she would reach her destined goal.—
                         At length,
One day, amidst their onward course, they see,
Or think they see, in farthest verge of sky,
Where heav'n and ocean meet,—a mound of foam;—
And then a blackened mass;—then foam again.
And as they near and nearer draw, they see
The ocean seething like a caldron vast,
And far beyond the rage of Scylla or
Charibdis known to seamen in the days
Of old. The breakers, mighty in their surge,
And awful in their roar, leap up and wet
The clouds. This was their destined goal; the rock,
The fatal rock where Satan should be chained.—
The sea then settles down to calm, the first
Time since that sea was sea, that rock was rock.
For God had stilled the wave as at the word
Of Jesus: "Peace, be still." They now prepare
To end their task. Their bark lies safely on
The lee.—They stand upon the rock, that mass
Of adamant, that peak of mountain in
The sea, upreaching from the depths below;

That rock, that has, for ages past, withstood
The ceaseless surge, the mighty wrath of storms.
And shall forever stand   and hold its head
Unbroken by their power.

                   The " chain " is bound
Thereto with brazen bolts   unbreakable
And incorrupt.—And now they seize on him
With fetters bound, and bring him struggling forth.
   He saw,—and deadly pale, he felt his knees
Together smite,—his heart within him sink.
He saw his fate, a fate he might have shunned,
But now *too late.*   They bind with lesser chains
Thrice round his neck, and thrice his body round,
And thrice round every limb.   Then lock and bolt
Them fast ; and these again to that " great chain "
In 'pocalypse revealed, and thither brought
By Michael at the word of God, just made
Forever fast to that dire rock.

                      'Tis done !
The chafing, deadly fiend is safe.—They loose
The fetters from his hands and feet ; and leave
Him to his fate ;—and then depart.—He waits,
In sullen mood, till their retiring bark
Is lost to sight on distant wave ;—then bounds
Amain   like bison late on prairie caught,
Or tiger recent from his jungle home.—
He bounds again, again ;—and tries his chain ;—
He chafes and foams, and tries again, again ;
But all in vain.

                 He there shall sit enchained
Till God's great Judgment Day ; then, brought before
His seat, shall hear his doom anew ; and be
Remanded back ; shall ever view his crimes

And con them o'er ; but unrepentant still.
There, there shall he abide   and feel the scourge ;
Yet curse, and curse his God   and upward look,
Bereft of hope, through ages without end.

Yes, chained forever on that lonely rock
In Hell's dread ocean, shall he waste his years :
And feel the beat upon his naked soul,
Of her tempestuous and eternal waves.

THE END.